D0109466

ORIENTAL RELIGIONS
IN
ROMAN PAGANISM

The Oriental Religions in Roman Paganism

By

Franz Cumont

With an Introductory Essay by

Grant Showerman

Authorized Translation

DOVER PUBLICATIONS

NEW YORK

Published in Canada by General Publishing Company, Ltd., 30 Lesmill Road, Don Mills, Toronto, Ontario.

Published in the United Kingdom by Constable and Company, Ltd., 10 Orange Street, London WC 2.

This Dover edition, first published in 1956, is an unabridged and unaltered republication of the first English translation of *Les religions orientales dans le paganisme romain* as originally published in 1911 by G. Routledge & Sons, Ltd.

Standard Book Number: 486-20321-2
Library of Congress Catalog Card Number: 58-259

Manufactured in the United States of America
Dover Publications, Inc.
180 Varick Street
New York, N. Y. 10014

TO MY TEACHER AND FRIEND
CHARLES MICHEL

TABLE OF CONTENTS.

INTRODUCTION.

THE SIGNIFICANCE OF FRANZ CUMONT'S WORK.

FRANZ CUMONT, born January 3, 1868, and educated at Ghent, Bonn, Berlin, and Paris, resides in Brussels, and has been Professor in the University of Ghent since 1892. His monumental work, *Textes et monuments figurés relatifs aux mystères de Mithra,* published in 1896 and 1899 in two volumes, was followed in 1902 by the separate publication, under the title *Les Mystères de Mithra,* of the second half of Vol. I, the *Conclusions* in which he interpreted the great mass of evidence contained in the remainder of the work. The year following, this book appeared in the translation of Thomas J. McCormack as *The Mysteries of Mithra,* published by the Open Court Publishing Company. M. Cumont's other work of prime interest to students of the ancient faiths, *Les religions orientales dans le paganisme romain,* appeared in 1906, was revised and issued in a second edition in 1909, and is now presented in English in the following pages.

M. Cumont is an ideal contributor to knowledge in his chosen field. As an investigator, he combines in one person Teutonic thoroughness and Gallic intuition. As a writer, his virtues are no less pronounced. Recognition of his mastery of an enormous array of detailed learning followed immediately on the publication of *Textes et monuments,* and the present series of essays, besides a numerous series of articles and monographs, makes manifest the same painstaking and thorough scholarship; but he is something more than the mere *savant* who has at command a vast and difficult body of knowledge. He is also the literary architect who builds up his material into well-ordered and graceful structure.

Above all, M. Cumont is an interpreter. In *The Mysteries of Mithra* he put into circulation, so to speak, the coin of the ideas he had minted in the patient and careful study of *Textes et Monuments*; and in the studies of *The Oriental Religions* he is giving to the wider public the interpretation of the larger and more comprehensive body of knowledge of which his acquaintance with the religion of Mithra is only a part, and against which as a background it stands. What his book *The Mysteries of Mithra* is to his special knowledge of Mithraism, *The Oriental Religions* is to his knowledge of the whole field. He is thus an example of the highest type of scholar—the exhaustive searcher after evidence, and the sympathetic interpreter who mediates between his subject and the lay intellectual life of his time.

And yet, admirable as is M. Cumont's presentation in *The Mysteries of Mithra* and *The Oriental Religions,* nothing is a greater mistake than to suppose that his popularizations are facile reading. The few specialists in ancient religions may indeed sail smoothly in the current of his thought; but the very nature of a subject which ramifies so extensively and so intricately into the whole of ancient life, concerning itself with practically all the manifestations of ancient civilization—

philosophy, religion, astrology, magic, mythology, literature, art, war, commerce, government—will of necessity afford some obstacle to readers unfamiliar with the study of religion.

It is in the hope of lessening somewhat this natural difficulty of assimilating M. Cumont's contribution to knowledge, and above all, to life, that these brief words of introduction are undertaken. The presentation in outline of the main lines of thought which underlie his conception of the importance of the Oriental religions in universal history may afford the uninitiated reader a background against which the author's depiction of the various cults of the Oriental group will be more easily and clearly seen.

M. Cumont's work, then, transports us in imagination to a time when Christianity was still—at least in the eyes of Roman pagans—only one of a numerous array of foreign Eastern religions struggling for recognition in the Roman world, and especially in the city of Rome. To understand the conditions under which the new faith finally triumphed, we should first realize the number of these religions, and the apparently chaotic condition of paganism when viewed as a system.

"Let us suppose," says M. Cumont, "that in modern Europe the faithful had deserted the Christian churches to worship Allah or Brahma, to follow the precepts of Confucius or Buddha, or to adopt the maxims of the Shinto; let us imagine a great confusion of all the races of the world in which Arabian mullahs, Chinese scholars, Japanese bonzes, Tibetan lamas and Hindu pundits should all be preaching fatalism and predestination, ancestor-worship and devotion to a deified sovereign, pessimism and deliverance through annihilation—a confusion in which all those priests should erect temples of exotic architecture in our cities and celebrate their disparate rites therein. Such a dream, which the future may perhaps realize, would offer a pretty accurate picture of the religious chaos in which the ancient world was struggling before the reign of Constantine."

But it is no less necessary to realize, in the second place, that, had there not been an essential solidarity of all these different faiths, the triumph of Christianity would have been achieved with much less difficulty and in much less time. We are not to suppose that religions are long-lived and tenacious unless they possess something vital which enables them to resist. In his chapter on "The Transformation of Roman Paganism," M. Cumont thus accounts for the vitality of the old faiths: "The mass of religions at Rome finally became so impregnated by neo-Platonism and Orientalism that paganism may be called a single religion with a fairly distinct theology, whose doctrines were somewhat as follows: adoration of the elements, especially the cosmic bodies; the reign of one God, eternal and omnipotent, with messenger attendants; spiritual interpretation of the gross rites yet surviving from primitive times; assurance of eternal felicity to the faithful; belief that the soul was on earth to be proved before its final return to the universal spirit, of which it was a spark; the existence of an abysmal abode for the evil, against whom the faithful must keep up an unceasing struggle; the destruction of the universe, the death of the wicked, and the eternal happiness of the good in a reconstructed world."*

If this formulation of pagan doctrine surprises those who have been told that paganism was "a fashion rather than a faith," and are accustomed to think of it in terms of Jupiter and Juno, Venus and Mars, and the other empty, cold, and formalized deities that have so long filled literature and art, it will be because they have failed to take into account that between Augustus and Constantine three hundred years elapsed, and are unfamiliar with the very natural fact that during all that long period the character of paganism was gradually undergoing change and growth. "The faith of the friends of Symmachus," M. Cumont tells us, "was much farther removed from the religious ideal of Augustus, although they would never have admitted it, than that of their opponents in the senate."

To what was due this change in the content of the pagan ideal, so great that the phraseology in which the ideal is described puts us in mind of Christian doctrine itself? First, answers M. Cumont, to neo-Platonism, which attempted the reconciliation of the antiquated religions with the advanced moral and intellectual ideas of its own time by spiritual interpretation of outgrown cult stories and cult practices. A second and more vital cause, however, wrought to bring about the same result. This was the invasion of the Oriental religions, and the slow working, from the advent of the Great Mother of the Gods in B. C. 204 to the downfall of paganism at the end of the fourth cen-

* This summary of M. Cumont's chapter is quoted from my review of the first edition of *Les religions orientales* in *Classical Philology*, III, 4, p. 467.

tury of the Christian era, of the leaven of Oriental sentiment. The cults of Asia and Egypt bridged the gap between the old religions and Christianity, and in such a way as to make the triumph of Christianity an evolution, not a revolution. The Great Mother and Attis, with self-consecration, enthusiasm, and asceticism; Isis and Serapis, with the ideals of communion and purification; Baal, the omnipotent dweller in the far-off heavens; Jehovah, the jealous God of the Hebrews, omniscient and omnipresent; Mithra, deity of the sun, with the Persian dualism of good and evil, and with after-death rewards and punishments—all these, and more, flowed successively into the channel of Roman life and mingled their waters to form the late Roman paganism which proved so pertinacious a foe to the Christian religion. The influence that underlay their pretensions was so real that there is some warrant for the view of Renan that at one time it was doubtful whether the current as it flowed away into the Dark Ages should be Mithraic or Christian.

The vitalization of the evidence regarding these cults is M. Cumont's great contribution. His perseverance in the accurate collection of material is equalled only by his power to see the real nature and effect of the religions of which he writes. Assuming that no religion can succeed merely because of externals, but must stand on some foundation of moral excellence, he shows how the pagan faiths were able to hold their own, and even to contest the ground with Christianity. These religions, he asserts, gave greater satisfaction first, to the senses and passions, secondly, to the intelligence, finally, and above all, to the conscience. "The spread of the Oriental religions"—again I quote a summary from *Classical Philology* — "was due to merit. In contrast to the cold and formal religions of Rome, the Oriental faiths, with their hoary traditions and basis of science and culture, their fine ceremonial, the excitement attendant on their mysteries, their deities with hearts of compassion, their cultivation of the social bond, their appeal to conscience and their promises of purification and reward in a future life, were personal rather than civic, and satisfied the individual soul.... With such a conception of latter-day paganism, we may more easily understand its strength and the bitter rivalry between it and the new faith, as well as the facility with which pagan society, once its cause was proved hopeless, turned to Christianity." The Oriental religions had made straight the way. Christianity triumphed after long conflict because its antagonists also were not without weapons from the armory of God. Both parties to the struggle had their loins girt about with truth, and both wielded the sword of the spirit; but the steel of the Christian was the more piercing, the breastplate of his righteousness was the stronger, and his feet were better shod with the preparation of the gospel of peace.

Nor did Christianity stop there. It took from its opponents their own weapons, and used them; the better elements of paganism were transferred to the new religion. "As the religious history of the empire is studied more closely," writes M. Cumont, "the triumph of the church will, in our opinion, appear more and more as the culmination of a long evolution of beliefs. We can understand the Christianity of the fifth century with its greatness and weaknesses, its spiritual exaltation and its puerile superstitions, if we know the moral antecedents of the world in which it developed "

M. Cumont is therefore a contributor to our appreciation of the continuity of history. Christianity was not a sudden and miraculous transformation, but a composite of slow and laborious growth. Its four centuries of struggle were not a struggle against an entirely unworthy religion, else would our faith in its divine warrant be diminished; it is to its own great credit, and also to the credit of the opponents that succumbed to it, that it finally overwhelmed them. To quote Emil Aust: "Christianity did not wake into being the religious sense, but it afforded that sense the fullest opportunity of being satisfied; and paganism fell because the less perfect must give place to the more perfect, not because it was sunken in sin and vice. It had out of its own strength laid out the ways by which it advanced to lose itself in the arms of Christianity, and to recognize this does not mean to minimize the significance of Christianity. We are under no necessity of artificially darkening the heathen world; the light of the Evangel streams into it brightly enough without this."*

Finally, the work of M. Cumont and others in the field of the ancient Oriental religions is not an isolated activity, but part of a larger intellectual movement. Their effort is only one manifestation of the interest of recent years in the study of universal religion; other manifestations of the same interest are to be seen in the histories of the Greek and Roman religions by

* *Die Religion der Römer,* p. 116. For the significance of the pagan faiths, see an essay on "The Ancient Religions in Universal History," *American Journal of Philology,* XXIX. 2, pp. 156-171.

Gruppe, Farnell, and Wissowa, in the anthropological labors of Tylor, Lang, and Frazer, in the publication of Reinach's *Orpheus,* in the study of comparative religion, and in such a phenomenon as a World's Parliament of Religions.

In a word, M. Cumont and his companion ancient Orientalists are but one brigade engaged in the modern campaign for the liberation of religious thought. His studies are therefore not concerned alone with paganism, nor alone with the religions of the ancient past; in common with the labors of students of modern religion, they touch our own faith and our own times, and are in vital relation with our philosophy of living, and consequently with our highest welfare. "To us moderns," says Professor Frazer in the preface to his *Golden Bough,* "a still wider vista is vouchsafed, a greater panorama is unrolled by the study which aims at bringing home to us the faith and the practice, the hopes and the ideals, not of two highly gifted races only, but of all mankind, and thus at enabling us to follow the long march, the slow and toilsome ascent, of humanity from savagery to civilization.... But the comparative study of the beliefs and institutions of mankind is fitted to be much more than a means of satisfying an enlightened curiosity and of furnishing materials for the researches of the learned. Well handled, it may become a powerful instrument to expedite progress...."

It is possible that all this might disquiet the minds of those who have been wont to assume perfection in the primitive Christian church, and who assume also that present-day Christianity is the ultimate form of the Christian religion. Such persons—if there are such—should rather take heart from the whole-souled devotion to truth everywhere to be seen in the works of scholars in ancient religion, and from their equally evident sympathy with all manifestations of human effort to establish the divine relation; but most of all from their universal testimony that for all time and in all places and under all conditions the human heart has felt powerfully the need of the divine relation. From the knowledge that the desire to get right with God—the common and essential element in all religions —has been the most universal and the most potent and persistent factor in past history, it is not far to the conviction that it will always continue to be so, and that the struggle toward the divine light of religion pure and undefiled will never perish from the earth.

GRANT SHOWERMAN.

THE UNIVERSITY OF WISCONSIN.

PREFACE.

IN November, 1905, the Collège de France honored
the writer by asking him to succeed M. Naville in
opening the series of lectures instituted by the Michonis
foundation. A few months later the "Hibbert Trust"
invited him to Oxford to develop certain subjects which
he had touched upon at Paris. In this volume have
been collected the contents of both series with the addition of a short bibliography and notes intended for
scholars desirous of verifying assertions made in the
text.[1] The form of the work has scarcely been changed,
but we trust that these pages, intended though they
were for oral delivery, will bear reading, and that the
title of these studies will not seem too ambitious for
what they have to offer. The propagation of the
Oriental religions, with the development of neo-Platonism, is the leading fact in the moral history of the
pagan empire. May this small volume on a great subject throw at least some light upon this truth, and may
the reader receive these essays with the same kind
interest shown by the audiences at Paris and Oxford.

The reader will please remember that the different
chapters were thought out and written as lectures. They
do not claim to contain a debit and credit account of
what the Latin paganism borrowed from or loaned to
the Orient. Certain well-known facts have been de-

liberately passed over in order to make room for others that are perhaps less known. We have taken liberties with our subject matter that would not be tolerated in a didactic treatise, but to which surely no one will object.

We are more likely to be reproached for an apparently serious omission. We have investigated only the internal development of paganism in the Latin world, and have considered its relation to Christianity only incidentally and by the way. The question is nevertheless important and has been the subject of celebrated lectures as well as of learned monographs and widely distributed manuals.[2] We wish to slight neither the interest nor the importance of that controversy, and it is not because it seemed negligible that we have not entered into it.

By reason of their intellectual bent and education the theologians were for a long time more inclined to consider the continuity of the Jewish tradition than the causes that disturbed it; but a reaction has taken place, and to-day they endeavor to show that the church has borrowed considerably from the conceptions and ritualistic ceremonies of the pagan mysteries. In spite of the prestige that surrounded Eleusis, the word "mysteries" calls up Hellenized Asia rather than Greece proper, because in the first place the earliest Christian communities were founded, formed and developed in the heart of Oriental populations, Semites, Phrygians and Egyptians. Moreover the religions of those people were much farther advanced, much richer in ideas and sentiments, more striking and stirring than the Greco-Latin anthropomorphism. Their liturgy always derives its inspiration from generally accepted beliefs about purification embodied in certain acts regarded as sanctifying. These facts were almost identical in the various sects. The new faith poured its revelation into the hallowed moulds of earlier religions because in that form alone could the world in which it developed receive its message.

This is approximately the point of view adopted by the latest historians.

But, however absorbing this important problem may be, we could not think of going into it, even briefly, in these studies on Roman paganism. In the Latin world the question assumes much more modest proportions, and its aspect changes completely. Here Christianity spread only after it had outgrown the embryonic state and really became established. Moreover like Christianity the Oriental mysteries at Rome remained for a long time chiefly the religion of a foreign minority. Did any exchange take place between these rival sects? The silence of the ecclesiastical writers is not sufficient reason for denying it. We dislike to acknowledge a debt to our adversaries, because it means that we recognize some value in the cause they defend, but I believe that the importance of these exchanges should not be exaggerated. Without a doubt certain ceremonies and holidays of the church were based on pagan models. In the fourth century Christmas was placed on the 25th of December because on that date was celebrated the birth of the sun (*Natalis Invicti*) who was born to a new life each year after the solstice.[3] Certain vestiges of the religions of Isis and Cybele besides other polytheistic practices perpetuated themselves in the adoration of local saints. On the other hand as soon as Christianity became a moral power in the world, it imposed itself even on its enemies. The Phrygian priests of the Great Mother openly opposed their celebration of the vernal equinox to the Christian Easter, and attributed to the blood shed in the tauro-bolium the redemptive power of the blood of the divine Lamb.[4]

All these facts constitute a series of very delicate problems of chronology and interrelation, and it would be rash to attempt to solve them *en bloc.* Probably there is a different answer in each particular case, and I am afraid that some cases must always remain un-solved. We may speak of "vespers of Isis" or of a "eucharist of Mithra and his companions," but only in the same sense as when we say "the vassal princes of the empire" or "Diocletian's socialism." These are tricks of style used to give prominence to a similarity and to establish a parallel strongly and closely. A word is not a demonstration, and we must be careful not to infer an influence from an analogy. Precon-ceived notions are always the most serious obstacles to an exact knowledge of the past. Some modern writers, like the ancient Church Fathers, are fain to see a sacrilegious parody inspired by the spirit of lies in the resemblance between the mysteries and the church ceremonies. Other historians seem disposed to agree with the Oriental priests, who claimed priority for their cults at Rome, and saw a plagiarism of their ancient rituals in the Christian ceremonies. It would appear that both are very much mistaken. Resem-blance does not necessarily presuppose imitation, and frequently a similarity of ideas and practices must be explained by common origin, exclusive of any borrow-ing.

An illustration will make my thought clearer. The votaries of Mithra likened the practice of their religion to military service. When the neophyte joined he was compelled to take an oath (*sacramentum*) similar to the one required of recruits in the army, and there is no doubt that an indelible mark was likewise branded on his body with a hot iron. The third degree of the mystical hierarchy was that of "soldier" (*miles*). Thenceforward the initiate belonged to the sacred militia of the invincible god and fought the powers of evil under his orders. All these ideas and institutions are so much in accord with what we know of Mazdean dualism, in which the entire life was conceived as a struggle against the malevolent spirits; they are so inseparable from the history even of Mithraism, which always was a soldiers' religion, that we cannot doubt they belonged to it before its appearance in the Occident.

On the other hand, we find similar conceptions in Christianity. The society of the faithful—the term is still in use—is the "Church Militant." During the first centuries the comparison of the church with an army was carried out even in details;[5] the baptism of the neophyte was the oath of fidelity to the flag taken by the recruits. Christ was the "emperor," the commander-in-chief, of his disciples, who formed cohorts triumphing under his command over the demons; the apostates were deserters; the sanctuaries, camps; the pious practices, drills and sentry-duty, and so on.

If we consider that the gospel preached peace, that for a long time the Christians felt a repugnance to military service, where their faith was threatened, we are tempted to admit *a priori* an influence of the belligerent cult of Mithra upon Christian thought.

But this is not the case. The theme of the *militia Christi* appears in the oldest ecclesiastical authors, in the epistles of St. Clement and even in those of St. Paul. It is impossible to admit an imitation of the Mithraic mysteries then, because at that period they had no importance whatever.

But if we extend our researches to the history of that notion, we shall find that, at least under the empire, the mystics of Isis were also regarded as forming sacred cohorts enlisted in the service of the goddess, that previously in the Stoic philosophy human existence was frequently likened to a campaign, and that even the astrologers called the man who submitted to destiny and renounced all revolt a "soldier of fate."[6]

This conception of life, especially of religious life, was therefore very popular from the beginning of our era. It was manifestly prior both to Christianity and to Mithraism. It developed in the military monarchies of the Asiatic Diadochi. Here the soldier was no longer a citizen defending his country, but in most instances a volunteer bound by a sacred vow to the person of his king. In the martial states that fought for the heritage of the Achemenides this personal devotion dominated or displaced all national feeling. We know the oaths taken by those subjects to their deified kings.[7] They agreed to defend and uphold them even at the cost of their own lives, and always to have the same friends and the same enemies as they; they dedicated to them not only their actions and words, but their very thoughts. Their duty was a complete abandonment of their personality in favor of those monarchs who were held the equals of the gods. The sacred *militia* of the mysteries was nothing but this civic morality viewed from the religious standpoint. It confounded loyalty with piety.

As we see, the researches into the doctrines or practices common to Christianity and the Oriental mysteries lead almost always beyond the limits of the Roman empire into the Hellenistic Orient. The religious conceptions which imposed themselves on Latin Europe under the Cæsars[8] were developed there, and it is there we must look for the key to enigmas still unsolved. It is true that at present nothing is more obscure than the history of the religions that arose in Asia when Greek culture came in contact with barbarian theology. It is rarely possible to formulate satisfactory conclusions with any degree of certainty, and before further discoveries are made we shall frequently be compelled to weigh contrasting probabilities. We must frequently throw out the sounding line into the shifting sea of possibility in order to find secure anchorage. But at any rate we perceive with sufficient distinctness the direction in which the investigations must be pursued.

It is our belief that the main point to be cleared up is the composite religion of those Jewish or Jewish-pagan communities, the worshipers of Hypsistos, the Sabbatists, the Sabaziasts and others in which the new creed took root during the apostolic age. In those communities the Mosaic law had become adapted to the sacred usages of the Gentiles even before the beginning of our era, and monotheism had made concessions to idolatry. Many beliefs of the ancient Orient, as for instance the ideas of Persian dualism regarding the infernal world, arrived in Europe by two roads, the more or less orthodox Judaism of the communities of the dispersion in which the gospel was accepted immediately, and the pagan mysteries imported from Syria or Asia Minor. Certain similarities that surprised and shocked the apologists will cease to look strange as soon as we reach the distant sources of the channels that reunited at Rome.

But these delicate and complicated researches into origins and relationships belong especially to the history of the Alexandrian period. In considering the Roman empire, the principal fact is that the Oriental religions propagated doctrines, previous to and later side by side with Christianity, that acquired with it universal authority at the decline of the ancient world. The preaching of the Asiatic priests also unwittingly prepared for the triumph of the church which put its stamp on the work at which they had unconsciously labored.

Through their popular propaganda they had completely disintegrated the ancient national faith of the Romans, while at the same time the Cæsars had gradually destroyed the political particularism. After their advent it was no longer necessary for religion to be connected with a state in order to become universal. Religion was no longer regarded as a public duty, but as a personal obligation; no longer did it subordinate the individual to the city-state, but pretended above all to assure his welfare in this world and especially in the world to come. The Oriental mysteries offered their votaries radiant perspectives of eternal happiness. Thus the focus of morality was changed. The aim became to realize the sovereign good in the life hereafter instead of in this world, as the Greek philosophy had done. No longer did man act in view of tangible real-

ities, but to attain ideal hopes. Existence in this life
was regarded as a preparation for a sanctified life, as
a trial whose outcome was to be either everlasting
happiness or everlasting pain.

As we see, the entire system of ethical values was
overturned.

The salvation of the soul, which had become the one
great human care, was especially promised in these
mysteries upon the accurate performance of the sacred
ceremonies. The rites possessed a power of purification and redemption. They made man better and freed
him from the dominion of hostile spirits. Consequently,
religion was a singularly important and absorbing
matter, and the liturgy could be performed only by a
clergy devoting itself entirely to the task. The Asiatic
gods exacted undivided service; their priests were no
longer magistrates, scarcely citizens. They devoted
themselves unreservedly to their ministry, and demanded of their adherents submission to their sacred
authority.

All these features that we are but sketching here,
gave the Oriental religions a resemblance to Christianity, and the reader of these studies will find many
more points in common among them. These analogies
are even more striking to us than they were in those
times because we have become acquainted in India and
China with religions very different from the Roman
paganism and from Christianity as well, and because
the relationships of the two latter strike us more
strongly on account of the contrast. These theological
similarities did not attract the attention of the ancients,
because they scarcely conceived of the existence of
other possibilities, while differences were what they

remarked especially. I am not at all forgetting how considerable these were. The principal divergence was that Christianity, by placing God in an ideal sphere beyond the confines of this world, endeavored to rid itself of every attachment to a frequently abject polytheism. But even if we oppose tradition, we cannot break with the past that has formed us, nor separate ourselves from the present in which we live. As the religious history of the empire is studied more closely, the triumph of the church will, in our opinion, appear more and more as the culmination of a long evolution of beliefs. We can understand the Christianity of the fifth century with its greatness and weaknesses, its spiritual exaltation and its puerile superstitions, if we know the moral antecedents of the world in which it developed. The faith of the friends of Symmachus was much farther removed from the religious ideal of Augustus, although they would never have admitted it, than that of their opponents in the senate. I hope that these studies will succeed in showing how the pagan religions from the Orient aided the long continued effort of Roman society, contented for many centuries with a rather insipid idolatry, toward more elevated and more profound forms of worship. Possibly their credulous mysticism deserves as much blame as is laid upon the theurgy of neo-Platonism, which drew from the same sources of inspiration, but like neo-Platonism it has strengthened man's feeling of eminent dignity by asserting the divine nature of the soul. By making inner purity the main object of earthly existence, they refined and exalted the psychic life and gave it an almost supernatural intensity, which until then was unknown in the ancient world.

PREFACE TO THE SECOND EDITION.

IN this second edition the eight lectures forming the reading matter of this book have suffered scarcely any change, and, excepting the chapter on Syria, the additions are insignificant. It would have been an easy matter to expand them, but I did not want these lectures to become erudite dissertations, nor the ideas which are the essential part of a sketch like the present to be overwhelmed by a multiplicity of facts. In general I have therefore limited myself to weeding out certain errors that were overlooked, or introduced, in the proofreading.

The notes, however, have been radically revised. I have endeavored to give expression to the suggestions or observations communicated to me by obliging readers; to mention new publications and to utilize the results of my own studies. The index makes it easy to find the subjects discussed.

And here I must again thank my friend Charles Michel, who undertook the tedious task of rereading the proofs of this book, and whose scrupulous and sagacious care has saved me from many and many a blunder.

F. C.

PARIS, FRANCE, February, 1909.

ROME AND THE ORIENT.

W E are fond of regarding ourselves as the heirs of
Rome, and we like to think that the Latin genius,
after having absorbed the genius of Greece, held an
intellectual and moral supremacy in the ancient world
similar to the one Europe now maintains, and that the
culture of the peoples that lived under the authority
of the Cæsars was stamped forever by their strong
touch. It is difficult to forget the present entirely and
to renounce aristocratic pretensions. We find it hard
to believe that the Orient has not always lived, to some
extent, in the state of humiliation from which it is
now slowly emerging, and we are inclined to ascribe
to the ancient inhabitants of Smyrna, Beirut or Alexandria the faults with which the Levantines of to-day
are being reproached. The growing influence of the
Orientals that accompanied the decline of the empire
has frequently been considered a morbid phenomenon
and a symptom of the slow decomposition of the ancient world. Even Renan does not seem to have been
sufficiently free from an old prejudice when he wrote
on this subject:[1] "That the oldest and most worn out
civilization should by its corruption subjugate the
younger was inevitable."

But if we calmly consider the real facts, avoiding
the optical illusion that makes things in our immediate

vicinity look larger, we shall form a quite different
opinion. It is beyond all dispute that Rome found the
point of support of its military power in the Occident.
The legions from the Danube and the Rhine were always braver, stronger and better disciplined than those
from the Euphrates and the Nile. But it is in the Orient, especially in these countries of "old civilization,"
that we must look for industry and riches, for technical
ability and artistic productions, as well as for intelligence and science, even before Constantine made it the
center of political power.

While Greece merely vegetated in a state of poverty,
humiliation and exhaustion; while Italy suffered de-
population and became unable to provide for her own
support; while the other countries of Europe were
hardly out of barbarism; Asia Minor, Egypt and Syria
gathered the rich harvests Roman peace made possible.
Their industrial centers cultivated and renewed all the
traditions that had caused their former celebrity. A
more intense intellectual life corresponded with the
economic activity of these great manufacturing and
exporting countries. They excelled in every profession
except that of arms, and even the prejudiced Romans
admitted their superiority. The menace of an Oriental
empire haunted the imaginations of the first masters
of the world. Such an empire seems to have been
the main thought of the dictator Cæsar, and the trium-
vir Antony almost realized it. Even Nero thought of
making Alexandria his capital. Although Rome, supported by her army and the right of might, retained
the political authority for a long time, she bowed to
the fatal moral ascendency of more advanced peoples.
Viewed from this standpoint the history of the empire

during the first three centuries may be summarized as a "peaceful infiltration" of the Orient into the Occident.[2] This truth has become evident since the various aspects of Roman civilization are being studied in greater detail; and before broaching the special subject of these studies we wish to review a few phases of the slow metamorphosis of which the propagation of the Oriental religions was one phenomenon.

In the first place the imitation of the Orient showed itself plainly in political institutions.[3] To be convinced of this fact it is sufficient to compare the government of the empire in the time of Augustus with what it had become under Diocletian. At the beginning of the imperial régime Rome ruled the world but did not govern it. She kept the number of her functionaries down to a minimum, her provinces were mere unorganized aggregates of cities where she only exercised police power, protectorates rather than annexed countries.[4] As long as law and order were maintained and her citizens, functionaries and merchants could transact their business, Rome was satisfied. She saved herself the trouble of looking after the public service by leaving broad authority to the cities that had existed before her domination, or had been modeled after her. The taxes were levied by syndicates of bankers and the public lands rented out. Before the reforms instituted by Augustus, even the army was not an organic and permanent force, but consisted theoretically of troops levied before a war and discharged after victory.

Rome's institutions remained those of a city. It was difficult to apply them to the vast territory she attempted to govern with their aid. They were a clumsy apparatus that worked only by sudden starts, a rudimentary system that could not and did not last.

What do we find three centuries later? A strongly centralized state in which an absolute ruler, worshiped like a god and surrounded by a large court, commanded a whole hierarchy of functionaries; cities divested of their local liberties and ruled by an omnipotent bureaucracy, the old capital herself the first to be dispossessed of her autonomy and subjected to prefects. Outside of the cities the monarch, whose private fortune was identical with the state finances, possessed immense domains managed by intendants and supporting a population of serf-colonists. The army was composed largely of foreign mercenaries, professional soldiers whose pay or bounty consisted of lands on which they settled. All these features and many others caused the Roman empire to assume the likeness of ancient Oriental monarchies.

It would be impossible to admit that like causes produce like results, and then maintain that a similarity is not sufficient proof of an influence in history. Wherever we can closely follow the successive transformations of a particular institution, we notice the action of the Orient and especially of Egypt. When Rome had become a great cosmopolitan metropolis like Alexandria, Augustus reorganized it in imitation of the capital of the Ptolemies. The fiscal reforms of the Cæsars like the taxes on sales and inheritances, the register of land surveys and the direct collection of taxes, were suggested by the very perfect financial system of the Lagides,[5] and it can be maintained that their government was the first source from which those of modern Europe were derived, through the medium of the Romans. The imperial *saltus,* superintended by a procurator and cultivated by metayers reduced to the state of serfs, was an imitation of the ones that the Asiatic potentates formerly cultivated through their agents.[6] It would be easy to increase this list of examples. The absolute monarchy, theocratic and bureaucratic at the same time, that was the form of government of Egypt, Syria and even Asia Minor during the Alexandrine period was the ideal on which the deified Cæsars gradually fashioned the Roman empire.

One cannot however deny Rome the glory of having elaborated a system of private law that was logically deduced from clearly formulated principles and was destined to become the fundamental law of all civilized communities. But even in connection with this private law, where the originality of Rome is uncontested and her preeminence absolute, recent researches have shown with how much tenacity the Hellenized Orient maintained its old legal codes, and how much resistance local customs, the woof of the life of nations, offered to unification. In truth, unification never was realized except in theory.[7] More than that, these researches have proved that the fertile principles of that provincial law, which was sometimes on a higher moral plane than the Roman law, reacted on the progressive transformation of the old *ius civile.* And how could it be otherwise? Were not a great number of famous jurists like Ulpian of Tyre and Papinian of Hemesa natives of Syria? And did not the law-school of Beirut constantly grow in importance after the third century, until during the fifth century it became the most brilliant center of legal education? Thus Levantines cultivated even the patrimonial field cleared by Scaevola and Labeo.[8]

In the austere temple of law the Orient held as yet only a minor position; everywhere else its authority was predominant. The practical mind of the Romans, which made them excellent lawyers, prevented them from becoming great scholars. They esteemed pure science but little, having small talent for it, and one notices that it ceased to be earnestly cultivated wherever their direct domination was established. The great astronomers, mathematicians, and physicians, like the originators or defenders of the great metaphysical systems, were mostly Orientals. Ptolemy and Plotinus were Egyptians, Porphyry and Iamblichus, Syrians, Dioscorides and Galen, Asiatics. All branches of learning were affected by the spirit of the Orient. The clearest minds accepted the chimeras of astrology and magic. Philosophy claimed more and more to derive its inspiration from the fabulous wisdom of Chaldea and Egypt. Tired of seeking truth, reason abdicated and hoped to find it in a revelation preserved in the mysteries of the barbarians. Greek logic strove to coordinate into an harmonious whole the confused traditions of the Asiatic religions.

Letters, as well as science, were cultivated chiefly by the Orientals. Attention has often been called to the fact that those men of letters that were considered the purest representatives of the Greek spirit under the empire belonged almost without exception to Asia Minor, Syria or Egypt. The rhetorician Dion Chrysostom came from Prusa in Bithynia, the satirist Lucian from Samosata in Commagene on the borders of the Euphrates. A number of other names could be cited.

From Tacitus and Suetonius down to Ammianus, there was not one author of talent to preserve in Latin the memory of the events that stirred the world of that period, but it was a Bithynian again, Dion Cassius of Nicea, who, under the Severi, narrated the history of the Roman people.

It is a characteristic fact that, besides this literature whose language was Greek, others were born, revived and developed. The Syriac, derived from the Aramaic which was the international language of earlier Asia, became again the language of a cultured race with Bardesanes of Edessa. The Copts remembered that they had spoken several dialects derived from the ancient Egyptian and endeavored to revive them. North of the Taurus even the Armenians began to write and polish their barbarian speech. Christian preaching, addressed to the people, took hold of the popular idioms and roused them from their long lethargy. Along the Nile as well as on the plains of Mesopotamia or in the valleys of Anatolia it proclaimed its new ideas in dialects that had been despised hitherto, and wherever the old Orient had not been entirely denationalized by Hellenism, it successfully reclaimed its intellectual autonomy.

A revival of native art went hand in hand with this linguistic awakening. In no field of intellect has the illusion mentioned above been so complete and lasting as in this one. Until a few years ago the opinion prevailed that an "imperial" art had come into existence in the Rome of Augustus and that thence its predominance had slowly spread to the periphery of the ancient world. If it had undergone some special modifications in Asia these were due to exotic influences, undoubtedly

Assyrian or Persian. Not even the important discoveries of M. de Vogüé in Hauran[9] were sufficient to prove the emptiness of a theory that was supported by our lofty conviction of European leadership.

To-day it is fully proven not only that Rome has given nothing or almost nothing to the Orientals but also that she has received quite a little from them. Impregnated with Hellenism, Asia produced an astonishing number of original works of art in the kingdoms of the Diadochs. The old processes, the discovery of which dates back to the Chaldeans, the Hittites or the subjects of the Pharaohs, were first utilized by the conquerors of Alexander's empire who conceived a rich variety of new types, and created an original style. But if during the three centuries preceding our era, sovereign Greece played the part of the demiurge who creates living beings out of preexisting matter, during the three following centuries her productive power became exhausted, her faculty of invention weakened, the ancient local traditions revolted against her empire and with the help of Christianity overcame it. Transferred to Byzantium they expanded in a new efflorescence and spread over Europe where they paved the way for the formation of the Romanesque art of the early Middle Ages.[10]

Rome, then, far from having established her suzerainty, was tributary to the Orient in this respect. The Orient was her superior in the extent and precision of its technical knowledge as well as in the inventive genius and ability of its workmen. The Cæsars were great builders but frequently employed foreign help. Trajan's principal architect, a magnificent builder, was a Syrian, Apollodorus of Damascus.[11]

Her Levantine subjects not only taught Italy the artistic solution of architectonic problems like the erection of a cupola on a rectangular or octagonal edifice, but also compelled her to accept their taste, and they saturated her with their genius. They imparted to her their love of luxuriant decoration, and of violent polychromy, and they gave religious sculpture and painting the complicated symbolism that pleased their abstruse and subtle minds.

In those times art was closely connected with industry, which was entirely manual and individual. They learned from each other, they improved and declined together, in short they were inseparable. Shall we call the painters that decorated the architecturally fantastic and airy walls of Pompeii in Alexandrian or perhaps Syrian taste artisans or artists? And how shall we classify the goldsmiths, Alexandrians also, who carved those delicate leaves, those picturesque animals, those harmoniously elegant or cunningly animated groups that cover the phials and goblets of Bosco Reale? And descending from the productions of the industrial arts to those of industry itself, one might also trace the growing influence of the Orient; one might show how the action of the great manufacturing centers of the East gradually transformed the material civilization of Europe; one might point out how the introduction into Gaul[12] of exotic patterns and processes changed the old native industry and gave its products a perfection and a popularity hitherto unknown. But I dislike to insist overmuch on a point apparently so foreign to the one now before us. It was important however to mention this subject at the beginning because in whatever direction scholars of to-day pursue their investigations they always notice Asiatic culture slowly supplanting that of Italy. The latter developed only by absorbing elements taken from the inexhaustible reserves of the "old civilizations" of which we spoke at the beginning. The Hellenized Orient imposed itself everywhere through its men and its works; it subjected its Latin conquerors to its ascendancy in the same manner as it dominated its Arabian conquerors later when it became the civilizer of Islam. But in no field of thought was its influence, under the empire, so decisive as in religion, because it finally brought about the complete destruction of the Greco-Latin paganism.[13]

The invasion of the barbarian religions was so open, so noisy and so triumphant that it could not remain unnoticed. It attracted the anxious or sympathetic attention of the ancient authors, and since the Renaissance modern scholars have frequently taken interest in it. Possibly however they did not sufficiently understand that this religious evolution was not an isolated and extraordinary phenomenon, but that it accompanied and aided a more general evolution, just as that aided it in turn. The transformation of beliefs was intimately connected with the establishment of the monarchy by divine right, the development of art, the prevailing philosophic tendencies, in fact with all the manifestations of thought, sentiment and taste.

We shall attempt to sketch this religious movement with its numerous and far-reaching ramifications. First we shall try to show what caused the diffusion of the Oriental religions. In the second place we shall examine those in particular that originated in Asia Minor, Egypt, Syria and Persia, and we shall endeavor to distinguish their individual characteristics and estimate their value. We shall see, finally, how the ancient idolatry was transformed and what form it assumed in its last struggle against Christianity, whose victory was furthered by Asiatic mysteries, although they opposed its doctrine.

• * * *

But before broaching this subject a preliminary question must be answered. Is the study which we have just outlined possible? What items will be of assistance to us in this undertaking? From what sources are we to derive our knowledge of the Oriental religions in the Roman empire?

It must be admitted that the sources are inadequate and have not as yet been sufficiently investigated.

Perhaps no loss caused by the general wreck of ancient literature has been more disastrous than that of the liturgic books of paganism. A few mystic formulas quoted incidentally by pagan or Christian authors and a few fragments of hymns in honor of the gods[14] are practically all that escaped destruction. In order to obtain an idea of what those lost rituals may have been one must turn to their imitations contained in the chorus of tragedies, and to the parodies comic authors sometimes made; or look up in books of magic the plagiarisms that writers of incantations may have committed.[15] But all this gives us only a dim reflection of the religious ceremonies. Shut out from the sanctuary like profane outsiders, we hear only the indistinct echo of the sacred songs and not even in imagination can we attend the celebration of the mysteries.

We do not know how the ancients prayed, we cannot penetrate into the intimacy of their religious life, and certain depths of the soul of antiquity we must leave unsounded. If a fortunate windfall could give us possession of some sacred book of the later paganism its revelations would surprise the world. We could witness the performance of those mysterious dramas whose symbolic acts commemorated the passion of the gods; in company with the believers we could sympathize with their sufferings, lament their death and share in the joy of their return to life. In those vast collections of archaic rites that hazily perpetuated the memory of abolished creeds we would find traditional formulas couched in obsolete language that was scarcely understood, naive prayers conceived by the faith of the earliest ages, sanctified by the devotion of past centuries, and almost ennobled by the joys and sufferings of past generations. We would also read those hymns in which philosophic thought found expression in sumptuous allegories[16] or humbled itself before the omnipotence of the infinite, poems of which only a few stoic effusions celebrating the creative or destructive fire, or expressing a complete surrender to divine fate can give us some idea.[17]

But everything is gone, and thus we lose the possibility of studying from the original documents the internal development of the pagan religions.

We should feel this loss less keenly if we possessed at least the works of Greek and Latin mythographers on the subject of foreign divinities like the voluminous books published during the second century by Eusebius and Pallas on the Mysteries of Mithra. But those works were thought devoid of interest or even dangerous by the devout Middle Ages, and they are not likely to have survived the fall of paganism. The treatises on mythology that have been preserved deal almost entirely with the ancient Hellenic fables made famous by the classic writers, to the neglect of the Oriental religions.[18]

As a rule, all we find in literature on this subject are a few incidental remarks and passing allusions. History is incredibly poor in that respect. This poverty of information was caused in the first place by a narrowness of view characteristic of the rhetoric cultivated by historians of the classical period and especially of the empire. Politics and the wars of the rulers, the dramas, the intrigues and even the gossip of the courts and of the official world were of much higher interest to them than the great economic or religious transformations. Moreover, there is no period of the Roman empire concerning which we are so little informed as the third century, precisely the one during which the Oriental religions reached the apogee of their power. From Herodianus and Dion Cassius to the Byzantines, and from Suetonius to Ammianus Marcellinus, all narratives of any importance have been lost, and this deplorable blank in historic tradition is particularly fatal to the study of paganism.

It is a strange fact that light literature concerned itself more with these grave questions. The rites of the exotic religions stimulated the imagination of the satirists, and the pomp of the festivities furnished the novelists with brilliant descriptive matter. Juvenal laughs at the mortifications of the devotees of Isis; in his *Necromancy* Lucian parodies the interminable purifications of the magi, and in the *Metamorphoses* Apuleius relates the various scenes of an initiation into the mysteries of Isis with the fervor of a neophyte and

the studied refinement of a rhetorician. But as a rule
we find only incidental remarks and superficial observations in the authors. Not even the precious treatise
On the Syrian Goddess, in which Lucian tells of a
visit to the temple of Hierapolis and repeats his conversation with the priests, has any depth. What he
relates is the impression of an intelligent, curious and
above all an ironical traveler.[19]

In order to obtain a more perfect initiation and a less
fragmentary insight into the doctrines taught by the
Oriental religions, we are compelled to turn to two
kinds of testimony, inspired by contrary tendencies, but
equally suspicious: the testimony of the philosophers,
and that of the fathers of the church. The Stoics and
the Platonists frequently took an interest in the religious beliefs of the barbarians, and it is to them that
we are indebted for the possession of highly valuable
data on this subject. Plutarch's treatise *Isis and Osiris*
is a source whose importance is appreciated even by
Egyptologists, whom it aids in reconstructing the legends of those divinities.[20] But the philosophers very
seldom expounded foreign doctrines objectively and
for their own sake. They embodied them in their systems as a means of proof or illustration; they surrounded them with personal exegesis or drowned them
in transcendental commentaries; in short, they claimed
to discover their own ideas in them. It is always difficult and sometimes impossible to distinguish the dogmas from the self-confident interpretations which are
usually as incorrect as possible.

The writings of the ecclesiastical authors, although
prejudiced, are very fertile sources of information, but
in perusing them one must guard against another kind

of error. By a peculiar irony of fate those controversialists are to-day in many instances our only aid in reviving the idolatry they attempted to destroy. Although the Oriental religions were the most dangerous and most persistent adversaries of Christianity, the works of the Christian writers do not supply as abundant information as one might suppose. The reason for this is that the fathers of the church often show a certain reserve in speaking of idolatry, and affect to recall its monstrosities only in guarded terms. Moreover, as we shall see later on,[21] the apologists of the fourth century were frequently behind the times as to the evolution of doctrines, and drawing on literary tradition, from epicureans and skeptics, they fought especially the beliefs of the ancient Grecian and Italian religions that had been abolished or were dying out, while they neglected the living beliefs of the contemporary world.

Some of these polemicists nevertheless directed their attacks against the divinities of the Orient and their Latin votaries. Either they derived their information from converts or they had been pagans themselves during their youth. This was the case with Firmicus Maternus who has written a bad treatise on astrology and finally fought the *Error of the Profane Religions.* However, the question always arises as to how much they can have known of the esoteric doctrines and the ritual ceremonies, the secret of which was jealously guarded. They boast so loudly of their power to disclose these abominations, that they incur the suspicion that the discretion of the initiates baffled their curiosity. In addition they were too ready to believe all the calumnies that were circulated against the pagan mysteries, calumnies directed against occult sects of all times and against the Christians themselves.

In short, the literary tradition is not very rich and frequently little worthy of belief. While it is comparatively considerable for the Egyptian religions because they were received by the Greek world as early as the period of the Ptolemies, and because letters and science were always cultivated at Alexandria, it is even less important for Phrygia, although Cybele was Hellenized and Latinized very early, and excepting the tract by Lucian on the goddess of Hierapolis it is almost nothing for the Syrian, Cappadocian and Persian religions.

The insufficiency of the data supplied by writers increases the value of information furnished by epigraphic and archeological documents, whose number is steadily growing. The inscriptions possess a certainty and precision that is frequently absent in the phrases of the writers. They enable one to draw important conclusions as to the dates of propagation and disappearance of the various religions, their extent, the quality and social rank of their votaries, the sacred hierarchy and sacerdotal personnel, the constitution of the religious communities, the offerings made to the gods, and the ceremonies performed in their honor; in short, conclusions as to the secular and profane history of these religions, and in a certain measure their ritual. But the conciseness of the lapidary style and the constant repetition of stereotyped formulas naturally render that kind of text hardly explicit and sometimes enigmatical. There are dedications like the *Nama Sebesio* engraved upon the great Mithra bas-relief preserved in the Louvre, that caused a number of dissertations to be written without any one explaining it. And besides, in a general way, epigraphy gives us but little information about the liturgy and almost nothing regarding the doctrines.

Archeology must endeavor to fill the enormous blanks left by the written tradition; the monuments, especially the artistic ones, have not as yet been collected with sufficient care nor interpreted with sufficient method. By studying the arrangement of the temples and the religious furniture that adorned them, one can at the same time determine part of the liturgic ceremonies which took place there. On the other hand, the critical interpretation of statuary relics enables us to reconstruct with sufficient correctness certain sacred legends and to recover part of the theology of the mysteries. Unlike Greek art, the religious art at the close of paganism did not seek, or sought only incidentally, to elevate the soul through the contemplation of an ideal of divine beauty. True to the traditions of the ancient Orient, it tried to edify and to instruct at the same time.[22] It told the history of the gods and the world in cycles of pictures, or it expressed through symbols the subtle conceptions of theology and even certain doctrines of profane science, like the struggle of the four elements; just as during the Middle Ages, so the artist of the empire interpreted the ideas of the clergy, teaching the believers by means of pictures and rendering the highest religious conceptions intelligible to the humblest minds. But to read this mystic book whose pages are scattered in our museums we must laboriously look for its key, and we cannot take for a guide and exegetist some Vincent de Beauvais of Diocletian's period[23] as when looking over the marvelous sculptured encyclopedias in our Gothic cathedrals. Our position is frequently similar to that of a scholar of the year 4000 who would undertake to write the history of the Passion from the pictures of the fourteen stations, or to study the veneration of the saints from the statues found in the ruins of our churches.

But, as far as the Oriental religions are concerned, the results of all the laborious investigations now being made in the classical countries can be indirectly controlled, and this is a great advantage. To-day we are tolerably well acquainted with the old religions of Egypt, Babylonia and Persia. We read and translate correctly the hieroglyphics of the Nile, the cuneiform tablets of Mesopotamia and the sacred books, Zend or Pahlavi, of Parseeism. Religious history has profited more by their deciphering than the history of politics or of civilization. In Syria also, the discovery of Aramaic and Phœnician inscriptions and the excavations made in temples have in a certain measure covered the deficiency of information in the Bible or in the Greek writers on Semitic paganism. Even Asia Minor, that is to say the uplands of Anatolia, is beginning to reveal herself to explorers although almost all the great sanctuaries, Pessinus, the two Comanas, Castabala, are as yet buried underground. We can, therefore, even now form a fairly exact idea of the beliefs of some of the countries that sent the Oriental mysteries to Rome. To tell the truth, these researches have not been pushed far enough to enable us to state precisely what form religion had assumed in those regions at the time they came into contact with Italy, and we should be likely to commit very strange errors, if we brought together practices that may have been separated by thousands of years. It is a task reserved for the future to establish a rigorous chronology in this matter, to determine the ultimate phase that the evolution of creeds in all regions of the Levant had reached at the beginning of our era, and to connect them without interruption of continuity to the mysteries practiced in the Latin world, the secrets of which archeological researches are slowly bringing to light.

We are still far from welding all the links of this long chain firmly together; the orientalists and the classical philologists cannot, as yet, shake hands across the Mediterranean. We raise only one corner of Isis's veil, and scarcely guess a part of the revelations that were, even formerly, reserved for a pious and chosen few. Nevertheless we have reached, on the road of certainty, a summit from which we can overlook the field that our successors will clear. In the course of these lectures I shall attempt to give a summary of the essential results achieved by the erudition of the nineteenth century and to draw from them a few conclusions that will, possibly, be provisional. The invasion of the Oriental religions that destroyed the ancient religions and national ideals of the Romans also radically transformed the society and government of the empire, and in view of this fact it would deserve the historian's attention even if it had not foreshadowed and prepared the final victory of Christianity.

WHY THE ORIENTAL RELIGIONS SPREAD.

WHEN, during the fourth century, the weakened empire split asunder like an overburdened scale whose beam is broken, this political divorce perpetuated a moral separation that had existed for a long time. The opposition between the Greco-Oriental and the Latin worlds manifests itself especially in religion and in the attitude taken by the central power toward it.

Occidental paganism was almost exclusively Latin under the empire. After the annexation of Spain, Gaul and Brittany, the old Iberian, Celtic and other religions were unable to keep up the unequal struggle against the more advanced religion of the conquerors. The marvelous rapidity with which the literature of the civilizing Romans was accepted by the subject peoples has frequently been pointed out. Its influence was felt in the temples as well as in the forum; it transformed the prayers to the gods as well as the conversation between men. Besides, it was part of the political program of the Cæsars to make the adoption of the Roman divinities general, and the government imposed the rules of its sacerdotal law as well as the principles of its public and civil law upon its new subjects. The municipal laws prescribed the election of pontiffs and augurs in common with the judicial duumvirs. In Gaul druidism, with its oral traditions embodied in

long poems, perished and disappeared less on account
of the police measures directed against it than in consequence of its voluntary relinquishment by the Celts,
as soon as they came under the ascendency of Latin
culture. In Spain it is difficult to find any traces of the
aboriginal religions. Even in Africa, where the Punic
religion was far more developed, it maintained itself
only by assuming an entirely Roman appearance. Baal
became Saturn and Eshmoun Æsculapius. It is doubtful if there was one temple in all the provinces of Italy
and Gaul where, at the time of the disappearance of
idolatry, the ceremonies were celebrated according to
native rites and in the local idiom. To this exclusive
predominance of Latin is due the fact that it remained
the only liturgic language of the Occidental church,
which here as in many other cases perpetuated a preexisting condition and maintained a unity previously
established. By imposing her speech upon the inhabitants of Ireland and Germany, Christian Rome simply
continued the work of assimilation in the barbarian
provinces subject to her influence that she had begun
while pagan.[1]

In the Orient, however, the churches that are separate from the Greek orthodoxy use, even to-day, a
variety of dialects calling to mind the great diversity
of races formerly subject to Rome. In those times
twenty varieties of speech translated the religious
thought of the peoples joined under the dominion of
the Cæsars. At the beginning of our era Hellenism
had not yet conquered the uplands of Anatolia,[2] nor
central Syria, nor the divisions of Egypt. Annexation
to the empire might retard and in certain regions
weaken the power of expansion of Greek civilization,

but it could not substitute Latin culture for it[3] except around the camps of the legions guarding the frontier and in a very few colonies. It especially benefitted the individuality of each region. The native religions retained all their prestige and independence. In their ancient sanctuaries that took rank with the richest and most famous of the world, a powerful clergy continued to practise ancestral devotions according to barbarian rites, and frequently in a barbarian tongue. The traditional liturgy, everywhere performed with scrupulous respect, remained Egyptian or Semitic, Phrygian or Persian, according to the locality.

Neither pontifical law nor augural science ever obtained credit outside of the Latin world. It is a characteristic fact that the worship of the deified emperors, the only official worship required of every one by the government as a proof of loyalty, should have originated of its own accord in Asia, received its inspiration from the purest monarchic traditions, and revived in form and spirit the veneration accorded to the Diadochi by their subjects.

Not only were the gods of Egypt and Asia never supplanted like those of Gaul or Spain, but they soon crossed the seas and gained worshipers in every Latin province. Isis and Serapis, Cybele and Attis, the Syrian Baals, Sabazius and Mithra were honored by brotherhoods of believers as far as the remotest limits of Germany. The Oriental reaction that we perceive from the beginning of our era, in studying the history of art, literature, and philosophy, manifested itself with incomparably greater power in the religious sphere. First, there was a slow infiltration of despised exotic religions, then, toward the end of the first cen-

tury, the Orontes, the Nile and the Halys, to use the
words of Juvenal, flowed into the Tiber, to the great
indignation of the old Romans.   Finally, a hundred
years later, an influx of Egyptian, Semitic and Persian beliefs and conceptions took place that threatened
to submerge all that the Greek and Roman genius had
laboriously built up.   What called forth and permitted
this spiritual commotion, of which the triumph of
Christianity was the outcome?   Why was the influence
of the Orient strongest in the religious field?   These
questions claim our attention.   Like all great phenomena of history, this particular one was determined by
a number of influences that concurred in producing it.
In the mass of half-known particulars that brought it
about, certain factors or leading causes, of which every
one has in turn been considered the most important,
may be distinguished.

If we yielded to the tendency of many excellent
minds of to-day and regarded history as the resultant
of economic and social forces, it would be easy to show
their influence in that great religious movement.   The
industrial and commercial preponderance of the Orient
was manifest, for there were situated the principal centers of production and export.   The ever increasing
traffic with the Levant induced merchants to establish
themselves in Italy, in Gaul, in the Danubian countries, in Africa and in Spain; in some cities they formed
real colonies.   The Syrian emigrants were especially
numerous.   Compliant, quick and diligent, they went
wherever they expected profit, and their colonies, scattered as far as the north of Gaul, were centers for the
religious propaganda of paganism just as the Jewish
communities of the Diaspora were for Christian preach-

ing. Italy not only bought her grain from Egypt, she
imported men also; she ordered slaves from Phrygia,
Cappadocia, Syria and Alexandria to cultivate her depopulated fields and perform the domestic duties in
her palaces. Who can tell what influence chamber-
maids from Antioch or Memphis gained over the minds
of their mistresses? At the same time the necessities
of war removed officers and men from the Euphrates
to the Rhine or to the outskirts of the Sahara, and
everywhere they remained faithful to the gods of their
far-away country. The requirements of the government transferred functionaries and their clerks, the
latter frequently of servile birth, into the most distant
provinces. Finally, the ease of communication, due
to the good roads, increased the frequency and extent
of travel.

Thus the exchange of products, men and ideas necessarily increased, and it might be maintained that theoc-
racy was a necessary consequence of the mingling of
the races, that the gods of the Orient followed the great
commercial and social currents, and that their establishment in the Occident was a natural result of the
movement that drew the excess population of the
Asiatic cities and rural districts into the less thickly
inhabited countries.

These reflections, which could be developed at some
length, surely show the way in which the Oriental religions spread. It is certain that the merchants acted
as missionaries in the seaports and places of commerce,
the soldiers on the frontiers and in the capital, the
slaves in the city homes,4 in the rural districts and in
public affairs. But while this acquaints us with the
means and the agents of the diffusion of those religions,

it tells us nothing of the reasons for their adoption by the Romans. We perceive the how, but not the why, of their sudden expansion. Especially imperfect is our understanding of the reasons for the difference between the Orient and the Occident pointed out above.

An example will make my meaning clear. A Celtic divinity, Epona,[5] was held in particular honor as the protectress of horses, as we all know. The Gallic horsemen worshiped her wherever they were cantoned; her monuments have been found scattered from Scotland to Transylvania. And yet, although this goddess enjoyed the same conditions as, for instance, Jupiter *Dolichenus* whom the cohorts of Commagene introduced into Europe, it does not appear that she ever received the homage of many strangers; it does not appear, above all, that druidism ever assumed the shape of "mysteries of Epona" into which Greeks and Romans would have asked to be initiated. It was too deficient in the intrinsic strength of the Oriental religions, to make proselytes.

Other historians and thinkers of to-day prefer to apply the laws of natural science to religious phenomena; and the theories about the variation of species find an unforeseen application here. It is maintained that the immigration of Orientals, of Syrians in particular, was considerable enough to provoke an alteration and rapid deterioration in the robust Italic and Celtic races. In addition, a social status contrary to nature, and a bad political régime effected the destruction of the strongest, the extermination of the best and the ascendancy of the worst elements of the population. This multitude, corrupted by deleterious cross-breeding and weakened by bad selection, became unable to oppose the invasion of the Asiatic chimeras and aberrations. A lowering of the intellectual level and the disappearance of the critical spirit accompanied the decline of morals and the weakening of character. In the evolution of beliefs the triumph of the Orient denoted a regression toward barbarism, a return to the remote origins of faith and to the worship of natural forces. This is a brief outline of explanations recently proposed and received with some favor.[6]

It cannot be denied that souls and morals appear to have become coarser during the Roman decline. Society as a whole was deplorably lacking in imagination, intellect and taste. It seemed afflicted with a kind of cerebral anemia and incurable sterility. The impaired reason accepted the coarsest superstitions, the most extreme asceticism and most extravagant theurgy. It resembled an organism incapable of defending itself against contagion. All this is partly true; but the theories summarized proceed from an incorrect conception of things; in reality they are based on the illusion that Asia, under the empire, was inferior to Europe. While the triumph of the Oriental religions sometimes assumed the appearance of an awakening of savagery, these religions in reality represented a more advanced type in the evolution of religious forms than the ancient national devotions. They were less primitive, less simple, and, if I may use the expression, provided with more organs than the old Greco-Roman idolatry. We have indicated this on previous occasions, and hope to bring it out with perfect clearness in the course of these studies.

It is hardly necessary to state that a great religious conquest can be explained only on moral grounds.

Whatever part must be ascribed to the instinct of imitation and the contagion of example, in the last analysis we are always face to face with a series of individual conversions. The mysterious affinity of minds is as much due to reflection as to the continued and almost unconscious influence of confused aspirations that produce faith. The obscure gestation of a new ideal is accomplished with pangs of anguish. Violent struggles must have disturbed the souls of the masses when they were torn away from their old ancestral religions, or more often from indifference, by those exacting gods who demanded a surrender of the entire person, a *devotion* in the etymological meaning of the word. The consecration to Isis of the hero of Apuleius was the result of a call, of an appeal, by the goddess who wanted the neophyte to enlist in her sacred militia.[7]

If it is true that every conversion involves a psychological crisis, a transformation of the intimate personality of the individual, this is especially true of the propagation of the Oriental religions. Born outside of the narrow limits of the Roman city, they grew up frequently in hostility to it, and were international, consequently individual. The bond that formerly kept devotion centered upon the city or the tribe, upon the *gens* or the family, was broken. In place of the ancient social groups communities of initiates came into existence, who considered themselves brothers no matter where they came from.[8] A god, conceived of as being universal, received every mortal as his child. Whenever these religions had any relation to the state they were no longer called upon to support old municipal or social institutions, but to lend their strength to the authority of a sovereign regarded as the eternal lord of the whole world jointly with God himself. In the circles of the mystics, Asiatics mingled with Romans, and slaves with high functionaries. The adoption of the same faith made the poor freedman the equal and sometimes the superior, of the decurion and the *clarissimus*. All submitted to the same rules and participated in the same festivities, in which the distinctions of an aristocratic society and the differences of blood and country were obliterated. The distinctions of race and nationality, of magistrate and father of a family, of patrician and plebeian, of citizen and foreigner, were abolished; all were but men, and in order to recruit members, those religions worked upon man and his character.

In order to gain the masses and the cream of Roman society (as they did for a whole century) the barbarian mysteries had to possess a powerful charm, they had to satisfy the deep wants of the human soul, and their strength had to be superior to that of the ancient Greco-Roman religion. To explain the reasons for their victory we must try to reveal the nature of this superiority—I mean their superiority in the struggle, without assuming innate superiority.

I believe that we can define it by stating that those religions gave greater satisfaction first, to the senses and passions, secondly, to the intelligence, finally, and above all, to the conscience.

In the first place, they appealed more strongly to the senses. This was their most obvious feature, and it has been pointed out more often than any other. Perhaps there never was a religion so cold and prosaic as the Roman. Being subordinated to politics, it sought,

above all, to secure the protection of the gods for the
state and to avert the effects of their malevolence by
the strict execution of appropriate practices. It entered
into a contract with the celestial powers from which
mutual obligations arose: sacrifices on one side, favors
on the other. The pontiffs, who were also magistrates,
regulated the religious practices with the exact precision of jurists;[9] as far as we know the prayers were all
couched in formulas as dry and verbose as notarial
instruments. The liturgy reminds one of the ancient
civil law on account of the minuteness of its prescriptions. This religion looked suspiciously at the abandonment of the soul to the ecstasies of devotion. It re-
pressed, by force if necessary, the exuberant manifestations of too ardent faith and everything that was
not in keeping with the grave dignity befitting the
relations of a *civis Romanus* with a god. The Jews
had the same scrupulous respect as the Romans for a
religious code and formulas of the past, "but in spite
of their dry and minute practices, the legalism of the
Pharisees stirred the heart more strongly than did
Roman formalism."[10]

Lacking the recognized authority of official creeds,
the Oriental religions had to appeal to the passions of
the individual in order to make proselytes. They attracted men first by the disturbing seductiveness of
their mysteries, where terror and hope were evoked in
turns, and charmed them by the pomp of their festivities and the magnificence of their processions. Men
were fascinated by the languishing songs and intoxi-
cating melodies. Above all these religions taught men
how to reach that blissful state in which the soul was
freed from the tyranny of the body and of suffering,

and lost itself in raptures. They led to ecstasy either by means of nervous tension resulting from continued maceration and fervent contemplation or by more material means like the stimulation of vertiginous dances and dizzy music, or even by the absorption of fermented liquors after a long abstinence,[11]as in the case of the priests of the Great Mother. In mysticism it is easy to descend from the sublime to the vile.

Even the gods, with whom the believers thought they were uniting themselves in their mystic outbursts, were more human and sometimes more sensual than those of the Occident. The latter had that quietude of soul in which the philosophic morality of the Greeks saw a privilege of the sage; in the serenity of Olympus they enjoyed perpetual youth; they were Immortals. The divinities of the Orient, on the contrary, suffered and died, but only to revive again.[12] Osiris, Attis and Adonis were mourned like mortals by wife or mistress, Isis, Cybele or Astarte. With them the mystics moaned for their deceased god and later, after he had revived, celebrated with exultation his birth to a new life. Or else they joined in the passion of Mithra, condemned to create the world in suffering. This common grief and joy were often expressed with savage violence, by bloody mutilations, long wails of despair, and extravagant acclamations. The manifestations of the extreme fanaticism of those barbarian races that had not been touched by Greek skepticism and the very ardor of their faith inflamed the souls of the multitudes attracted by the exotic gods.

The Oriental religions touched every chord of sensibility and satisfied the thirst for religious emotion that the austere Roman creed had been unable to quench.

But at the same time they satisfied the intellect more fully, and this is my second point.

In very early times Greece—later imitated by Rome —became resolutely rationalistic: her greatest originality lies here. Her philosophy was purely laical; thought was unrestrained by any sacred tradition; it even pretended to pass judgment upon these traditions and condemned or approved of them. Being sometimes hostile, sometimes indifferent and some times conciliatory, it always remained independent of faith. But while Greece thus freed herself from the fetters of a superannuated mythology, and openly and boldly constructed those systems of metaphysics by means of which she claimed to solve the enigmas of the universe, her religion lost its vitality and dried up because it lacked the strengthening nourishment of reflection. It became a thing devoid of sense, whose *raison d'être* was no longer understood; it embodied dead ideas and an obsolete conception of the world. In Greece as well as at Rome it was reduced to a collection of unintelligible rites, scrupulously and mechanically reproduced without addition or omission because they had been practised by the ancestors of long ago, and formulas hallowed by the *mos maiorum,* that were no longer understood or sincerely cherished. Never did a people of advanced culture have a more infantile religion.

The Oriental civilizations on the contrary were sacerdotal in character. As in medieval Europe, the scholars of Asia and Egypt were priests. In the temples the nature of the gods and of man were not the only subjects of discussion; mathematics, astronomy, medicine, philology and history were also studied. The successors of Berosus, a priest from Babylonia, and

Manetho, a priest from Heliopolis, were considered deeply versed in all intellectual disciplines as late as the time of Strabo.[13]

This state of affairs proved detrimental to the progress of science. Researches were conducted according to preconceived ideas and were perverted through strange prejudices. Astrology and magic were the monstrous fruit of a hybrid union. But all this certainly gave religion a power it had never possessed either in Greece or Rome.

All results of observation, all conquests of thought, were used by an erudite clergy to attain the principal object of their activities, the solution of the problem of the destiny of man and matter, and of the relations of heaven and earth. An ever enlarging conception of the universe kept transforming the modes of belief. Faith presumed to enslave both physics and metaphysics. The credit of every discovery was given to the gods. Thoth in Egypt and Bel in Chaldea were the revealers not only of theology and the ritual, but of all human knowledge.[14] The names of the Oriental Hipparchi and Euclids who solved the first problems of astronomy and geometry were unknown; but a confused and grotesque literature made use of the name and authority of Hermes Trismegistus. The doctrines of the planetary spheres and the opposition of the four elements were made to support systems of anthropology and of morality; the theorems of astronomy were used to establish an alleged method of divination; formulas of incantation, supposed to subject divine powers to the magician, were combined with chemical experiments and medical prescriptions.

This intimate union of erudition and faith continued

in the Latin world.   Theology became more and more
a process of deification of the principles or agents discovered by science and a worship of time regarded as
the first cause, the stars whose course determined the
events of this world, the four elements whose innumerable combinations produced the natural phenomena,
and especially the sun which preserved heat, fertility
and life.   The dogmas of the mysteries of Mithra were,
to a certain extent, the religious expression of Roman
physics and astronomy.   In all forms of pantheism the
knowledge of nature appears to be inseparable from
that of God.[15]   Art itself complied more and more
with the tendency to express erudite ideas by subtle
symbolism, and it represented in allegorical figures the
relations of divine powers and cosmic forces, like the
sky, the earth, the ocean, the planets, the constellations
and the winds.   The sculptors engraved on stone everything man thought and taught.   In a general way the
belief prevailed that redemption and salvation depended
on the revelation of certain truths, on a knowledge of
the gods, of the world and of our person, and piety
became gnosis.[16]

But, you will say, since in the classic age philosophy
also claimed to lead to morality through instruction
and to acquaint man with the supreme good, why did
it yield to Oriental religions that were in reality neither
original nor innovating?   Quite right, and if a powerful rationalist school, possessed of a good critical
method, had led the minds, we may believe that it
would have checked the invasion of the barbarian mysteries or at least limited their field of action.   However,
as has frequently been pointed out, even in ancient
Greece the philosophic critics had very little hold on

popular religion obstinately faithful to its inherited superstitious forms. But how many second century minds shared Lucian's skepticism in regard to the dogmatic systems! The various sects were fighting each other for ever so long without convincing one another of their alleged error. The satirist of Samosata enjoyed opposing their exclusive pretensions while he himself reclined on the "soft pillow of doubt." But only intelligent minds could delight in doubt or surrender to it; the masses wanted certainties. There was nothing to revive confidence in the power of a decrepit and threadbare science. No great discovery transformed the conception of the universe. Nature no longer betrayed her secrets, the earth remained unexplored and the past inscrutable. Every branch of knowledge was forgotten. The world cursed with sterility, could but repeat itself; it had the poignant appreciation of its own decay and impotence. Tired of fruitless researches, the mind surrendered to the necessity of believing. Since the intellect was unable to formulate a consistent rule of life faith alone could supply it, and the multitudes gravitated toward the temples, where the truths taught to man in earlier days by the Oriental gods were revealed. The stanch adherence of past generations to beliefs and rites of unlimited antiquity seemed to guarantee their truth and efficacy. This current was so strong that philosophy itself was swept toward mysticism and the neo-Platonist school became a theurgy.

The Oriental mysteries, then, could stir the soul by arousing admiration and terror, pity and enthusiasm in turn. They gave the intellect the illusion of learned depth and absolute certainty and finally—our third

point—they satisfied conscience as well as passion and
reason. Among the complex causes that guaranteed
their domination, this was without doubt the most
effective.

In every period of their history the Romans, unlike
the Greeks in this respect, judged theories and institutions especially by their practical results. They always had a soldier's and business man's contempt for
metaphysicians. It is a matter of frequent observation
that the philosophy of the Latin world neglected metaphysical speculations and concentrated its attention on
morals, just as later the Roman church left to the subtle
Hellenes the interminable controversies over the essence of the divine logos and the double nature of
Christ. Questions that could rouse and divide her were
those having a direct application to life, like the doctrine of grace.

The old religion of the Romans had to respond to
this demand of their genius. Its poverty was honest.[17]
Its mythology did not possess the poetic charm of that
of Greece, nor did its gods have the imperishable beauty
of the Olympians, but they were more moral, or at least
pretended to be. A large number were simply personified qualities, like chastity and piety. With the aid of
the censors they imposed the practice of the national
virtues, that is to say of the qualities useful to society,
temperance, courage, chastity, obedience to parents and
magistrates, reverence for the oath and the law, in fact,
the practice of every form of patriotism. During the
last century of the republic the pontiff Scaevola, one
of the foremost men of his time, rejected as futile the
divinities of fable and poetry, as superfluous or ob-
noxious those of the philosophers and the exegetists,

and reserved all his favors for those of the statesmen, as the only ones fit for the people.[18] These were the ones protecting the old customs, traditions and frequently even the old privileges. But in the perpetual flux of things conservatism ever carries with it a germ of death. Just as the law failed to maintain the integrity of ancient principles, like the absolute power of the father of the family, principles that were no longer in keeping with the social realities, so religion witnessed the foundering of a system of ethics contrary to the moral code that had slowly been established. The idea of collective responsibility contained in a number of beliefs is one instance. If a vestal violated her vow of chastity the divinity sent a pest that ceased only on the day the culprit was punished. Sometimes the angry heavens granted victory to the army only on condition that a general or soldier dedicate himself to the infernal gods as an expiatory victim. However, through the influence of the philosophers and the jurists the conviction slowly gained ground that each one was responsible for his own misdeeds, and that it was not equitable to make a whole city suffer for the crime of an individual. People ceased to admit that the gods crushed the good as well as the wicked in one punishment. Often, also, the divine anger was thought to be as ridiculous in its manifestations as in its cause. The rural superstitions of the country districts of Latium continued to live in the pontifical code of the Roman people. If a lamb with two heads or a colt with five legs was born, solemn supplications were prescribed to avert the misfortunes foreboded by those terrifying prodigies.[19]

All these puerile and monstrous beliefs that burdened

the religion of the Latins had thrown it into disrepute. Its morality no longer responded to the new conception of justice beginning to prevail. As a rule Rome remedied the poverty of her theology and ritual by taking what she needed from the Greeks. But here this resource failed her because the poetic, artistic and even intellectual religion of the Greeks was hardly moral. And the fables of a mythology jeered at by the philosophers, parodied on the stage and put to verse by libertine poets were anything but edifying.

Moreover—this was its second weakness—whatever morality it demanded of a pious man went unrewarded. People no longer believed that the gods continually intervened in the affairs of men to reveal hidden crimes and to punish triumphant vice, or that Jupiter would hurl his thunderbolt to crush the perjurer. At the time of the proscriptions and the civil wars under Nero or Commodus it was more than plain that power and possessions were for the strongest, the ablest or even the luckiest, and not for the wisest or the most pious. The idea of reward or punishment beyond the grave found little credit. The notions of future life were hazy, uncertain, doubtful and contradictory. Everybody knows Juvenal's famous lines: "That there are manes, a subterranean kingdom, a ferryman with a long pole, and black frogs in the whirlpools of the Styx; that so many thousand men could cross the waves in a single boat, to-day even children refuse to believe."[20]

After the fall of the republic indifference spread, the temples were abandoned and threatened to tumble into ruins, the clergy found it difficult to recruit members, the festivities, once so popular, fell into desuetude, and

Varro, at the beginning of his *Antiquities,* expressed his fear lest "the gods might perish, not from the blows of foreign enemies, but from very neglect on the part of the citizens."[21]   It is well known that Augustus, prompted by political rather than by religious reasons, attempted to revive the dying religion.   His religious reforms stood in close relation to his moral legislation and the establishment of the imperial dignity.   Their tendency was to bring the people back to the pious practice of ancient virtues but also to chain them to the new political order.   The alliance of throne and altar in Europe dates from that time.

This attempted reform failed entirely.   Making religion an auxiliary to moral policing is not a means of establishing its empire over souls.   Formal reverence for the official gods is not incompatible with absolute and practical skepticism.   The restoration attempted by Augustus is nevertheless very characteristic because it is so consistent with the Roman spirit which by temperament and tradition demanded that religion should support morality and the state.

The Asiatic religions fulfilled the requirements.   The change of régime, although unwelcome, brought about a change of religion.   The increasing tendency of Cæsarism toward absolute monarchy made it lean more and more upon the Oriental clergy.   True to the traditions of the Achemenides and the Pharaohs, those priests preached doctrines tending to elevate the sovereign above humanity, and they supplied the emperors with dogmatic justification for their despotism.[22]

It is a noteworthy fact that the rulers who most loudly proclaimed their autocratic pretentions, like Domitian and Commodus, were also those that favored foreign creeds most openly.

But his selfish support merely sanctioned a power already established. The propaganda of the Oriental religions was originally democratic and sometimes even revolutionary like the Isis worship. Step by step they advanced, always reaching higher social classes and appealing to popular conscience rather than to the zeal of functionaries.

As a matter of fact all these religions, except that of Mithra, seem at first sight to be far less austere than the Roman creed. We shall have occasion to note that they contained coarse and immodest fables and atrocious or vile rites. The Egyptian gods were expelled from Rome by Augustus and Tiberius on the charge of being immoral, but they were called immoral principally because they opposed a certain conception of the social order. They gave little attention to the public interest but attached considerable importance to the inner life and consequently to the value of the individual. Two new things, in particular, were brought to Italy by the Oriental priests: mysterious methods of purification, by which they claimed to wash away the impurities of the soul, and the assurance that a blessed immortality would be the reward of piety.[23]

These religions pretended to restore lost purity[24] to the soul either through the performance of ritual ceremonies or through mortifications and penance. They had a series of ablutions and lustrations supposed to restore original innocence to the mystic. He had to wash himself in the sacred water according to certain prescribed forms. This was really a magic rite, because bodily purity acted sympathetically upon the soul, or

else it was a real spiritual disinfection with the water
driving out the evil spirits that had caused pollution.
The votary, again, might drink or besprinkle himself
with the blood of a slaughtered victim or of the priests
themselves, in which case the prevailing idea was that
the liquid circulating in the veins was a vivifying principle capable of imparting a new existence.[25] These
and similar rites[26] used in the mysteries were supposed
to regenerate the initated person and to restore him to
an immaculate and incorruptible life.[27]

Purgation of the soul was not effected solely by
liturgic acts but also by self-denial and suffering.[28]
The meaning of the term *expiatio* changed. Expiation,
or atonement, was no longer accomplished by the exact
performance of certain ceremonies pleasing to the gods
and required by a sacred code like a penalty for dam-
ages, but by privation and personal suffering. Abstinence, which prevented the introduction of deadly
elements into the system, and chastity, which preserved
man from pollution and debility, became means of
getting rid of the domination of the evil powers and of
regaining heavenly favor.[29] Macerations, laborious
pilgrimages, public confessions, sometimes flagellations
and mutilations, in fact all forms of penance and mortifications uplifted the fallen man and brought him
nearer to the gods. In Phrygia a sinner would write
his sin and the punishment he suffered upon a stela for
every one to see and would return thanks to heaven
that his prayer of repentance had been heard.[30] The
Syrian, who had offended his goddess by eating her
sacred fish, dressed in sordid rags, covered himself with
a sack and sat in the public highway humbly to proclaim his misdeed in order to obtain forgiveness.[31]

"Three times, in the depths of winter," says Juvenal, "the devotee of Isis will dive into the chilly waters of the Tiber, and shivering with cold, will drag herself around the temple upon her bleeding knees; if the goddess commands, she will go to the outskirts of Egypt to take water from the Nile and empty it within the sanctuary."[32]   This shows the introduction into Europe of Oriental asceticism.

But there were impious acts and impure passions that contaminated and defiled the soul.   Since this infection could be destroyed only by expiations prescribed by the gods, the extent of the sin and the character of the necessary penance had to be estimated.   It was the priest's prerogative to judge the misdeeds and to impose the penalties.   This circumstance gave the clergy a very different character from the one it had at Rome.   The priest was no longer simply the guardian of sacred traditions, the intermediary between man or the state and the gods, but also a spiritual guide.   He taught his flock the long series of obligations and restrictions for shielding their weakness from the attacks of evil spirits.   He knew how to quiet remorse and scruples, and to restore the sinner to spiritual calm.   Being versed in sacred knowledge, he had the power of reconciling the gods.   Frequent sacred repasts maintained a spirit of fellowship among the mystics of Cybele, Mithra or the Baals,[33] and a daily service unceasingly revived the faith of the Isis worshipers.   In consequence, the clergy were entirely absorbed in their holy office and lived only for and by their temples.   Unlike the sacerdotal colleges of Rome in which the secular and religious functions were not yet clearly differentiated,[34] they were not an

administrative commission ruling the sacred affairs of
the state under the supervision of the senate; they
formed what might almost be called a caste of recluses
distinguished from ordinary men by their insignia, garb,
habits and food, and constituting an independent body
with a hierarchy, formulary and even councils of their
own.[35] They did not return to every-day duties as
private citizens or to the direction of public affairs as
magistrates as the ancient pontiffs had done after the
solemn festival service.

We can readily understand that these beliefs and institutions were bound to establish the Oriental religions
and their priests on a strong basis. Their influence
must have been especially powerful at the time of the
Cæsars. The laxity of morals at the beginning of our
era has been exaggerated but it was real. Many un-
healthy symptoms told of a profound moral anarchy
weighing on a weakened and irresolute society. The
farther we go toward the end of the empire the more
its energy seems to fail and the character of men to
weaken. The number of strong healthy minds incapable of a lasting aberration and without need of
guidance or comfort was growing ever smaller. We
note the spread of that feeling of exhaustion and debility which follows the aberrations of passion, and the
same weakness that led to crime impelled men to seek
absolution in the formal practices of asceticism. They
applied to the Oriental priests for spiritual remedies.

People flattered themselves that by performing the
rites they would attain a condition of felicity after
death. All barbarian mysteries pretended to reveal to
their adherents the secret of blessed immortality. Participation in the occult ceremonies of the sect was a

chief means of salvation.[36] The vague and dishearten-
ing beliefs of ancient paganism in regard to life after
death were transformed into the firm hope of a well-
defined form of happiness.[37]

This faith in a personal survival of the soul and even
of the body was based upon a strong instinct of human
nature, the instinct of self-preservation. Social and
moral conditions in the empire during its decline gave
it greater strength than it had ever possessed before.[38]
The third century saw so much suffering, anguish and
violence, so much unnecessary ruin and so many un-
punished crimes, that the Roman world took refuge in
the expectation of a better existence in which all the
iniquity of this world would be retrieved. No earthly
hope brightened life. The tyranny of a corrupt bureaucracy choked all disposition for political progress.
Science stagnated and revealed no more unknown
truths. Growing poverty discouraged the spirit of
enterprise. The idea gained ground that humanity
was afflicted with incurable decay, that nature was
approaching her doom and that the end of world was
near.[39] We must remember all these causes of dis-
couragement and despondency to understand the power
of the idea, expressed so frequently, that the spirit
animating man was forced by bitter necessity to im-
prison itself in matter and that it was delivered from
its carnal captivity by death. In the heavy atmosphere
of a period of oppression and impotence the dejected
soul longed with incredible ardor to fly to the radiant
abode of heaven.

To recapitulate, the Oriental religions acted upon
the senses, the intellect and the conscience at the same
time, and therefore gained a hold on the entire man.

Compared with the ancient creeds, they appear to have
offered greater beauty of ritual, greater truth of doctrine and a far superior morality. The imposing ceremonial of their festivities and the alternating pomp and
sensuality, gloom and exaltation of their services appealed especially to the simple and the humble, while
the progressive revelation of ancient wisdom, inherited
from the old and distant Orient, captivated the cultured mind. The emotions excited by these religions
and the consolations offered strongly attracted the women, who were the most fervent and generous followers and most passionate propagandists[40] of the religions of Isis and Cybele. Mithra was worshiped
almost exclusively by men, whom he subjected to a
rigid moral discipline. Thus souls were gained by the
promise of spiritual purification and the prospect of
eternal happiness.

The worship of the Roman gods was a civic duty, the
worship of the foreign gods the expression of a personal belief. The latter were the objects of the
thoughts, feelings and intimate aspirations of the individual, not merely of the traditional and, one might
say, functional adoration of the citizen. The ancient
municipal devotions were connected with a number of
earthly interests that helped to support each other.
They were one of various forms of family spirit and
patriotism and guaranteed the prosperity of the community. The Oriental mysteries, directing the will
toward an ideal goal and exalting the inner spirit, were
less mindful of economic utility, but they could produce
that vibration of the moral being that caused emotions,
stronger than any rational faculty, to gush forth from
the depths of the soul. Through a sudden illumination

they furnished the intuition of a spiritual life whose intensity made all material happiness appear insipid and contemptible. This stirring appeal of supernatural life made the propaganda irresistible. The same ardent enthusiasm guaranteed at the same time the uncontested domination of neo-Platonism among the philosophers. Antiquity expired and a new era was born.

ASIA MINOR.

THE first Oriental religion adopted by the Romans was that of the goddess of Phrygia, whom the people of Pessinus and Mount Ida worshiped, and who received the name of *Magna Mater deum Idea* in the Occident. Its history in Italy covers six centuries, and we can trace each phase of the transformation that changed it in the course of time from a collection of very primitive nature beliefs into a system of spiritualized mysteries used by some as a weapon against Christianity. We shall now endeavor to outline the successive phases of that slow metamorphosis.

This religion is the only one whose success in the Latin world was caused originally by a mere chance circumstance. In 205 B. C., when Hannibal, vanquished but still threatening, made his last stand in the mountains of Bruttium, repeated torrents of stones frightened the Roman people. When the books were officially consulted in regard to this prodigy they promised that the enemy would be driven from Italy if the Great Mother of Ida could be brought to Rome. Nobody but the Sibyls themselves had the power of averting the evils prophesied by them. They had come to Italy from Asia Minor, and in this critical situation their sacred poem recommended the practice of their native religion as a remedy. In token of his friendship, King Attalus presented the ambassadors of the senate with the black aerolite, supposed to be the abode of the goddess, that this ruler had shortly before transferred from Pessinus to Pergamum. According to the mandate of the oracle the stone was received at Ostia by the best citizen of the land, an honor accorded to Scipio Nasica—and carried by the most esteemed matrons to the Palatine, where, hailed by the cheers of the multitude and surrounded by fumes of incense, it was solemnly installed (Nones of April, 204). This triumphal entry was later glorified by marvelous legends, and the poets told of edifying miracles that had occurred during Cybele's voyage. In the same year Scipio transferred the seat of war to Africa, and Hannibal, compelled to meet him there, was beaten at Zama. The prediction of the Sybils had come true and Rome was rid of the long Punic terror. The foreign goddess was honored in recognition of the service she had rendered. A temple was erected to her on the summit of the Palatine, and every year a celebration enhanced by scenic plays, the *ludi Megalenses,* commemorated the date of dedication of the sanctuary and the arrival of the goddess (April 4th-10th).

What was this Asiatic religion that had suddenly been transferred into the heart of Rome by an extraordinary circumstance? Even then it could look back upon a long period of development. It combined beliefs of various origin. It contained primitive usages of the religion of Anatolia, some of which have survived to this day in spite of Christianity and Islam. Like the Kizil-Bash peasants of to-day, the ancient inhabitants of the peninsula met on the summits of mountains covered with woods no ax had desecrated, and celebrated their festal days.[1] They believed that Cybele resided on the high summits of Ida and Berecyntus, and the perennial pines, in conjunction with the prolific and early maturing almond tree, were the sacred trees of Attis. Besides trees, the country people worshiped stones, rocks or meteors that had fallen from the sky like the one taken from Pessinus to Pergamum and thence to Rome. They also venerated certain animals, especially the most powerful of them all, the lion, who may at one time have been the totem of savage tribes.[2] In mythology as well as in art the lion remained the riding or driving animal of the Great Mother. Their conception of the divinity was indistinct and impersonal. A goddess of the earth, called Mâ or Cybele, was revered as the fecund mother of all things, the "mistress of the wild beasts"[3] that inhabit the woods. A god Attis, or Papas, was regarded as her husband, but the first place in this divine household belonged to the woman, a reminiscence of the period of matriarchy.[4]

When the Phrygians at a very early period came from Thrace and inserted themselves like a wedge in the old Anatolian races, they adopted the vague deities of their new country by identifying them with their own, after the habit of pagan nations. Thus Attis became one with the Dionysus-Sabazius of the conquerors, or at least assumed some of his characteristics. This Thracian Dionysus was a god of vegetation. Foucart has thus admirably pictured his savage nature: "Wooded summits, deep oak and pine forests, ivy-clad caverns were at all times his favorite haunts. Mortals who were anxious to know the powerful divinity ruling these solitudes had to observe the life of his kingdom, and to guess the god's nature from the phenomena through which he manifested his power. Seeing the creeks descend in noisy foaming cascades, or hearing the roaring of steers in the uplands and the strange sounds of the wind-beaten forests, the Thracians thought they heard the voice and the calls of the lord of that empire, and imagined a god who was fond of extravagant leaps and of wild roaming over the wooded mountains. This conception inspired their religion, for the surest way for mortals to ingratiate themselves with a divinity was to imitate him, and as far as possible to make their lives resemble his. For this reason the Thracians endeavored to attain the divine delirium that transported their Dionysus, and hoped to realize their purpose by following their invisible yet ever-present lord in his chase over the mountains."[5]

In the Phrygian religion we find the same beliefs and rites, scarcely modified at all, with the one difference that Attis, the god of vegetation, was united to the goddess of the earth instead of living "in sullen loneliness." When the tempest was beating the forests of the Berecyntus or Ida, it was Cybele traveling about in her car drawn by roaring lions mourning her lover's death. A crowd of worshipers followed her through woods and thickets, mingling their shouts with the shrill sound of flutes, with the dull beat of tambourines, with the rattling of castanets and the dissonance of brass cymbals. Intoxicated with shouting and with uproar of the instruments, excited by their impetuous advance, breathless and panting, they surrendered to the raptures of a sacred enthusiasm. Catullus has left us a dramatic description of this divine ecstasy.[6]

The religion of Phrygia was perhaps even more violent than that of Thrace. The climate of the Anatolian uplands is one of extremes. Its winters are rough, long and cold, the spring rains suddenly develop a vigorous vegetation that is scorched by the hot summer sun. The abrupt contrasts of a nature generous and sterile, radiant and bleak in turn, caused excesses of sadness and joy that were unknown in temperate and smiling regions, where the ground was never buried under snow nor scorched by the sun. The Phrygians mourned the long agony and death of the vegetation, but when the verdure reappeared in March they surrendered to the excitement of a tumultuous joy. In Asia savage rites that had been unknown in Thrace or practiced in milder form expressed the vehemence of those opposing feelings. In the midst of their orgies, and after wild dances, some of the worshipers voluntarily wounded themselves and, becoming intoxicated with the view of the blood, with which they besprinkled their altars, they believed they were uniting themselves with their divinity. Or else, arriving at a paroxysm of frenzy, they sacrificed their virility to the gods as certain Russian dissenters still do to-day. These men became priests of Cybele and were called Galli. Violent ecstasis was always an endemic disease in Phrygia. As late as the Antonines, montanist prophets that arose in that country attempted to introduce it into Christianity.

All these excessive and degrading demonstrations of an extreme worship must not cause us to slight the power of the feeling that inspired it. The sacred ecstasy, the voluntary mutilations and the eagerly sought sufferings manifested an ardent longing for deliverance from subjection to carnal instincts, and a fervent desire to free the soul from the bonds of matter. The ascetic tendencies went so far as to create a kind of begging monachism—the *métragyrtes*. They also harmonized with some of the ideas of renunciation taught by Greek philosophy, and at an early period Hellenic theologians took an interest in this devotion that attracted and repelled them at the same time. Timotheus the Eumolpid, who was one of the founders of the Alexandrian religion of Serapis, derived the inspiration for his essays on religious reform, among other sources, from the ancient Phrygian myths. Those thinkers undoubtedly succeeded in making the priests of Pessinus themselves admit many speculations quite foreign to the old Anatolian nature worship. The votaries of Cybele began at a very remote period to practise "mysteries"[7] in which the initiates were made acquainted, by degrees, with a wisdom that was always considered divine, but underwent peculiar variations in the course of time.

* * *

Such is the religion which the rough Romans of the Punic wars accepted and adopted. Hidden under theological and cosmological doctrines it contained an ancient stock of very primitive and coarse religious ideas, such as the worship of trees, stones and animals. Besides this superstitious fetichism it involved ceremonies that were both· sensual and ribald, including all the wild and mystic rites of the bacchanalia which the public authorities were to prohibit a few years later.

When the senate became better acquainted with the divinity imposed upon it by the Sibyls, it must have been quite embarrassed by the present of King Attalus.

The enthusiastic transports and the somber fanaticism of the Phrygian worship contrasted violently with the calm dignity and respectable reserve of the official religion, and excited the minds of the people to a dangerous degree. The emasculated Galli were the objects of contempt and disgust and what in their own eyes was a meritorious act was made a crime punishable by law, at least under the empire.[8] The authorities hesitated between the respect due to the powerful goddess that had delivered Rome from the Carthaginians and the reverence for the *mos maiorum.* They solved the difficulty by completely isolating the new religion in order to prevent its contagion. All citizens were forbidden to join the priesthood of the foreign goddess or to participate in her sacred orgies. The barbarous rites according to which the Great Mother was to be worshiped were performed by Phrygian priests and priestesses. The holidays celebrated in her honor by the entire nation, the *Megalensia,* contained no Oriental feature and were organized in conformity with Roman traditions.

A characteristic anecdote told by Diodorus[9] shows what the public feeling was towards this Asiatic worship at the end of the republic. In Pompey's time a high priest from Pessinus came to Rome, presented himself at the forum in his sacerdotal garb, a golden diadem and a long embroidered robe—and pretending that the statue of his goddess had been profaned demanded public expiation. But a tribune forbade him to wear the royal crown, and the populace rose against him in a mob and compelled him to seek refuge in his house. Although apologies were made later, this story shows how little the people of that period felt

the veneration that attached to Cybele and her clergy
after a century had passed.

Kept closely under control, the Phrygian worship
led an obscure existence until the establishment of the
empire. That closed the first period of its history at
Rome. It attracted attention only on certain holidays,
when its priests marched the streets in procession,
dressed in motley costumes, loaded with heavy jewelry,
and beating tambourines. On those days the senate
granted them the right to go from house to house to
collect funds for their temples. The remainder of the
year they confined themselves to the sacred enclosure
of the Palatine, celebrating foreign ceremonies in a foreign language. They aroused so little notice during
this period that almost nothing is known of their practices or of their creed. It has even been maintained
that Attis was not worshiped together with his companion, the Great Mother, during the times of the republic, but this is undoubtedly wrong, because the two
persons of this divine couple must have been as inseparable in the ritual as they were in the myths.[10]

But the Phrygian religion kept alive in spite of police
surveillance, in spite of precautions and prejudices; a
breach had been made in the cracked wall of the old
Roman principles, through which the entire Orient
finally gained ingress.

Directly after the fall of the republic a second divinity from Asia Minor, closely related to the Great
Mother, became established in the capital. During the
wars against Mithridates the Roman soldiers learned
to revere Mâ, the great goddess of the two Comanas,
who was worshiped by a whole people of hierodules in
the ravines of the Taurus and along the banks of the

Iris. Like Cybele she was an ancient Anatolian divinity and personified fertile nature. Her worship, however, had not felt the influence of Thrace, but rather that of the Semites and the Persians,[11] like the entire religion of Cappadocia. It is certain that she was identical with the Anâhita of the Mazdeans, who was of much the same nature.

The rites of her cult were even more sanguinary and savage than those of Pessinus, and she had assumed or preserved a warlike character that gave her a resemblance to the Italian Bellona. The dictator Sulla, to whom this invincible goddess of combats had appeared in a dream, was prompted by his superstition to introduce her worship into Rome. The terrible ceremonies connected with it produced a deep impression. Clad in black robes, her "fanatics," as they were called, would turn round and round to the sound of drums and trumpets, with their long, loose hair streaming, and when vertigo seized them and a state of anesthesia was attained, they would strike their arms and bodies great blows with swords and axes. The view of the running blood excited them, and they besprinkled the statue of the goddess and her votaries with it, or even drank it. Finally a prophetic delirium would overcome them, and they foretold the future.

This ferocious worship aroused curiosity at first, but it never gained great consideration. It appears that the Cappadocian Bellona joined the number of divinities that were subordinated to the *Magna Mater* and, as the texts put it, became her follower (*pedisequa*).[12] The brief popularity enjoyed by this exotic *Mâ* at the beginning of our era shows, nevertheless, the growing influence of the Orient, and of the religions of Asia Minor in particular.

After the establishment of the empire the apprehensive distrust in which the worship of Cybele and Attis had been held gave way to marked favor and the original restrictions were withdrawn. Thereafter Roman citizens were chosen for *archigalli,* and the holidays of the Phrygian deities were solemnly and officially celebrated in Italy with even more pomp than had been displayed at Pessinus.

According to Johannes Lydus, the Emperor Claudius was the author of this change. Doubts have been expressed as to the correctness of the statement made by this second-rate compiler, and it has been claimed that the transformation in question took place under the Antonines. This is erroneous. The testimony of inscriptions corroborates that of the Byzantine writer.[13] In spite of his love of archaism, it was Claudius who permitted this innovation to be made, and we believe that we can divine the motives of his action.

Under his predecessor, Caligula, the worship of Isis had been authorized after a long resistance. Its stirring festivities and imposing processions gained considerable popularity. This competition must have been disastrous to the priests of the *Magna Mater,* who were secluded in their temple on the Palatine, and Caligula's successor could not but grant to the Phrygian goddess, so long established in the city, the favor accorded the Egyptian divinity who had been admitted into Rome but very recently. In this way Claudius prevented too great an ascendency in Italy of this second stranger and supplied a distributary to the current of popular superstition. Isis must have been held under great suspicion by a ruler who clung to old national institutions.[14]

The Emperor Claudius introduced a new cycle of holidays that were celebrated from March 15th to March 27th, the beginning of spring at the time of the revival of vegetation, personified in Attis. The various acts of this grand mystic drama are tolerably well known. The prelude was a procession of *cannophori* or reed-bearers on the fifteenth; undoubtedly they commemorated Cybele's discovery of Attis, who, according to the legends, had been exposed while a child on the banks of the Sangarius, the largest river of Phrygia, or else this ceremony may have been the transformation of an ancient phallephory intended to guarantee the fertility of the fields.[15] The ceremonies proper began with the equinox. A pine was felled and transferred to the temple of the Palatine by a brotherhood that owed to this function its name of "tree-bearers" (*dendrophori*). Wrapped like a corpse in woolen bands and garlands of violets, this pine represented Attis dead. This god was originally only the spirit of the plants, and the honors given to the "March-tree"[16] in front of the imperial palace perpetuated a very ancient agrarian rite of the Phrygian peasants. The next day was a day of sadness and abstinence on which the believers fasted and mourned the defunct god. The twenty-fourth bore the significant name of *Sanguis* in the calendars. We know that it was the celebration of the funeral of Attis, whose manes were appeased by means of libations of blood, as was done for any mortal. Mingling their piercing cries with the shrill sound of flutes, the Galli flagellated themselves and cut their flesh, and neophytes performed the supreme sacrifice with the aid of a sharp stone, being insensible to pain in their frenzy.[17] Then followed a mysterious vigil during which the mystic was supposed to be united as a new Attis with the great goddess.[18] On March 25th there was a sudden transition from the shouts of despair to a delirious jubilation, the *Hilaria*. With springtime Attis awoke from his sleep of death, and the joy created by his resurrection burst out in wild merry-making, wanton masquerades, and luxurious banquets. After twenty-four hours of an indispensable rest (*requietio*), the festivities wound up, on the twenty-seventh, with a long and gorgeous procession through the streets of Rome and surrounding country districts. Under a constant rain of flowers the silver statue of Cybele was taken to the river Almo and bathed and purified according to an ancient rite (*lavatio*).

The worship of the Mother of the Gods had penetrated into the Hellenic countries long before it was received at Rome, but in Greece it assumed a peculiar form and lost most of its barbarous character. The Greek mind felt an unconquerable aversion to the dubious nature of Attis. The *Magna Mater,* who is thoroughly different from her Hellenized sister, penetrated into all Latin provinces and imposed herself upon them with the Roman religion. This was the case in Spain, Brittany, the Danubian countries, Africa and especially in Gaul.[19] As late as the fourth century the car of the goddess drawn by steers was led in great state through the fields and vineyards of Autun in order to stimulate their fertility.[20] In the provinces the *dendrophori,* who carried the sacred pine in the spring festivities, formed associations recognized by the state. These associations had charge of the work of our modern fire departments, besides their religious mission. In case of necessity these woodcutters and carpenters, who knew how to fell the divine tree of Attis, were also able to cut down the timbers of burning buildings. All over the empire religion and the brotherhoods connected with it were under the high supervision of the quindecimvirs of the capital, who gave the priests their insignia. The sacerdotal hierarchy and the rights granted to the priesthood and believers were minutely defined in a series of senate decrees. These Phrygian divinities who had achieved full naturalization and had been placed on the official list of gods, were adopted by the populations of the Occident as Roman gods together with the rest. This propagation was clearly different from that of any other Oriental religion, for here the action of the government aided the tendencies that attracted the devout masses to these Asiatic divinities.

This popular zeal was the result of various causes. Ancient authors describe the impression produced upon the masses by those magnificent processions in which Cybele passed along on her car, preceded by musicians playing captivating melodies, by priests wearing gorgeous costumes covered with amulets, and by the long line of votaries and members of the fraternities, all barefoot and wearing their insignia. All this, however, created only a fleeting and exterior impression upon the neophyte, but as soon as he entered the temple a deeper sensation took hold of him. He heard the pathetic story of the goddess seeking the body of her lover cut down in the prime of his life like the grass of the fields. He saw the bloody funeral services in which the cruel death of the young man was mourned,

and heard the joyful hymns of triumph, and the gay
songs that greeted his return to life. By a skilfully
arranged gradation of feelings the onlookers were uplifted to a state of rapturous ecstasy. Feminine devotion in particular found encouragement and enjoyment
in these ceremonies, and the Great Mother, the fecund
and generous goddess, was always especially worshiped
by the women.

Moreover, people founded great hopes on the pious
practice of this religion. Like the Thracians, the Phrygians began very early to believe in the immortality of
the soul. Just as Attis died and came to life again
every year, these believers were to be born to new life
after their death. One of the sacred hymns said:
"Take courage, oh mystics, because the god is saved;
and for you also will come salvation from your trials."[21]
Even the funeral ceremonies were affected by the
strength of that belief. In some cities, especially at
Amphipolis in Macedonia, graves have been found
adorned with earthenware statuettes representing the
shepherd Attis;[22] and even in Germany the gravestones are frequently decorated with the figure of a
young man in Oriental costume, leaning dejectedly upon
a knotted stick (*pedum*), who represented the same
Attis. We are ignorant of the conception of immortality held by the Oriental disciples of the Phrygian
priests. Maybe, like the votaries of Sabazius, they
believed that the blessed ones were permitted to participate with Hermes Psychopompos in a great celestial feast, for which they were prepared by the
sacred repasts of the mysteries.[23]

Another agent in favor of this imported religion was, as we have stated above, the fact of its official recognition. This placed it in a privileged position among Oriental religions, at least at the beginning of the imperial régime. It enjoyed a toleration that was neither precarious nor limited; it was not subjected to arbitrary police measures nor to coercion on the part of magistrates; its fraternities were not continually threatened with dissolution, nor its priests with expulsion. It was publicly authorized and endowed, its holidays were marked in the calendars of the pontiffs, its associations of dendrophori were organs of municipal life in Italy and in the provinces, and had a corporate entity.

Therefore it is not surprising that other foreign religions, after being transferred to Rome, sought to avert the dangers of an illicit existence by an alliance with the Great Mother. The religion of the latter frequently consented to agreements and compromises, from which it gained in reality as much as it gave up. In exchange for material advantages it acquired complete moral authority over the gods that accepted its protection. Thus Cybele and Attis absorbed a majority of the divinities from Asia Minor that had crossed the Ionian Sea. Their clergy undoubtedly intended to establish a religion complex enough to enable the emigrants from every part of the vast peninsula, slaves, merchants, soldiers, functionaries, scholars, in short, people of all classes of society, to find their national and favorite devotions in it. As a matter of fact no other Anatolian god could maintain his independence side by side with the deities of Pessinus.[24]

We do not know the internal development of the

Phrygian mysteries sufficiently to give details of the addition of each individual part. But we can prove that in the course of time certain religions were added to the one that had been practised in the temple of the Palatine ever since the republic.

In the inscriptions of the fourth century, Attis bears the cognomen of *menotyrannus*. At that time this name was undoubtedly understood to mean "lord of the months," because Attis represented the sun who entered a new sign of the zodiac every month.[25] But that was not the original meaning of the term. *"Mèn tyrannus"* appears with quite a different meaning in many inscriptions found in Asia Minor. *Tyrannos,** "lord," is a word taken by the Greeks from the Lydian, and the honorable title of "tyrant" was given to Mèn, an old barbarian divinity worshiped by all Phrygia and surrounding regions.[26] The Anatolian tribes from Caria to the remotest mountains of Pontus worshiped a lunar god under that name who was supposed to rule not only the heavens but also the underworld, because the moon was frequently brought into connection with the somber kingdom of the dead. The growth of plants and the increase of cattle and poultry were ascribed to his celestial influence, and the villagers invoked his protection for their farms and their district. They also placed their rural burial grounds under the safeguard of this king of shadows. No god enjoyed greater popularity in the country districts.

This powerful divinity penetrated into Greece at an early period. Among the mixed populations of the Ægean seaports, in the Piræus, at Rhodes, Delos and Thasos, religious associations for his worship were

* Τύραννος.

founded. In Attica the presence of the cult can be traced back to the fourth century, and its monuments rival those of Cybele in number and variety. In the Latin Occident, however, no trace of it can be found, because it had been absorbed by the worship of *Magna Mater*. In Asia itself, Attis and Mèn were sometimes considered identical, and this involved the Roman world in a complete confusion of those two persons, who in reality were very different. A marble statue discovered at Ostia represents Attis holding the lunar crescent, which was the characteristic emblem of Mèn. His assimilation to the "tyrant" of the infernal regions transformed the shepherd of Ida into a master of the underworld, an office that he combined with his former one as author of resurrection.

A second title that was given to him reveals another influence. A certain Roman inscription is dedicated to Attis the Supreme.[27]* This epithet is very significant. In Asia Minor "Hypsistos" was the appellation used to designate the god of Israel.[28] A number of pagan thiasi had arisen who, though not exactly submitting to the practice of the synagogue, yet worshiped none but the Most High, the Supreme God, the Eternal God, God the Creator, to whom every mortal owed service. These must have been the attributes ascribed to Cybele's companion by the author of the inscription, because the verse continues :† "To thee, who containest and maintainest all things."[29] Must we then believe that Hebraic monotheism had some influence upon the mysteries of the Great Mother? This is not at all improbable. We know that numerous Jewish colonies were established in Phrygia by the Seleucides, and that

* Ἄττει ὑψίστῳ.   † καὶ συνέχοντι τὸ πᾶν.

these expatriated Jews agreed to certain compromises
in order to conciliate their hereditary faith with that of
the pagans in whose midst they lived. It is also possible that the clergy of Pessinus suffered the ascendancy
of the Biblical theology. Under the empire Attis and
Cybele became the "almighty gods" (*omnipotentes*)
par excellence, and it is easy to see in this new conception a leaning upon Semitic or Christian doctrines,
more probably upon Semitic ones.[30]

We shall now take up the difficult question of the
influence of Judaism upon the mysteries during the
Alexandrian period and at the beginning of the empire.
Many scholars have endeavored to define the influence
exercised by the pagan beliefs on those of the Jews; it
has been shown how the Israelitic monotheism became
Hellenized at Alexandria and how the Jewish propaganda attracted proselytes who revered the one God,
without, however, observing all the prescriptions of the
Mosaic law. But no successful researches have been
made to ascertain how far paganism was modified
through an infiltration of Biblical ideas. Such a modification must necessarily have taken place to some extent. A great number of Jewish colonies were scattered everywhere on the Mediterranean, and these were
long animated with such an ardent spirit of proselytism
that they were bound to impose some of their conceptions on the pagans that surrounded them. The magical
texts which are almost the only original literary documents of paganism we possess, clearly reveal this mixture of Israelitic theology with that of other peoples.
In them we frequently find names like Iao (Yahveh),
Sabaoth, or the names of angels side by side with those
of Egyptian or Greek divinities. Especially in Asia

Minor, where the Israelites formed a considerable and influential element of the population, an intermingling of the old native traditions and the religion of the strangers from the other side of the Taurus must have occurred.

This mixture certainly took place in the mysteries of Sabazius, the Phrygian Jupiter or Dionysus.[31] They were very similar to those of Attis, with whom he was frequently confounded. By means of an audacious etymology that dates back to the Hellenistic period, this old Thraco-Phrygian divinity has been identified with "Yahveh Zebaoth," the Biblical "Lord of Hosts." The corresponding expression* in the Septuagint has been regarded as the equivalent of the *kurios Sabazios*† of the barbarians. The latter was worshiped as the supreme, almighty and holy Lord. In the light of a new interpretation the purifications practised in the mysteries were believed to wipe out the hereditary impurity of a guilty ancestor who had aroused the wrath of heaven against his posterity, much as the original sin with which Adam's disobedience had stained the human race was to be wiped out. The custom observed by the votaries of Sabazius of dedicating votive hands which made the liturgic sign of benediction with the first three fingers extended (the *benedictio latina* of the church) was probably taken from the ritual of the Semitic temples through the agency of the Jews. The initiates believed, again like the Jews, that after death their good angel (*angelus bonus*) would lead them to the banquet of the eternally happy, and the everlasting joys of these banquets were anticipated on earth by the liturgic repasts. This celestial feast can

* κύριος Σαβαώθ.   † κύριος Σαβάζιος.

be seen in a fresco painting on the grave of a priest of Sabazius called Vincentius, who was buried in the Christian catacomb of Prætextatus, a strange fact for which no satisfactory explanation has as yet been furnished. Undoubtedly he belonged to a Jewish-pagan sect that admitted neophytes of every race to its mystic ceremonies. In fact, the church itself formed a kind of secret society sprung from the synagogue but distinct from it, in which Gentiles and the Children of Israel joined in a common adoration.

If it is a fact, then, that Judaism influenced the worship of Sabazius, it is very probable that it influenced the cult of Cybele also, although in this case the influence cannot be discerned with the same degree of certainty. The religion of the Great Mother did not receive rejuvenating germs from Palestine only, but it was greatly changed after the gods of more distant Persia came and joined it. In the ancient religion of the Achemenides, Mithra, the genius of light, was coupled with Anâhita, the goddess of the fertilizing waters. In Asia Minor the latter was assimilated with the fecund Great Mother, worshiped all over the peninsula,[32] and when at the end of the first century of our era the mysteries of Mithra spread over the Latin provinces, its votaries built their sacred crypts in the shadow of the temples of the *Magna Mater*.

Everywhere in the empire the two religions lived in intimate communion. By ingratiating themselves with the Phrygian priests, the priests of Mithra obtained the support of an official institution and shared in the protection granted by the state. Moreover, men alone could participate in the secret ceremonies of the Persian liturgy, at least in the Occident. Other mysteries, to which women could be admitted, had therefore to be added in order to complete them, and so the mysteries of Cybele received the wives and daughters of the Mithraists.

This union had even more important consequences for the old religion of Pessinus than the partial infusion of Judaic beliefs had had. Its theology gained a deeper meaning and an elevation hitherto unknown, after it had adopted some of the conceptions of Mazdaism.

The introduction of the taurobolium in the ritual of the *Magna Mater,* where it appeared after the middle of the first century, was probably connected with this transformation. We know the nature of this sacrifice, of which Prudentius gives a stirring description based on personal recollection of the proceeding. On an open platform a steer was killed, and the blood dropped down upon the mystic, who was standing in an excavation below. "Through the thousand crevices in the wood," says the poet, "the bloody dew runs down into the pit. The neophyte receives the falling drops on his head, clothes and body. He leans backward to have his cheeks, his ears, his lips and his nostrils wetted ; he pours the liquid over his eyes, and does not even spare his palate, for he moistens his tongue with blood and drinks it eagerly."33 After submitting to this repulsive sprinkling he offered himself to the veneration of the crowd. They believed that he was purified of his faults, and had become the equal of the deity through his red baptism.

Although the origin of this sacrifice that took place in the mysteries of Cybele at Rome is as yet shrouded in obscurity, recent discoveries enable us to trace back very closely the various phases of its development. In accordance with a custom prevalent in the entire Orient at the beginning of history, the Anatolian lords were fond of pursuing and lassoing wild buffalos, which they afterwards sacrificed to the gods. Beasts caught during a hunt were immolated, and frequently also prisoners of war. Gradually the savagery of this primitive rite was modified until finally nothing but a circus play was left. During the Alexandrian period people were satisfied with organizing a *corrida* in the arena, in the course of which the victim intended for immolation was seized. This is the proper meaning of the terms taurobolium and criobolium,* which had long been enigmas,[34] and which denoted the act of catching a steer or a ram by means of a hurled weapon, probably the thong of a lasso. Without doubt even this act was finally reduced to a mere sham under the Roman empire, but the weapon with which the animal was slain always remained a hunting weapon, a sacred boar spear.[35]

The ideas on which the immolation was based were originally just as barbarous as the sacrifice itself. It is a matter of general belief among savage peoples that one acquires the qualities of an enemy slain in battle or of a beast killed in the chase by drinking or washing in the blood, or by eating some of the viscera of the body. The blood especially has often been considered as the seat of vital energy. By moistening his body with the blood of the slaughtered steer, the neophyte believed that he was transfusing the strength of the formidable beast into his own limbs.

This naive and purely material conception was soon

* ταυροβόλιον, κριοβόλιον.

modified and refined. The Thracians brought into
Phrygia, and the Persian magi into Cappadocia, the
fast spreading belief in the immortality of mankind.
Under their influence, especially under that of Mazdaism, which made the mythical steer the author of creation and of resurrection, the old savage practice assumed a more spiritual and more elevated meaning.
By complying with it, people no longer thought they
were acquiring the buffalo's strength; the blood, as
the principle of life, was no longer supposed to renew
physical energy, but to cause a temporary or even an
eternal rebirth of the soul. The descent into the pit
was regarded as burial, a melancholy dirge accompanied the burial of the old man who had died. When
he emerged purified of all his crimes by the sprinkling
of blood and raised to a new life, he was regarded as
the equal of a god, and the crowd worshiped him from
a respectful distance.[36]

The vogue obtained in the Roman empire by the
practice of this repugnant rite can only be explained
by the extraordinary power ascribed to it. He who submitted to it was *in aeternum renatus*,[37] according to
the inscriptions.

We could also outline the transformation of other
Phrygian ceremonies, of which the spirit and sometimes the letter slowly changed under the influence of
more advanced moral ideas. This is true of the sacred
feasts attended by the initiates. One of the few liturgic formulas antiquity has left us refers to these Phrygian banquets. One hymn says: "I have eaten from the
tambourine, I have drunk from the cymbal, I have become a mystic of Attis." The banquet, which is found
in several Oriental religions, was sometimes simply the

external sign indicating that the votaries of the same divinity formed one large family. Admitted to the sacred table, the neophyte was received as the guest of the community and became a brother among brothers. The religious bond of the thiasus or *sodalicium* took the place of the natural relationship of the family, the *gens* or the clan, just as the foreign religion replaced the worship of the domestic hearth.

Sometimes other effects were expected of the food eaten in common. When the flesh of some animal supposed to be of a divine nature was eaten, the votary believed that he became identified with the god and that he shared in his substance and qualities. In the beginning the-Phrygian priests probably attributed the first of these two meanings to their barbarous communions.[38] Towards the end of the empire, moral ideas were particularly connected with the assimilation of sacred liquor and meats taken from the tambourine and cymbal of Attis. They became the staff of the spiritual life and were to sustain the votary in his trials; at that period he considered the gods as especially "the guardians of his soul and thoughts."[39]

As we see, every modification of the conception of the world and of man in the society of the empire had its reflection in the doctrine of the mysteries. Even the conception of the old deities of Pessinus was constantly changing. When astrology and the Semitic religions caused the establishment of a solar henotheism as the leading religion at Rome, Attis was considered as the sun, "the shepherd of the twinkling stars." He was identified with Adonis, Bacchus, Pan, Osiris and Mithra; he was made a "polymorphous"[40] being in which all celestial powers manifested themselves in turn; a *pantheos* who wore the crown of rays and the lunar crescent at the same time, and whose various emblems expressed an infinite multiplicity of functions.

When neo-Platonism was triumphing, the Phrygian fable became the traditional mould into which subtle exegetists boldly poured their philosophic speculations on the creative and stimulating forces that were the principles of all material forms, and on the deliverance of the divine soul that was submerged in the corruption of this earthly world. In his hazy oration on the Mother of the Gods, Julian lost all notion of reality on account of his excessive use of allegory and was swept away by an extravagant symbolism.[41]

Any religion as susceptible to outside influences as this one was bound to yield to the ascendancy of Christianity. From the explicit testimony of ecclesiastical writers we know that attempts were made to oppose the Phrygian mysteries to those of the church. It was maintained that the sanguinary purification imparted by the taurobolium was more efficacious than baptism. The food that was taken during the mystic feasts was likened to the bread and wine of the communion; the Mother of the Gods was undoubtedly placed above the Mother of God, whose son also had risen again. A Christian author, writing at Rome about the year 375, furnishes some remarkable information on this subject. As we have seen, a mournful ceremony was celebrated on March 24th, the *dies sanguinis* in the course of which the *galli* shed their blood and sometimes mutilated themselves in commemoration of the wound that had caused Attis's death, ascribing an expiatory and atoning power to the blood thus shed. The pagans claimed that the church had copied their most sacred rites by placing her Holy Week at the vernal equinox in commemoration of the sacrifice of the cross on which the divine Lamb, according to the church, had redeemed the human race. Indignant at these blasphemous pretensions, St. Augustine tells of having known a priest of Cybele who kept saying: *Et ipse Pileatus christianus est*—"and even the god with the Phrygian cap [i. e., Attis] is a Christian."[42]

But all efforts to maintain a barbarian religion stricken with moral decadence were in vain. On the very spot on which the last taurobolia took place at the end of the fourth century, in the *Phrygianum,* stands to-day the basilica of the Vatican.

* * *

There is no Oriental religion whose progressive evolution we could follow at Rome so closely as the cult of Cybele and Attis, none that shows so plainly one of the reasons that caused their common decay and disappearance. They all dated back to a remote period of barbarism, and from that savage past they inherited a number of myths the odium of which could be masked but not eradicated by philosophical symbolism, and practices whose fundamental coarseness had survived from a period of rude nature worship, and could never be completely disguised by means of mystic interpretations. Never was the lack of harmony greater between the moralizing tendencies of theologians and the cruel shamelessness of tradition. A god held up as the august lord of the universe was the pitiful and abject hero of an obscene love affair; the taurobolium, performed to satisfy man's most exalted aspirations for spiritual purification and immortality, looked like a shower bath of blood and recalled cannibalistic orgies. The men of letters and senators attending those mysteries saw them performed by painted eunuchs, ill reputed for their infamous morals, who went through dizzy dances similar to those of the dancing dervishes and the Aissaouas. We can imagine the repugnance these ceremonies caused in everybody whose judgment had not been destroyed by a fanatical devotion. Of no other pagan superstition do the Christian polemicists speak with such profound contempt, and there is undoubtedly a reason for their attitude. But they were in a more fortunate position than their pagan antagonists; their doctrine was not burdened with barbarous traditions dating back to times of savagery; and all the ignominies that stained the old Phrygian religion must not prejudice us against it nor cause us to slight the long continued efforts that were made to refine it gradually and to mould it into a form that would fulfil the new demands of morality and enable it to follow the laborious march of Roman society on the road of religious progress.

EGYPT.

W E know more about the religion of the early
Egyptians than about any other ancient religion.
Its development can be traced back three or four thousand years; we can read its sacred texts, mythical
narratives, hymns, rituals, and the Book of the Dead
in the original, and we can ascertain its various ideas
as to the nature of the divine powers and of future
life. A great number of monuments have preserved
for our inspection the pictures of divinities and representations of liturgic scenes, while numerous inscriptions and papyri enlighten us in regard to the sacerdotal organization of the principal temples. It would
seem that the enormous quantity of documents of all
kinds that have been deciphered in the course of nearly
an entire century should have dispelled every uncertainty about the creed of ancient Egypt, and should
have furnished exact information with regard to the
sources and original character of the worship which
the Greeks and the Romans borrowed from the subjects
of the Ptolemies.

And yet, this is not the case. While of the four
great Oriental religions which were transplanted into
the Occident, the religion of Isis and Serapis is the one
whose relation to the ancient belief of the mother
country we can establish with greatest accuracy, we

know very little of its first form and of its nature before the imperial period, when it was held in high esteem.

One fact, however, appears to be certain. The Egyptian worship that spread over the Greco-Roman world came from the Serapeum founded at Alexandria by Ptolemy Soter, somewhat in the manner of Judaism that emanated from the temple of Jerusalem. But the earliest history of that famous sanctuary is surrounded by such a thick growth of pious legends, that the most sagacious investigators have lost their way in it. Was Serapis of native origin, or was he imported from Sinope or Seleucia, or even from Babylon? Each of these opinions has found supporters very recently. Is his name derived from that of the Egyptian god Osiris-Apis, or from that of the Chaldean deity Sar-Apsi? *Grammatici certant.*[1]

Whichever solution we may adopt, one fact remains, namely, that Serapis and Osiris were either immediately identified or else were identical from the beginning. The divinity whose worship was started at Alexandria by Ptolemy was the god that ruled the dead and shared his immortality with them. He was fundamentally an Egyptian god, and the most popular of the deities of the Nile. Herodotus says that Isis and Osiris were revered by every inhabitant of the country, and their traditional holidays involved secret ceremonies whose sacred meaning the Greek writer dared not reveal.[2]

Recognizing their Osiris in Serapis, the Egyptians readily accepted the new cult. There was a tradition that a new dynasty should introduce a new god or give a sort of preeminence to the god of its own district. From time immemorial politics had changed the government of heaven when changing that of earth. Under the Ptolemies the Serapis of Alexandria naturally became one of the principal divinities of the country, just as the Ammon of Thebes had been the chief of the celestial hierarchy under the Pharaohs of that city, or as, under the sovereigns from Sais, the local Neith had the primacy. At the time of the Antonines there were forty-two Serapeums in Egypt.[3]

But the purpose of the Ptolemies was not to add one more Egyptian god to the countless number already worshiped by their subjects. They wanted this god to unite in one common worship the two races inhabiting the kingdom, and thus to further a complete fusion. The Greeks were obliged to worship him side by side with the natives. It was a clever political idea to institute a Hellenized Egyptian religion at Alexandria. A tradition mentioned by Plutarch[4] has it that Manetho, a priest from Heliopolis, a man of advanced ideas, together with Timotheus, a Eumolpid from Eleusis, thought out the character that would best suit the newcomer. The result was that the composite religion founded by the Lagides became a combination of the old creed of the Pharaohs and the Greek mysteries.

First of all, the liturgic language was no longer the native idiom but Greek. This was a radical change. The philosopher Demetrius of Phalerum, who had been cured of blindness by Serapis, composed poems in honor of the god that were still sung under the Cæsars several centuries later.[5] We can easily imagine that the poets, who lived on the bounty of the Ptolemies, vied with each other in their efforts to celebrate their benefactors' god, and the old rituals that were translated from the Egyptian were also enriched with edifying bits of original inspiration. A hymn to Isis, found on a marble monument in the island of Andros,[6] gives us some idea of these sacred compositions, although it is of more recent date.

In the second place, the artists replaced the old hieratic idols by more attractive images and gave them the beauty of the immortals. It is not known who created the figure of Isis draped in a linen gown with a fringed cloak fastened over the breast, whose sweet meditative, graciously maternal face is a combination of the ideals imagined for Hera and Aphrodite. But we know the sculptor of the first statue of Serapis that stood in the great sanctuary of Alexandria until the end of paganism. This statue, the prototype of all the copies that have been preserved, is a colossal work of art made of precious materials by a famous Athenian sculptor named Bryaxis, a contemporary of Scopas. It was one of the last divine creations of Hellenic genius. The majestic head, with its somber and yet benevolent expression, with its abundance of hair, and with a crown in the shape of a bushel, bespoke the double character of a god ruling at the same time both the fertile earth and the dismal realm of the dead.[7]

As we see, the Ptolemies had given their new religion a literary and artistic shape that was capable of attracting the most refined and cultured minds. But the adaptation to the Hellenic feeling and thinking was not exclusively external. Osiris, the god whose worship was thus renewed, was more adapted than any other to lend his authority to the formation of a syncretic faith. At a very early period, in fact before the time of Herodotus, Osiris had been identified with Dionysus, and Isis with Demeter. M. Foucart has en-

deavored to prove in an ingenious essay that this assimilation was not arbitrary, that Osiris and Isis came
into Crete and Attica during the prehistoric period,
and that they were mistaken for Dionysus and Demeter[8]
by the people of those regions. Without going back
to those remote ages, we shall merely say with him
that the mysteries of Dionysus were connected with
those of Osiris by far-reaching affinities, not simply by
superficial and fortuitous resemblances. Each commemorated the history of a god governing both vegetation and the underworld at the same time, who was
put to death and torn to pieces by an enemy, and
whose scattered limbs were collected by a goddess,
after which he was miraculously revived. The Greeks
must have been very willing to adopt a worship in
which they found their own divinities and their own
myths again with something more poignant and more
magnificent added. It is a very remarkable fact that
of all the many deities worshiped by the Egyptian districts those of the immediate neighborhood, or if you
like, the cycle of Osiris, his wife Isis, their son Harpocrates and their faithful servant Anubis, were the only
ones that were adopted by the Hellenic populations.
All other heavenly or infernal spirits worshiped by the
Egyptians remained strangers to Greece.[9]

In the Greco-Latin literature we notice two opposing attitudes toward the Egyptian religion. It was
regarded as the highest and the lowest of religions at
the same time, and as a matter of fact there was an
abyss between the always ardent popular beliefs and the
enlightened faith of the official priests. The Greeks
and Romans gazed with admiration upon the splendor
of the temples and ceremonial, upon the fabulous an-

tiquity of the sacred traditions and upon the erudition
of a clergy possessed of a wisdom that had been revealed by divinity. In becoming the disciples of that
clergy, they imagined they were drinking from the
pure fountain whence their own myths had sprung.
They were overawed by the pretensions of a clergy
that prided itself on a past in which it kept on living,
and they strongly felt the attraction of a marvelous
country where everything was mysterious, from the
Nile that had created it to the hieroglyphs engraved
upon the walls of its gigantic edifices.[10] At the same
time they were shocked by the coarseness of its fetichism and by the absurdity of its superstitions. Above
all they felt an unconquerable repulsion at the worship
of animals and plants, which had always been the most
striking feature of the vulgar Egyptian religion and
which, like all other archaic devotions, seems to have
been practised with renewed fervor after the accession
of the Saite dynasty. The comic writers and the
satirists never tired of scoffing at the adorers of the
cat, the crocodile, the leek and the onion. Juvenal
says ironically: "O holy people, whose very kitchen-
gardens produce gods."[11] In a general way, this
strange people, entirely separated from the remainder
of the world, were regarded with about the same kind
of feeling that Europeans entertained toward the Chinese for a long time.

A purely Egyptian worship would not have been acceptable to the Greco-Latin world. The main merit
of the mixed creation of the political genius of the
Ptolemies consisted in the rejection or modification
of everything repugnant or monstrous like the phallo-
phories of Abydos, and in the retention of none but

stirring or attractive elements. It was the most civilized of all barbarian religions; it retained enough of the exotic element to arouse the curiosity of the Greeks, but not enough to offend their delicate sense of proportion, and its success was remarkable.

It was adopted wherever the authority or the prestige of the Lagides was felt, and wherever the relations of Alexandria, the great commercial metropolis, extended. The Lagides induced the rulers and the nations with whom they concluded alliances to accept it. King Nicocreon introduced it into Cyprus after having consulted the oracle of the Serapeum,[12] and Agathocles introduced it into Sicily, at the time of his marriage with the daughter-in-law of Ptolemy I (298).[13] At Antioch, Seleucus Callinicus built a sanctuary for the statue of Isis sent to him from Memphis by Ptolemy Euergetes.[14] In token of his friendship Ptolemy Soter introduced his god Serapis into Athens, where the latter had a temple at the foot of the Acropolis[15] ever after, and Arsinoë, his mother or wife, founded another at Halicarnassus, about the year 307.[16] In this manner the political activity of the Egyptian dynasty was directed toward having the divinities, whose glory was in a certain measure connected with that of their house, recognized everywhere. Through Apuleius we know that under the empire the priests of Isis mentioned the ruling sovereign first of all in their prayers.[17] And this was simply an imitation of the grateful devotion which their predecessors had felt toward the Ptolemies.

Protected by the Egyptian squadrons, sailors and merchants propagated the worship of Isis, the goddess of navigators, simultaneously on the coasts of Syria,

Asia Minor and Greece, in the islands of the Archipelago,[18] and as far as the Hellespont and Thrace.[19] At Delos, where the inscriptions enable us to study this worship somewhat in detail, it was not merely practised by strangers, but the very sacerdotal functions were performed by members of the Athenian aristocracy. A number of funereal bas-reliefs, in which the deified dead wears the *calathos* of Serapis on his head, prove the popularity of the belief in future life propagated by these mysteries. According to the Egyptian faith he was identified with the god of the dead.[20]

Even after the splendor of the court of Alexandria had faded and vanished; even after the wars against Mithridates and the growth of piracy had ruined the traffic of the Ægean Sea, the Alexandrian worship was too deeply rooted in the soil of Greece to perish, although it became endangered in certain seaports like Delos. Of all the gods of the Orient, Isis and Serapis were the only ones that retained a place among the great divinities of the Hellenic world until the end of paganism.[21]

* * *

It was this syncretic religion that came to Rome after having enjoyed popularity in the eastern Mediterranean. Sicily and the south of Italy were more than half Hellenized, and the Ptolemies had diplomatic relations with these countries, just as the merchants of Alexandria had commercial relations with them. For this reason the worship of Isis spread as rapidly in those regions as on the coasts of Ionia or in the Cyclades.[22] It was introduced into Syracuse and Catana during the earliest years of the third century by Agathocles. The Serapeum of Pozzuoli, at that time the busiest seaport of Campania, was mentioned in a city ordinance of the year 105 B. C.[23] About the same time an Iseum was founded at Pompeii, where the decorative frescos attest to this day the power of expansion possessed by the Alexandrian culture.

After its adoption by the southern part of the Italian peninsula, this religion was bound to penetrate rapidly to Rome. Ever since the second century before our era, it could not help but find adepts in the chequered multitude of slaves and freedmen. Under the Antonines the college of the *pastophori* recalled that it had been founded in the time of Sulla.[24] In vain did the authorities try to check the invasion of the Alexandrian gods. Five different times, in 59, 58, 53, and 48 B. C., the senate ordered their altars and statues torn down,[25] but these violent measures did not stop the diffusion of the new beliefs. The Egyptian mysteries were the first example at Rome of an essentially popular religious movement that was triumphant over the continued resistance of the public authorities and the official clergy.

Why was this Egyptian worship the only one of all Oriental religions to suffer repeated persecutions? There were two motives, one religious and one political.

In the first place, this cult was said to exercise a corrupting influence perversive of piety. Its morals were loose, and the mystery surrounding it excited the worst suspicions. Moreover, it appealed violently to the emotions and senses. All these factors offended the grave decency that a Roman was wont to maintain in the presence of the gods. The innovators had every defender of the *mos maiorum* for an adversary.

In the second place, this religion had been founded, supported and propagated by the Ptolemies; it came from a country that was almost hostile to Italy during the last period of the republic;[26] it issued from Alexandria, whose superiority Rome felt and feared. Its secret societies, made up chiefly of people of the lower classes, might easily become clubs of agitators and haunts of spies. All these motives for suspicion and hatred were undoubtedly more potent in exciting persecution than the purely theological reasons, and persecution was stopped or renewed according to the vicissitudes of general politics.

As we have stated, the chapels consecrated to Isis were demolished in the year 48 B. C. After Cæsar's death, the triumvirs decided in 43 B. C. to erect a temple in her honor out of the public funds, undoubtedly to gain the favor of the masses. This action would have implied official recognition, but the project appears never to have been executed. If Antony had succeeded at Actium, Isis and Serapis would have entered Rome in triumph, but they were vanquished with Cleopatra; and when Augustus had become the master of the empire, he professed a deep aversion for the gods of his former enemies. Moreover, he could not have suffered the intrusion of the Egyptian clergy into the Roman sacerdotal class, whose guardian, restorer and chief he was. In 28 B. C. an ordinance was issued forbidding the erecting of altars to the Alexandrian divinities inside the sacred enclosure of the *pomerium,* and seven years later Agrippa extended this prohibitive regulation to a radius of a thousand paces around the

city. Tiberius acted on the same principle and in 19
A. D. instituted the bloodiest persecution against the
priests of Isis that they ever suffered, in consequence
of a scandalous affair in which a matron, a noble and
some priests of Isis were implicated.

All these police measures, however, were strangely
ineffectual. The Egyptian worship was excluded from
Rome and her immediate neighborhood in theory if
not in fact, but the rest of the world remained open to
its propaganda.[27]

With the beginning of the empire it slowly invaded
the center and the north of Italy and spread into the
provinces. Merchants, sailors, slaves, artisans, Egyptian men of letters, even the discharged soldiers of the
three legions cantoned in the valley of the Nile contributed to its diffusion. It entered Africa by way of
Carthage, and the Danubian countries through the
great emporium of Aquileia. The new province of
Gaul was invaded through the valley of the Rhone.
At that period many Oriental emigrants went to seek
their fortunes in these new countries. Intimate relations existed between the cities of Arles and Alexandria, and we know that a colony of Egyptian Greeks,
established at Nimes by Augustus, took the gods of
their native country thither.[28] At the beginning of our
era there set in that great movement of conversion
that soon established the worship of Isis and Serapis
from the outskirts of the Sahara to the vallum of
Britain, and from the mountains of Asturias to the
mouths of the Danube.

The resistance still offered by the central power could
not last much longer. It was impossible to dam in this
overflowing stream whose thundering waves struck the

shaking walls of the *pomerium* from every side. The
prestige of Alexandria seemed invincible. At that period the city was more beautiful, more learned, and
better policed than Rome. She was the model capital,
a standard to which the Latins strove to rise. They
translated the works of the scholars of Alexandria,
imitated her authors, invited her artists and copied her
institutions. It is plain that they had also to undergo
the ascendancy of her religion. As a matter of fact,
her fervent believers maintained her sanctuaries, despite
the law, on the very Capitol. Under Cæsar, Alexandrian astronomers had reformed the calendar of the
pontiffs, and Alexandrian priests soon marked the dates
of Isis holidays upon it.

The decisive step was taken soon after the death
of Tiberius. Caligula erected the great temple of Isis
Campensis on the Campus Martius probably in the
year 38.[29] In order to spare the sacerdotal suscepti-
bilities, he founded it outside of the sacred enclosure
of the city of Servius. Later Domitian made one of
Rome's most splendid monuments of that temple. From
that time Isis and Serapis enjoyed the favor of every
imperial dynasty, the Flavians as well as the Antonines
and the Severi. About the year 215 Caracalla built
an Isis temple, even more magnificent than that of
Domitian, on the Quirinal, in the heart of the city, and
perhaps another one on the Coelian. As the apologist
Minucius Felix states, the Egyptian gods had become
entirely Roman.[30]

The climax of their power seems to have been
reached at the beginning of the third century; later on
the popular vogue and official support went to other
divinities, like the Syrian Baals and the Persian Mith-

ras. The progress of Christianity also deprived them of their power, which was, however, still considerable until the end of the ancient world. The Isis processions that marched the streets of Rome were described by an eye witness as late as the year 394,[31] but in 391 the patriarch Theophilus had consigned the Serapeum of Alexandria to the flames, having himself struck the first blow with an ax against the colossal statue of the god that had so long been the object of a superstitious veneration. Thus the prelate destroyed the "very head of idolatry," as Rufinus put it.[32]

As a matter of fact, idolatry received its death blow. The worship of the gods of the Ptolemies died out completely between the reigns of Theodosius and Justinian,[33] and in accordance with the sad prophecy of Hermes Trismegistus[34] Egypt, Egypt herself, lost her divinities and became a land of the dead. Of her religions nothing remained but fables that were no longer believed, and the only thing that reminded the barbarians who came to inhabit the country of its former piety, were words engraved on stone.

* * *

This rapid sketch of the history of Isis and Serapis shows that these divinities were worshiped in the Latin world for more than five centuries. The task of pointing out the transformations of the cult during that long period, and the local differences there may have been in the various provinces, is reserved for future researches. These will undoubtedly find that the Alexandrian worship did not become Latinized under the empire, but that its Oriental character became more and more pronounced. When Domitian restored the Iseum of the Campus Martius and that of Beneventum, he

transferred from the valley of the Nile sphinxes, cyno-
cephali and obelisks of black or pink granite bearing
borders of hieroglyphics of Amasis, Nectanebos or even
Rameses II.   On other obelisks that were erected in
the propyleums even the inscriptions of the emperors
were written in hieroglyphics.[35]   Half a century later
that true dilettante, Hadrian, caused the luxuries of
Canopus to be reproduced, along with the vale of
Tempe, in his immense villa at Tibur, to enable him
to celebrate his voluptuous feasts under the friendly
eyes of Serapis.   He extolled the merits of the deified
Antinous in inscriptions couched in the ancient language of the Pharaohs, and set the fashion of statues
hewn out of black basalt in the Egyptian style.[36]   The
amateurs of that period affected to prefer the hieratic
rigidity of the barbarian idols to the elegant freedom
of Alexandrian art.   Those esthetic manifestations
probably corresponded to religious prejudices, and the
Latin worship always endeavored to imitate the art of
temples in the Nile valley more closely than did the
Greek.   This evolution was in conformity with all the
tendencies of the imperial period.

By what secret virtue did the Egyptian religion exercise this irresistible influence over the Roman world?
What new elements did those priests, who made proselytes in every province, give the Roman world?   Did
the success of their preaching mean progress or retrogression from the standard of the ancient Roman
faith?   These are complex and delicate questions that
would require minute analysis and cautious treatment
with a constant and exact observation of shades.   I am
compelled to limit myself to a rapid sketch, which, I

fear, will appear rather dry and arbitrary, like every
generalization.

The particular doctrines of the mysteries of Isis and
Serapis in regard to the nature and power of the gods
were not, or were but incidentally, the reasons for the
triumph of these mysteries. It has been said that the
Egyptian theology always remained in a "fluid state,"[37]
or better in a state of chaos. It consisted of an amal-
gamation of disparate legends, of an aggregate of particular cults, as Egypt herself was an aggregate of a
number of districts. This religion never formulated
a coherent system of generally accepted dogmas. It
permitted the coexistence of conflicting conceptions
and traditions, and all the subtlety of its clergy never
accomplished, or rather never began, the task of fusing
those irreconcilable elements into one harmonious synthesis.[38] For the Egyptians there was no principle of
contradiction. All the heterogeneous beliefs that ever
obtained in the various districts during the different
periods of a very long history, were maintained con-
currently and formed an inextricable confusion in the
sacred books.

About the same state of affairs prevailed in the Occidental worship of the Alexandrian divinities. In the
Occident, just as in Egypt, there were "prophets" in
the first rank of the clergy, who learnedly discussed
religion, but never taught a theological system that
found universal acceptance. The sacred scribe Cheremon, who became Nero's tutor, recognized the stoical
theories in the sacerdotal traditions of his country.[39]
When the eclectic Plutarch speaks of the character of
the Egyptian gods, he finds it agrees surprisingly with
his own philosophy,[40] and when the neo-Platonist Iam-

blichus examines them, their character seems to agree
with his doctrines. The hazy ideas of the Oriental
priests enabled every one to see in them the phantoms
he was pursuing. The individual imagination was given
ample scope, and the dilettantic men of letters rejoiced
in molding these malleable doctrines at will. They
were not outlined sharply enough, nor were they formulated with sufficient precision to appeal to the multitude. The gods were everything and nothing; they
got lost in a *sfumato*. A disconcerting anarchy and
confusion prevailed among them. By means of a scientific mixture of Greek, Egyptian and Semitic elements "Hermetism"[41] endeavored to create a theological system that would be acceptable to all minds, but
it seems never to have imposed itself generally on the
Alexandrian mysteries which were older than itself,
and furthermore it could not escape the contradictions
of Egyptian thought. The religion of Isis did not gain
a hold on the soul by its dogmatism.

It must be admitted, however, that, owing to its extreme flexibility, this religion was easily adapted to
the various centers to which it was transferred, and that
it enjoyed the valuable advantage of being always in
perfect harmony with the prevailing philosophy. Moreover, the syncretic tendencies of Egypt responded admirably to those that began to obtain at Rome. At a
very early period henotheistic theories had been favorably received in sacerdotal circles, and while crediting
the god of their own temple with supremacy, the priests
admitted that he might have a number of different
personalities, under which he was worshiped simultaneously. In this way the unity of the supreme being
was affirmed for the thinkers, and polytheism with its

intangible traditions maintained for the masses. In the same manner Isis and Osiris had absorbed several local divinities under the Pharaohs, and had assumed a complex character that was capable of indefinite extension. The same process continued under the Ptolemies when the religion of Egypt came into contact with Greece. Isis was identified simultaneously with Demeter, Aphrodite, Hera, Semele, Io, Tyche, and others. She was considered the queen of heaven and hell, of earth and sea. She was "the past, the present and the future,"[42] "nature the mother of things, the mistress of the elements, born at the beginning of the centuries."[43] She had numberless names, an infinity of different aspects and an inexhaustible treasure of virtues. In short, she became a pantheistic power that was everything in one, *una quae est omnia*.[44]

The authority of Serapis was no less exalted, and his field no less extensive. He also was regarded as a universal god of whom men liked to say that he was "unique."* In him all energies were centered, although the functions of Zeus, of Pluto or of Helios were especially ascribed to him. For many centuries Osiris had been worshiped at Abydos both as author of fecundity and lord of the underworld,[45] and this double character early caused him to be identified with the sun, which fertilizes the earth during its diurnal course and travels through the subterranean realms at night. Thus the conception of this nature divinity, that had already prevailed along the Nile, accorded without difficulty with the solar pantheism that was the last form of Roman paganism. This theological system, which did not gain the upper hand in the Occident until the sec-

* Εἷς Ζεὺς Σάραπις.

ond century of our era, was not brought in by Egypt. It did not have the exclusive predominance there that it had held under the empire, and even in Plutarch's time it was only one creed among many.[46]   The deciding influence in this matter was exercised by the Syrian Baals and the Chaldean astrology.

The theology of the Egyptian mysteries, then, followed rather than led the general influx of ideas.   The same may be said of their ethics.   It did not force itself upon the world by lofty moral precepts, nor by a sublime ideal of holiness.   Many have admired the edifying list in the Book of the Dead, that rightfully or otherwise sets forth the virtues which the deceased claims to have practised in order to obtain a favorable judgment from Osiris.   If one considers the period in which it appears, this ethics is undoubtedly very elevated, but it seems rudimentary and even childish if one compares it with the principles formulated by the Roman jurists, to say nothing of the minute psychological analyses of the Stoic casuists.   In this range of ideas also, the maintenance of the most striking contrasts characterizes Egyptian mentality, which was never shocked by the cruelties and obscenities that sullied the mythology and the ritual.   Like Epicurus at Athens, some of the sacred texts actually invited the believers to enjoy life before the sadness of death.[47]

Isis was not a very austere goddess at the time she entered Italy.   Identified with Venus, as Harpocrates was with Eros, she was honored especially by the women with whom love was a profession.   In Alexandria, the city of pleasure, she had lost all severity, and at Rome this good goddess remained very indulgent to human weaknesses.   Juvenal harshly refers to

her as a procuress,[48] and her temples had a more than
doubtful reputation, for they were frequented by young
men in quest of gallant adventures. Apuleius himself
chose a lewd tale in which to display his fervor as an
initiate.

But we have said that Egypt was full of contradictions, and when a more exacting morality demanded
that the gods should make man virtuous, the Alexandrian mysteries offered to satisfy that demand.

At all times the Egyptian ritual attributed considerable importance to purity, or, to use a more adequate
term, to cleanliness. Before every ceremony the officiating priest had to submit to ablutions, sometimes
to fumigations or anointing, and to abstain from certain foods and from incontinence for a certain time.
Originally no moral idea was connected with this purification. It was considered a means of exorcising
malevolent demons or of putting the priest into a state
in which the sacrifice performed by him could have
the expected effect. It was similar to the diet, shower-
baths and massage prescribed by physicians for physical health. The internal status of the officiating person
was a matter of as much indifference to the celestial
spirits as the actual worth of the deceased was to
Osiris, the judge of the underworld. All that was
necessary to have him open the fields of Aalu to the
soul was to pronounce the liturgic formulas, and if
the soul declared its innocence in the prescribed terms
its word was readily accepted.

But in the Egyptian religion, as in all the religions
of antiquity,[49] the original conception was gradually
transformed and a new idea slowly took its place.
The sacramental acts of purification were now ex-

pected to wipe out moral stains, and people became convinced that they made man better. The devout female votaries of Isis, whom Juvenal[50] pictures as breaking the ice to bathe in the Tiber, and crawling around the temple on their bleeding knees, hoped to atone for their sins and to make up for their shortcomings by means of these sufferings.

When a new ideal grew up in the popular conscience during the second century, when the magicians themselves became pious and serious people, free from passions and appetites, and were honored because of the dignity of their lives more than for their white linen robes,[51] then the virtues of which the Egyptian priests enjoined the practice also became less external. Purity of the heart rather than cleanliness of the body was demanded. Renunciation of sensual pleasures was the indispensable condition for the knowledge of divinity, which was the supreme good.[52] No longer did Isis favor illicit love. In the novel by Xenophon of Ephesus (about 280 A. D.) she protects the heroine's chastity against all pitfalls and assures its triumph. According to the ancient belief man's entire existence was a preparation for the formidable judgment held by Serapis after death, but to have him decide in favor of the mystic, it was not enough to know the rites of the sect; the individual life had to be free from crime; and the master of the infernal regions assigned everybody a place according to his deserts.[53] The doctrine of future retribution was beginning to develop.

However, in this regard, as in their conception of the divinity, the Egyptian mysteries followed the general progress of ideas more than they directed it. Phi-

losophy transformed them, but found in them little
inspiration.

*   *   *

How could a religion, of which neither the theology
nor the ethics was really new, stir up at the same time
so much hostility and fervor among the Romans?
To many minds of to-day theology and ethics constitute religion, but during the classical period it was
different, and the priests of Isis and Serapis conquered
souls mainly by other means. They seduced them by
the powerful attraction of the ritual and retained them
by the marvelous promises of their doctrine of immortality.

To the Egyptians ritual had a value far superior to
that we ascribe to it to-day. It had an operative
strength of its own that was independent of the in-
tentions of the officiating priest. The efficacy of prayer
depended not on the inner disposition of the believer,
but on the correctness of the words, gestures and intonation. Religion was not clearly differentiated from
magic. If a divinity was invoked according to the
correct forms, especially if one knew how to pronounce
its real name, it was compelled to act in conformity
to the will of its priest. The sacred words were an
incantation that compelled the superior powers to obey
the officiating person, no matter what purpose he had
in view. With the knowledge of the liturgy men acquired an immense power over the world of spirits.
Porphyry was surprised and indignant because the
Egyptians sometimes dared to threaten the gods in
their orations.[54] In the consecrations the priest's sum-
mons compelled the gods to come and animate their

statues, and thus his voice created divinities,[55] as originally the almighty voice of Thoth had created the world.[56]

The ritual that conferred such superhuman power[57] developed in Egypt into a state of perfection, completeness and splendor unknown in the Occident. It possessed a unity, a precision and a permanency that stood in striking contrast to the variety of the myths, the uncertainty of the dogmas and the arbitrariness of the interpretations. The sacred books of the Greco-Roman period are a faithful reproduction of the texts that were engraved upon the walls of the pyramids at the dawn of history, notwithstanding the centuries that had passed. Even under the Cæsars the ancient ceremonies dating back to the first ages of Egypt, were scrupulously performed because the smallest word and the least gesture had their importance.

This ritual and the attitude toward it found their way for the most part into the Latin temples of Isis and Serapis. This fact has long been ignored, but there can be no doubt about it. A first proof is that the clergy of those temples were organized just like those of Egypt during the period of the Ptolemies.[58] There was a hierarchy presided over by a high priest, which consisted of *prophetes* skilled in the sacred science, *stolistes,* or *ornatrices,*[59] whose office it was to dress the statues of the gods, *pastophori* who carried the sacred temple plates in the processions, and so on, just as in Egypt. As in their native country, the priests were distinguished from common mortals by a tonsure, by a linen tunic, and by their habits as well as by their garb. They devoted themselves entirely to their ministry and had no other profession. This sacerdotal body always remained Egyptian in character, if not in nationality, because the liturgy it had to perform remained so. In a similar manner the priests of the Baals were Syrians,[60] because they were the only ones that knew how to honor the gods of Syria.

In the first place a daily service had to be held just as in the Nile valley. The Egyptian gods enjoyed a precarious immortality, for they were liable to destruction and dependent on necessities. According to a very primitive conception that always remained alive, they had to be fed, clothed and refreshed every day or else perish. From this fact arose the necessity of a liturgy that was practically the same in every district. It was practised for thousands of years and opposed its unaltering form to the multiplicity of legends and local beliefs.[61]

This daily liturgy was translated into Greek, perhaps later into Latin also; it was adapted to the new requirements by the founders of the Serapeum, and faithfully observed in the Roman temples of the Alexandrian gods. The essential ceremony always was the opening (*apertio*)[62] of the sanctuary. At dawn the statue of the divinity was uncovered and shown to the community in the *naos*, that had been closed and sealed during the night.[63] Then, again as in Egypt, the priest lit the sacred fire and offered libations of water supposed to be from the deified Nile,[64] while he chanted the usual hymns to the sound of flutes. Finally, "erect upon the threshold"—I translate literally from Porphyry—"he awakens the god by calling to him in the Egyptian language."[65] As we see, the god was revived by the sacrifice and, as under the Pharaohs, awoke from his slumber at the calling of

his name. As a matter of fact the name was indis-
solubly connected with the personality; he who could
pronounce the exact name of an individual or of a
divinity was obeyed as a master by his slave.[66] This
fact made it necessary to maintain the original form
of that mysterious word. There was no other motive
for the introduction of a number of barbarian appel-
latives into the magical incantations.

It is also probable that the toilet of the statue was
made every day, that its body and head were dressed,[67]
as in the Egyptian ritual. We have seen that the
ornatrices or *stolistes* were especially entrusted with
these duties. The idol was covered with sumptuous
raiment and ornamented with jewels and gems. An
inscription furnishes us with an inventory of the jewels
worn by an Isis of ancient Cadiz;[68] her ornaments
were more brilliant than those of a Spanish madonna.

During the entire forenoon, from the moment that
a noisy acclamation had greeted the rising of the sun,
the images of the gods were exposed to the silent adoration of the initiates.[69] Egypt is the country whence
contemplative devotion penetrated into Europe. Then,
in the afternoon, a second service was held to close
the sanctuary.[70]

The daily liturgy must have been very absorbing.
This innovation in the Roman paganism was full of
consequences. No longer were sacrifices offered to
the god on certain occasions only, but twice a day
elaborate services were held. As with the Egyptians,
whom Herodotus had termed the most religious of all
peoples,[71] devotion assumed a tendency to fill out the
whole existence and to dominate private and public
interests. The constant repetition of the same prayers

kept up and renewed faith, and, we might say, people
lived continually under the eyes of the gods.

Besides the daily rites of the Abydos liturgy the
holidays marking the beginning of the different seasons were celebrated at the same date every year.[72]
It was the same in Italy. The calendars have preserved the names of several of them, and of one, the
Navigium Isidis, the rhetorician Apuleius[73] has left
us a brilliant description on which, to speak with the
ancients, he emptied all his color tubes. On March
5th, when navigation reopened after the winter months,
a gorgeous procession[74] marched to the coast, and a
ship consecrated to Isis, the protectress of sailors, was
launched. A burlesque group of masked persons
opened the procession, then came the women in white
gowns strewing flowers, the *stolistes* waving the garments of the goddess and the *dadophori* with lighted
torches. After these came the *hymnodes,* whose songs
mingled in turn with the sharp sound of the cross-
flutes and the ringing of the brass timbrels; then the
throngs of the initiates, and finally the priests, with
shaven heads and clad in linen robes of a dazzling
white, bearing the images of animal-faced gods and
strange symbols, as for instance a golden urn containing the sacred water of the Nile. The procession
stopped in front of altars[75] erected along the road,
and on these altars the sacred objects were uncovered
for the veneration of the faithful. The strange and
sumptuous magnificence of these celebrations made a
deep impression on the common people who loved
public entertainments.

But of all the celebrations connected with the worship of Isis the most stirring and the most suggestive

was the commemoration of the "Finding of Osiris" (*Inventio,* Εὕρεσις). Its antecedents date back to remote antiquity. Since the time of the twelfth dynasty, and probably much earlier, there had been held at Abydos and elsewhere a sacred performance similar to the mysteries of our Middle Ages, in which the events of Osiris's passion and resurrection were reproduced. We are in possession of the ritual of those performances.[76] Issuing from the temple, the god fell under Set's blows; around his body funeral lamentations were simulated, and he was buried according to the rites; then Set was vanquished by Horus, and Osiris, restored to life, reentered his temple triumphant over death.

The same myth was represented in almost the same manner at Rome at the beginning of each November.[77] While the priests and the believers moaned and lamented, Isis in great distress sought the divine body of Osiris, whose limbs had been scattered by Typhon. Then, after the corpse had been found, rehabilitated and revived, there was a long outburst of joy, an exuberant jubilation that rang through the temples and the streets so loudly that it annoyed the passers-by.

This mingled despair and enthusiasm acted as strongly upon the feelings of the believers as did the spring-holiday ceremony in the Phrygian religion, and it acted through the same means. Moreover, there was an esoteric meaning attached to it that none but the pious elect understood. Besides the public ceremonies there was a secret worship to which one was admitted only after a gradual initiation. The hero of Apuleius had to submit to the ordeal three times in order to obtain the whole revelation. In Egypt the clergy communicated certain rites and interpretations only upon a promise not to reveal them. In fact this was the case in the worship of Isis at Abydos and elsewhere.[78] When the Ptolemies regulated the Greek ritual of their new religion, it assumed the form of the mysteries spread over the Hellenic world and became very like those of Eleusis. The hand of the Eumolpid Timotheus is noticeable in this connection.[79]

But while the ceremonial of the initiations and even the production of the liturgic drama were thus adapted to the religious habits of the Greeks, the doctrinal contents of the Alexandrian mysteries remained purely Egyptian. The old belief that immortality could be secured by means of an identification of the deceased with Osiris or Serapis never died out.

Perhaps in no other people did the epigram of Fustel de Coulanges find so complete a verification as in the Egyptians: "Death was the first mystery; it started man on the road to the other mysteries."[80] Nowhere else was life so completely dominated by preoccupation with life after death; nowhere else was such minute and complicated care taken to secure and perpetuate another existence for the deceased. The funeral literature, of which we have found a very great number of documents, had acquired a development equaled by no other, and the architecture of no other nation can exhibit tombs comparable with the pyramids or the rock-built sepulchers of Thebes.

This constant endeavor to secure an after-existence for one's self and relatives manifested itself in various ways, but it finally assumed a concrete form in the worship of Osiris. The fate of Osiris, the god who died and returned to life, became the prototype of the fate of every human being that observed the funeral rites. "As truly as Osiris lives," says an Egyptian text, "he also shall live; as truly as Osiris is not dead, shall he not die; as truly as Osiris is not annihilated, shall he not be annihilated."[81]

If, then, the deceased had piously served Osiris-Serapis, he was assimilated to that god, and shared his immortality in the underworld, where the judge of the dead held forth. He lived not as a tenuous shade or as a subtle spirit, but in full possession of his body as well as of his soul. That was the Egyptian doctrine, and that certainly was also the doctrine of the Greco-Latin mysteries.[82]

Through the initiation the mystic was born again, but to a superhuman life, and became the equal of the immortals.[83] In his ecstasy he imagined that he was crossing the threshold of death and contemplating the gods of heaven and hell face to face.[84] If he had accurately followed the prescriptions imposed upon him by Isis and Serapis through their priests, those gods prolonged his life after his decease beyond the duration assigned to it by destiny, and he participated eternally in their beatitude and offered them his homage in their realm.[85] The "unspeakable pleasure" he felt when contemplating the sacred images in the temple[86] became perpetual rapture when he was in the divine presence instead of in the presence of the image, and drawn close to divinity his thirsting soul enjoyed the delights of that ineffable beauty.[87]

When the Alexandrian mysteries spread over Italy under the republic, no religion had ever brought to mankind so formal a promise of blest immortality as these, and this, more than anything else, lent them an irresistible power of attraction. Instead of the vague and contradictory opinions of the philosophers in regard to the destiny of the soul, Serapis offered certainty founded on divine revelation corroborated by the faith of the countless generations that had adhered to it. What the votaries of Orpheus had confusedly discovered through the veil of the legends, and taught to Magna Grecia,[88] namely, that this earthly life was a trial, a preparation for a higher and purer life, that the happiness of an after-life could be secured by means of rites and observances revealed by the gods themselves, all this was now preached with a firmness and precision hitherto unknown. These eschatological doctrines in particular, helped Egypt to conquer the Latin world and especially the miserable masses, on whom the weight of all the iniquities of Roman society rested heavily.

* * *

The power and popularity of that belief in future life has left traces even in the French language, and in concluding this study, from which I have been compelled to exclude every picturesque detail, I would like to point out how a French word of to-day dimly perpetuates the memory of the old Egyptian ideas.

During the cold nights of their long winters the Scandinavians dreamed of a Walhalla where the deceased warriors sat in well-closed brilliantly illuminated halls, warming themselves and drinking the strong liquor served by the Valkyries; but under the burning sky of Egypt, near the arid sand where thirst kills the traveler, people wished that their dead might find a limpid spring in their future wanderings to assuage the heat that devoured them, and that they might be refreshed by the breezes of the north wind.[89]   Even at Rome the adherents of the Alexandrian gods frequently inscribed the following wish on their tombs: "May Osiris give you fresh water."[90]   Soon this water became, in a figurative sense, the fountain of life pouring out immortality to thirsting souls.   The metaphor obtained such popularity that in Latin *refrigerium* became synonymous with comfort and happiness.   The term retained this meaning in the liturgy of the church,[91] and for that reason people continue to pray for spiritual *rafraîchissement* of the dead although the Christian paradise has very little resemblance to the fields of Aalu.

SYRIA.

THE religions of Syria never had the same solidarity in the Occident as those from Egypt or Asia Minor. From the coasts of Phœnicia and the valleys of Lebanon, from the borders of the Euphrates and the oases of the desert, they came at various periods, like the successive waves of the incoming tide, and existed side by side in the Roman world without uniting, in spite of their similarities. The isolation in which they remained and the persistent adherence of their believers to their particular rites were a consequence and reflection of the disunited condition of Syria herself, where the different tribes and districts remained more distinct than anywhere else, even after they had been brought together under the domination of Rome. They doggedly preserved their local gods and Semitic dialects.

It would be impossible to outline each one of these religions in detail at this time and to reconstruct their history, because our meager information would not permit it, but we can indicate, in a general way, how they penetrated into the Occidental countries at various periods, and we can try to define their common characteristics by showing what new elements the Syrian paganism brought to the Romans.

The first Semitic divinity to enter Italy was *Atar-*

gatis, frequently mistaken for the Phœnician Astarte, who had a famous temple at Bambyce or Hierapolis, not far from the Euphrates, and was worshiped with her husband, Hadad, in a considerable part of Syria besides. The Greeks considered her as the principal Syrian goddess,* and in the Latin countries she was commonly known as *dea Syria,* a name corrupted into *Iasura* by popular use.

We all remember the unedifying descriptions of her itinerant priests that Lucian and Apuleius[1] have left. Led by an old eunuch of dubious habits, a crowd of painted young men marched along the highways with an ass that bore an elaborately adorned image of the goddess. Whenever they passed through a village or by some rich villa, they went through their sacred exercises. To the shrill accompaniment of their Syrian flutes they turned round and round, and with their heads thrown back fluttered about and gave vent to hoarse clamors until vertigo seized them and insensibility was complete. Then they flagellated themselves wildly, struck themselves with swords and shed their blood in front of a rustic crowd which pressed closely about them, and finally they took up a profitable collection from the wondering spectators. They received jars of milk and wine, cheeses, flour, bronze coins of small denominations and even some silver pieces, all of which disappeared in the folds of their capacious robes. If opportunity presented they knew how to increase their profits by means of clever thefts or by making commonplace predictions for a moderate consideration.

This picturesque description, based on a novel by

* Συρία θεά.

Lucius of Patras, is undoubtedly extreme. It is difficult to believe that the sacerdotal corps of the goddess of Hierapolis should have consisted only of charlatans and thieves. But how can the presence in the Occident of that begging and low nomadic clergy be explained?

It is certain that the first worshipers of the Syrian goddess in the Latin world were slaves. During the wars against Antiochus the Great a number of prisoners were sent to Italy to be sold at public auction, as was the custom, and the first appearance in Italy of the *Chaldaei*[2] has been connected with that event. The *Chaldaei* were Oriental fortune-tellers who asserted that their predictions were based on the Chaldean astrology. They found credulous clients among the farm laborers, and Cato gravely exhorts the good landlord to oust them from his estate.[3]

Beginning with the second century before Christ, merchants began to import Syrian slaves. At that time Delos was the great trade center in this human commodity, and in that island especially Atargatis was worshiped by citizens of Athens and Rome.[4] Trade spread her worship in the Occident.[5] We know that the great slave revolution that devastated Sicily in 134 B. C. was started by a slave from Apamea, a votary of the Syrian goddess. Simulating divine madness, he called his companions to arms, pretending to act in accordance with orders from heaven.[6] This detail, which we know by chance, shows how considerable a proportion of Semites there was in the gangs working the fields, and how much authority Atargatis enjoyed in the rural centers. Being too poor to build temples for their national goddess, those agricultural laborers

waited with their devotions until a band of itinerant
galli passed through the distant hamlet where the lot
of the auction had sent them. The existence of those
wandering priests depended, therefore, on the number
of fellow-countrymen they met in the rural districts,
who supported them by sacrificing a part of their poor
savings.

Towards the end of the republic those diviners
appear to have enjoyed rather serious consideration
at Rome. It was a pythoness from Syria that advised
Marius on the sacrifices he was to perform.[7]

Under the empire the importation of slaves increased. Depopulated Italy needed more and more
foreign hands, and Syria furnished a large quota of
the forced immigration of cultivators. But those
Syrians, quick and intelligent as they were strong
and industrious, performed many other functions.
They filled the countless domestic positions in the
palaces of the aristocracy and were especially appreciated as litter-bearers.[8] The imperial and municipal
administrations, as well as the big contractors to whom
customs and the mines were farmed out, hired or
bought them in large numbers, and even in the remotest border provinces the *Syrus* was found serving
princes, cities or private individuals. The worship
of the Syrian goddess profited considerably by the
economic current that continually brought new worshipers. We find her mentioned in the first century
of our era in a Roman inscription referring in precise
terms to the slave market, and we know that Nero
took a devout fancy to the stranger that did not, however, last very long.[9] In the popular Trastevere quarter
she had a temple until the end of paganism.[10]

During the imperial period, however, the slaves were no longer the only missionaries that came from Syria, and Atargatis was no longer the only divinity from that country to be worshiped in the Occident. The propagation of the Semitic worship progressed for the most part in a different manner under the empire.

At the beginning of our era the Syrian merchants, *Syri negotiatores,* undertook a veritable colonization of the Latin provinces.[11] During the second century before Christ the traders of that nation had established settlements along the coast of Asia Minor, on the Piraeus, and in the Archipelago. At Delos, a small island but a large commercial center, they maintained several associations that worshiped their national gods, in particular Hadad and Atargatis. But the wars that shook the Orient at the end of the republic, and above all the growth of piracy, ruined maritime commerce and stopped emigration. This began again with renewed vigor when the establishment of the empire guaranteed the safety of the seas and when the Levantine traffic attained a development previously unknown. We can trace the history of the Syrian establishments in the Latin provinces from the first to the seventh century, and recently we have begun to appreciate their economic, social and religious importance at its true value.

The Syrians' love of lucre was proverbial. Active, compliant and able, frequently little scrupulous, they knew how to conclude first small deals, then larger ones, everywhere. Using the special talents of their race to advantage, they succeeded in establishing themselves on all coasts of the Mediterranean, even in

Spain.[12] At Malaga an inscription mentions a cor-
poration formed by them. The Italian ports where
business was especially active, Pozzuoli, Ostia, later
Naples, attracted them in great numbers. But they
did not confine themselves to the seashore; they penetrated far into the interior of the countries, wherever
they hoped to find profitable trade. They followed the
commercial highways and traveled up the big rivers.
By way of the Danube they went as far as Pannonia,
by way of the Rhone they reached Lyons. In Gaul
they were especially numerous. In this new country
that had just been opened to commerce fortunes could
be made rapidly   A rescript discovered on the range
of the Lebanon is addressed to sailors from Arles,
who had charge of the transportation of grain, and in
the department of Ain a bilingual epitaph has been
found mentioning a merchant of the third century,
Thaïm or Julian, son of Saad, decurion of the city
of Canatha in Syria, who owned two factories in the
Rhone basin, where he handled goods from Aqui-
tania.[13] Thus the Syrians spread over the entire province as far as Treves, where they had a strong colony.
Not even the barbarian invasions of the fifth century
stopped their immigration. Saint Jerome describes
them traversing the entire Roman world amidst the
troubles of the invasion, prompted by the lust of gain
to defy all dangers. In the barbarian society the part
played by this civilized and city-bred element was even
more considerable. Under the Merovingians in about
591 they had sufficient influence at Paris to have one
of their number elected bishop and to gain possession
of all ecclesiastical offices. Gregory of Tours tells
how King Gontrand, on entering the city of Orleans

in 585, was received by a crowd praising him "in the
language of the Latins, the Jews and the Syrians."[14]
The merchant colonies existed until the Saracen cor-
sairs destroyed the commerce of the Mediterranean.

Those establishments exercised a strong influence
upon the economic and material life of the Latin provinces, especially in Gaul. As bankers the Syrians
concentrated a large share of the money business in
their hands and monopolized the importing of the valuable Levantine commodities as well as of the articles
of luxury; they sold wines, spices, glassware, silks
and purple fabrics, also objects wrought by goldsmiths,
to be used as patterns by the native artisans. Their
moral and religious influence was not less considerable:
for instance, it has been shown that they furthered
the development of monastic life during the Christian
period, and that the devotion to the crucifix[15] that
grew up in opposition to the monophysites, was introduced into the Occident by them. During the first
five centuries Christians felt an unconquerable repugnance to the representation of the Saviour of the
world nailed to an instrument of punishment more
infamous than the guillotine of to-day. The Syrians
were the first to substitute reality in all its pathetic
horror for a vague symbolism.

In pagan times the religious ascendency of that
immigrant population was no less remarkable. The
merchants always took an interest in the affairs of
heaven as well as in those of earth. At all times Syria
was a land of ardent devotion, and in the first century
its children were as fervid in propagating their barbarian gods in the Occident as after their conversion
they were enthusiastic in spreading Christianity as far

as Turkestan and China. As soon as the merchants had established their places of business in the islands of the Archipelago during the Alexandrian period, and in the Latin period under the empire, they founded chapels in which they practised their exotic rites.

It was easy for the divinities of the Phœnician coast to cross the seas. Among them were Adonis, whom the women of Byblos mourned; Balmarcodes, "the Lord of the dances," who came from Beirut; Marna, the master of rain, worshiped at Gaza; and Maiuma,[16] whose nautical holiday was celebrated every spring on the coast near Ostia as well as in the Orient.

Besides these half Hellenized religions, others of a more purely Semitic nature came from the interior of the country, because the merchants frequently were natives of the cities of the *Hinterland*, as for instance Apamea or Epiphanea in Coele-Syria, or even of villages in that flat country. As Rome incorporated the small kingdoms beyond the Lebanon and the Orontes that had preserved a precarious independence, the current of emigration increased. In 71 Commagene, which lies between the Taurus and the Euphrates, was annexed by Vespasian, a little later the dynasties of Chalcis and Emesa were also deprived of their power. Nero, it appears, took possession of Damascus; half a century later Trajan established the new province of Arabia in the south (106 A. D.), and the oasis of Palmyra, a great mercantile center, lost its autonomy at the same time. In this manner Rome extended her direct authority as far as the desert, over countries that were only superficially Hellenized, and where the native devotions had preserved all their savage fervor. From that time constant communication was established between Italy and those regions which had heretofore been almost inaccessible. As roads were built commerce developed, and together with the interests of trade the needs of administration created an incessant exchange of men, of products and of beliefs between those out-of-the-way countries and the Latin provinces.

These annexations, therefore, were followed by a renewed influx of Syrian divinities into the Occident. At Pozzuoli, the last port of call of the Levantine vessels, there was a temple to the Baal of Damascus (*Jupiter Damascenus*) in which leading citizens officiated, and there were altars on which two golden camels[17] were offered to Dusares, a divinity who had come from the interior of Arabia. They kept company with a divinity of more ancient repute, the Hadad of Baabek - Heliopolis (*Jupiter Heliopolitanus*), whose immense temple, considered one of the world's wonders,[18] had been restored by Antoninus Pius, and may still be seen facing Lebanon in majestic elegance. Heliopolis and Beirut had been the most ancient colonies founded by Augustus in Syria. The god of Heliopolis participated in the privileged position granted to the inhabitants of those two cities, who worshiped in a common devotion,[19] and he was naturalized as a Roman with greater ease than the others.

The conquest of all Syria as far as Euphrates and the subjection of even a part of Mesopotamia aided the diffusion of the Semitic religions in still another manner. From these regions, which were partly inhabited by fighting races, the Cæsars drew recruits for the imperial army. They levied a great number of legionaries, but especially auxiliary troops, who were transferred to the frontiers. Troopers and foot-soldiers from those provinces furnished important contingents to the garrisons of Europe and Africa. For instance, a cohort of one thousand archers from Emesa was established in Pannonia, another of archers from Damascus in upper Germany; Mauretania received irregulars from Palmyra, and bodies of troops levied in Ituraea, on the outskirts of the Arabian desert, were encamped in Dacia, Germany, Egypt and Cappadocia at the same time. Commagene alone furnished no less than six cohorts of five hundred men each that were sent to the Danube and into Numidia.[20]

The number of inscriptions consecrated by soldiers proves both the ardor of their faith and the diversity of their beliefs. Like the sailors of to-day who are transferred to strange climes and exposed to incessant danger, they were constantly inclined to invoke the protection of heaven, and remained attached to the gods who seemed to remind them in their exile of the distant home country. Therefore it is not surprising that the Syrians who served in the army should have practised the religion of their Baals in the neighborhood of their camps. In the north of England, near the wall of Hadrian, an inscription in verse in honor of the goddess of Hierapolis has been found; its author was a prefect, probably of a cohort of Hamites stationed at this distant post.[21]

Not all the soldiers, however, went to swell the ranks of believers worshiping divinities that had long been adopted by the Latin world, as did that officer. They also brought along new ones that had come from a still greater distance than their predecessors, in fact

from the outskirts of the barbarian world, because
from those regions in particular trained men could
be obtained. There were, for instance, *Baltis,* an "Our
Lady" from Osroene beyond the Euphrates;[22] *Aziz,*
the "strong god" of Edessa, who was identified with
the star Lucifer;[23] *Malakbel,* the "Lord's messenger,"
patron of the soldiers from Palmyra, who appeared
with several companions at Rome, in Numidia and in
Dacia.[24] The most celebrated of those gods then was
the Jupiter of Doliche, a small city of Commagene,
that owed its fame to him. Because of the troops
coming from that region, this obscure Baal, whose
name is mentioned by no author, found worshipers in
every Roman province as far as Africa, Germany and
Brittany. The number of known inscriptions consecrated to him exceeds a hundred, and it is still growing. Being originally nothing but a god of lightning,
represented as brandishing an ax, this local genius
of the tempest was elevated to the rank of tutelary
divinity of the imperial armies.[25]

The diffusion of the Semitic religions in Italy that
commenced imperceptibly under the republic became
more marked after the first century of our era. Their
expansion and multiplication were rapid, and they
attained the apogee of their power during the third
century. Their influence became almost predominant
when the accession of the Severi lent them the support
of a court that was half Syrian. Functionaries of all
kinds, senators and officers, vied with each other in
devotion to the patron gods of their sovereigns, gods
which the sovereigns patronized in turn. Intelligent
and ambitious princesses like Julia Domna, Julia
Maesa, Julia Mammea, whose ascendency was very

considerable, became propagators of their national religion. We all know the audacious pronunciamento of the year 218 that placed upon the throne the fourteen-year-old emperor Heliogabalus, a worshiper of the Baal of Emesa. His intention was to give supremacy over all other gods to his barbarian divinity, who had heretofore been almost unknown. The ancient authors narrate with indignation how this crowned priest attempted to elevate his black stone, the coarse idol brought from Emesa, to the rank of supreme divinity of the empire by subordinating the whole ancient pantheon to it; they never tire of giving revolting details about the dissoluteness of the debaucheries for which the festivities of the new *Sol invictus Elagabal* furnished a pretext.[26] However, the question arises whether the Roman historians, being very hostile to that foreigner who haughtily favored the customs of his own country, did not misrepresent or partly misunderstand the facts. Heliogabalus's attempt to have his god recognized as supreme, and to establish a kind of monotheism in heaven as there was monarchy on earth, was undoubtedly too violent, awkward and premature, but it was in keeping with the aspirations of the time, and it must be remembered that the imperial policy could find the support of powerful Syrian colonies not only at Rome but all over the empire.

Half a century later Aurelian[27] was inspired by the same idea when he created a new worship, that of the "Invincible Sun." Worshiped in a splendid temple, by pontiffs equal in rank to those of ancient Rome, having magnificent plays held in his honor every fourth year, *Sol invictus* was also elevated to the supreme rank in the divine hierarchy, and became the special protector of the emperors and the empire. The country where Aurelian found the pattern he sought to reproduce, was again Syria. Into the new sanctuary he transferred the images of Bel and Helios, taken from Palmyra, after it had fallen before his arms.

* * *

The sovereigns, then, twice attempted to replace the Capitoline Jupiter by a Semitic god and to make a Semitic religion the principal and official religion of the Romans. They proclaimed the fall of the old Latin idolatry and the accession of a new paganism taken from Syria. What was the superiority attributed to the creeds of that country? Why did even an Illyrian general like Aurelian look for the most perfect type of pagan religion in that country? That is the problem to be solved, but it must remain unsolved unless an exact account is given of the fate of the Syrian beliefs under the empire.

That question has not as yet been very completely elucidated. Besides the superficial opuscule of Lucian on the *dea Syria,* we find scarcely any reliable information in the Greek or Latin writers. The work by Philo of Byblos is a euhemeristic interpretation of an alleged Phœnician cosmogony, and a composition of little merit. Neither have we the original texts of the Semitic liturgies, as we have for Egypt. Whatever we have learned we owe especially to the inscriptions, and while these furnish highly valuable indications as to the date and area of expansion of these religions, they tell us hardly anything about their doctrines. Light on this subject may be expected from the excavations that are being made in the great sanctuaries of Syria, and also from a more exact interpretation of the sculptured monuments that we now possess in great numbers, especially those of Jupiter Dolichenus.

Some characteristics of the Semitic paganism, however, are known at present, and it must be admitted that it would appear at a disadvantage if judged by those noticeable features that first attract our attention. It had retained a stock of very primitive ideas and some aboriginal nature worship that had lasted through many centuries and was to persist, in part, under Christianity and Islam until the present day.[28] Such were the worship of high elevations on which a rustic enclosure sometimes marked the limits of the consecrated territory; the worship of the waters that flow to the sea, the streams that arise in the mountains, the springs that gush out of the soil, the ponds, the lakes and the wells, into all of which offerings were thrown with the idea either of venerating in them the thirst-quenching liquid or else the fecund nature of the earth; the worship of the trees that shaded the altars and that nobody dared to fell or mutilate; the worship of stones, especially of the rough stones called bethels that were regarded, as their name (*beth-El*) indicates, as the residence of the god, or rather, as the matter in which the god was embodied.[29] Aphrodite Astarte was worshiped in the shape of a conical stone at Paphos, and a black aerolite covered with projections and depressions to which a symbolic meaning was attributed represented Elagabal, and was transferred from Emesa to Rome, as we have said.

The animals, as well as inanimate things, received their share of homage. Remnants of the old Semitic zoolatry perpetuated themselves until the end of paganism and even later. Frequently the gods were repre-

sented standing erect on animals. Thus the Dolichean
Baal stood on a steer, and his spouse on a lion. Around
certain temples there were sacred parks, in which savage beasts roamed at liberty,[30] a reminder of the time
when they were considered divine. Two animals especially were the objects of universal veneration, the
pigeon and the fish. Vagrant multitudes of pigeons
received the traveler landing at Ascalon,[31] and they
played about the enclosures of all the temples of Astarte[32] in flocks resembling white whirlwinds. The
pigeon belonged, properly speaking, to the goddess
of love, whose symbol it has remained above all to the
people worshiping that goddess.

> "Quid referam ut volitet crebras intacta per urbes
> Alba Palaestino sancta columba Syro?"[33]

The fish was sacred to Atargatis, who undoubtedly
had been represented in that shape at first, as Dagon
always was.[34] The fish were kept in ponds in the
proximity of the temples.[35] A superstitious fear prevented people from touching them, because the goddess
punished the sacrilegious by covering their bodies
with ulcers and tumors.[36] At certain mystic repasts,
however, the priests and initiates consumed the forbidden food in the belief that they were absorbing the
flesh of the divinity herself. That worship and its
practices, which were spread over Syria, probably suggested the ichthus symbolism in the Christian period.[37]

However, over this lower and primordial stratum
that still cropped out here and there, other less rudimentary beliefs had formed. Besides inanimate objects
and animals, the Syrian paganism worshiped personal
divinities especially. The character of the gods that
were originally adored by the Semitic tribes has been

ingeniously reconstructed.[38]   Each tribe had its Baal
and Baalat who protected it and whom only its members were permitted to worship.   The name of *Ba'al,*
"master," summarizes the conception people had of
him.   In the first place he was regarded as the sovereign of his votaries, and his position in regard to
them was that of an Oriental potentate towards his
subjects; they were his servants, or rather his slaves.[39]
The Baal was at the same time the "master" or pro-
prietor of the country in which he resided and which
he made fertile by causing springs to gush from its
soil.   Or his domain was the firmament and he was
the *dominus caeli,* whence he made the waters fall to
the roar of tempests.   He was always united with a
celestial or earthly "queen" and, in the third place,
he was the "lord" or husband of the "lady" associated
with him.   The one represented the male, the other
the female principle; they were the authors of all
fecundity, and as a consequence the worship of the
divine couple often assumed a sensual and voluptuous
character.

As a matter of fact, immorality was nowhere so
flagrant as in the temples of Astarte, whose female
servants honored the goddess with untiring ardor.   In
no country was sacred prostitution so developed as in
Syria, and in the Occident it was to be found practically only where the Phœnicians had imported it, as
on Mount Eryx.   Those aberrations, that were kept
up until the end of paganism,[40] probably have their
explanation in the primitive constitution of the Semitic
tribe, and the religious custom must have been originally one of the forms of exogamy, which compelled
the woman to unite herself first with a stranger.[41]

As a second blemish, the Semitic religions practised human immolations longer than any other religion, sacrificing children and grown men in order to please sanguinary gods. In spite of Hadrian's prohibition of those murderous offerings,[42] they were maintained in certain clandestine rites and in the lowest practices of magic, up to the fall of the idols, and even later. They corresponded to the ideas of a period during which the life of a captive or slave had no greater value than that of an animal.

These sacred practices and many others, on which Lucian complacently enlarges in his opuscule on the goddess of Hierapolis, daily revived the habits of a barbarous past in the temples of Syria. Of all the conceptions that had successively dominated the country, none had completely disappeared. As in Egypt, beliefs of very different date and origin coexisted, without any attempt to make them agree, or without success when the task was undertaken. In these beliefs zoolatry, litholatry and all the other nature worships outlived the savagery that had created them. More than anywhere else the gods had remained the chieftains of clans[43] because the tribal organizations of Syria were longer lived and more developed than those of any other region. Under the empire many districts were still subjected to the tribal régime and commanded by "ethnarchs" or "phylarchs."[44] Religion, which sacrificed the lives of the men and the honor of the women to the divinity, had in many regards remained on the moral level of unsocial and sanguinary tribes. Its obscene and atrocious rites called forth exasperated indignation on the part of

the Roman conscience when Heliogabalus attempted
to introduce them into Italy with his Baal of Emesa.

* * *

How, then, can one explain the fact that in spite of
all, the Syrian gods imposed themselves upon the
Occident and made even the Cæsars accept them? The
reason is that the Semitic paganism can no more be
judged by certain revolting practices, that perpetuated
in the heart of civilization the barbarity and puerilities
of an uncultivated society, than the religion of the
Nile can be so judged. As in the case of Egypt we
must distinguish between the sacerdotal religion and
the infinitely varied popular religion that was embodied in local customs. Syria possessed a number of
great sanctuaries in which an educated clergy medi-
tated and expatiated upon the nature of the divine
beings and on the meaning of traditions inherited from
remote ancestors. As their own interests demanded,
that clergy constantly amended the sacred traditions
and modified their spirit when the letter was immutable, in order to make them agree with the new
aspirations of a more advanced period. They had
their mysteries and their initiates to whom they revealed a wisdom that was above the vulgar beliefs of
the masses.[45]

Frequently we can draw diametrically opposite conclusions from the same principle. In that manner the
old idea of *tabu,* that seems to have transformed the
temples of Astarte into houses of debauchery, also
became the source of a severe code of morals. The
Semitic tribes were haunted with the fear of the tabu.
A multitude of things were either impure or sacred
because, in the original confusion, those two notions

had not been clearly differentiated. Man's ability to
use the products of nature to satisfy his needs, was
thus limited by a number of prohibitions, restrictions
and conditions. He who touched a forbidden object
was soiled and corrupted, his fellows did not associate
with him and he could no longer participate in the
sacrifices. In order to wipe out the blemish, he had
recourse to ablutions and other ceremonies known to
the priests. Purity, that had originally been considered simply physical, soon became ritualistic and finally
spiritual. Life was surrounded by a network of circumstances subject to certain conditions, every vio-
lation of which meant a fall and demanded penance.
The anxiety to remain constantly in a state of holiness
or regain that state when it had been lost, filled one's
entire existence. It was not peculiar to the Semitic
tribes, but they ascribed a prime importance to it.[46]
And the gods, who necessarily possessed this quality
in an eminent degree, were holy beings ($\H{\alpha}\gamma\iota o\iota$)[47] *par
excellence*.

In this way principles of conduct and dogmas of
faith have frequently been derived from instinctive
and absurd old beliefs. All theological doctrines that
were accepted in Syria modified the prevailing ancient
conception of the Baals. But in our present state of
knowledge it is very difficult indeed to determine the
shares that the various influences contributed, from
the conquests of Alexander to the Roman domination,
to make the Syrian paganism what it became under
the Cæsars. The civilization of the Seleucid empire
is little known, and we cannot determine what caused
the alliance of Greek thought with the Semitic traditions.[48] The religions of the neighboring nations

also had an undeniable influence. Phœnicia and Lebanon remained moral tributaries of Egypt long after they had liberated themselves from the suzerainty of the Pharaohs. The theogony of Philo of Byblos took gods and myths from that country, and at Heliopolis Hadad was honored "according to Egyptian rather than Syrian rite."[49] The rigorous monotheism of the Jews, who were dispersed over the entire country, must also have acted as an active ferment of transformation.[50] But it was Babylon that retained the intellectual supremacy, even after its political ruin. The powerful sacerdotal caste ruling it did not fall with the independence of the country, and it survived the conquests of Alexander as it had previously lived through the Persian domination. The researches of Assyriologists have shown that its ancient worship persisted under the Seleucides, and at the time of Strabo the "Chaldeans" still discussed cosmology and first principles in the rival schools of Borsippa and Orchoë.[51] The ascendancy of that erudite clergy affected all surrounding regions; it was felt by Persia in the east, Cappadocia in the north, but more than anywhere else by the Syrians, who were connected with the Oriental Semites by bonds of language and blood. Even after the Parthians had wrested the valley of the Euphrates from the Seleucides, relations with the great temples of that region remained uninterrupted. The plains of Mesopotamia, inhabited by races of like origin, extended on both sides of an artificial border line; great commercial roads followed the course of the two rivers flowing into the Persian Gulf or cut across the desert, and the pilgrims came to Babylon, as Lucian tells us, to perform their devotions to the Lady of Bambyce.[52]

Ever since the Captivity, constant spiritual relations had existed between Judaism and the great religious metropolis. At the birth of Christianity they manifested themselves in the rise of gnostic sects in which the Semitic mythology formed strange combinations with Jewish and Greek ideas and furnished the foundation for extravagant superstructures.[53] Finally, during the decline of the empire, it was Babylon again from which emanated Manicheism, the last form of idolatry received in the Latin world. We can imagine how powerful the religious influence of that country on the Syrian paganism must have been.

That influence manifested itself in various ways. First, it introduced new gods. In this way Bel passed from the Babylonian pantheon into that of Palmyra and was honored throughout northern Syria.[54] It also caused ancient divinities to be arranged in new groups. To the primitive couple of the Baal and the Baalat a third member was added in order to form one of those triads dears to Chaldean theology. This took place at Hierapolis as well as at Heliopolis, and the three gods of the latter city, Hadad, Atargatis and Simios, became Jupiter, Venus and Mercury in Latin inscriptions.[55] Finally, and most important, astrolatry wrought radical changes in the characters of the celestial powers, and, as a further consequence, in the entire Roman paganism. In the first place it gave them a second personality in addition to their own nature. The sidereal myths superimposed themselves upon the agrarian myths, and gradually obliterated them. Astrology, born on the banks of the Euphrates, imposed itself in Egypt upon the haughty and unapproachable clergy of the most conservative of all nations.[56] Syria re-

ceived it without reserve and surrendered uncondi-
tionally;[57] numismatics and archeology as well as
literature prove this. King Antiochus of Commagene,
for instance, who died 34 B. C., built himself a monumental tomb on a spur of the Taurus, in which he
placed his horoscope, designed on a large bas-relief,
beside the images of his ancestral divinities.[58]

The importance which the introduction of the Syrian religions into the Occident has for us consists
therefore in the fact that indirectly they brought certain theological doctrines of the Chaldeans with them,
just as Isis and Serapis carried beliefs of old Egypt
from Alexandria to the Occident. The Roman empire
received successively the religious tribute of the two
great nations that had formerly ruled the Oriental
world. It is characteristic that the god Bel whom
Aurelian brought from Asia to set up as the protector
of his states, was in reality a Babylonian who had
emigrated to Palmyra,[59] a cosmopolitan center apparently predestined by virtue of its location to become the intermediary between the civilizations of the
Euphrates and the Mediterranean.

The influence exercised by the speculations of the
Chaldeans upon Greco-Roman thought can be asserted
positively, but cannot as yet be strictly defined. It
was at once philosophic and religious, literary and
popular. The entire neo-Platonist school used the
names of those venerable masters, but it cannot be
determined how much it really owes to them. A
selection of poems that has often been quoted since
the third century, under the title of "Chaldaic Oracles"*
combines the ancient Hellenic theories with a fantastic

* Λόγια Χαλδαϊκά.

mysticism that was certainly imported from the Orient. It is to Babylonia what the literature of Hermes Trismegistus is to Egypt, and it is equally difficult to determine the nature of the ingredients that the author put into his sacred compositions. But at an earlier date the Syrian religions had spread far and wide in the Occident ideas conceived on the distant banks of the Euphrates. I shall try to indicate briefly what their share in the pagan syncretism was.

We have seen that the gods from Alexandria gained souls especially by the promise of blessed immortality. Those from Syria must also have satisfied doubts tormenting all the minds of that time. As a matter of fact the old Semitic ideas on man's fate in after-life were little comforting. We know how sad, dull and hopeless their conception of life after death was. The dead descended into a subterranean realm where they led a miserable existence, a weak reflection of the one they had lost; since they were subject to wants and suffering, they had to be supported by funeral offerings placed on their sepulchers by their descendants. Those ancient beliefs and customs were found also in primitive Greece and Italy.

This rudimentary eschatology, however, gave way to quite a different conception, one that was closely related to the Chaldean astrology, and which spread over the Occident towards the end of the republic. According to this doctrine the soul returned to heaven after death, to live there among the divine stars. While it remained on earth it was subject to all the bitter necessities of a destiny determined by the revolutions of the stars; but when it ascended into the upper regions, it escaped that fate and even the limits of time;

it shared equally in the immortality of the sidereal gods that surrounded it.[60] In the opinion of some, the soul was attracted by the rays of the sun, and after passing through the moon, where it was purified, it lost itself in the shining star of day.[61] Another more purely astrological theory, that was undoubtedly a development of the former, taught that the soul descended to earth from the heights of heaven by passing through the spheres of the seven planets. During its passage it acquired the dispositions and qualities proper to each planet. After death it returned to its original abode by the same route. To get from one sphere to another, it had to pass a door guarded by a commandant* [62] Only the souls of initiates knew the password that made those incorruptible guardians yield, and under the conduct of a psychopompus[63] they ascended safely from zone to zone. As the soul rose it divested itself of the passions and qualities it had acquired on its descent to the earth as though they were garments, and, free from sensuality, it penetrated into the eighth heaven to enjoy everlasting happiness as a subtle essence.

Perhaps this doctrine, undoubtedly of Babylonian origin, was not generally accepted by the Syrian religions, as it was by the mysteries of Mithra, but these religions, impregnated with astrology, certainly propagated the belief that the souls of those worshipers that had led pious lives were elevated to the heights of heaven, where an apotheosis made them the equals of the luminous gods.[64] Under the empire this doctrine slowly supplanted all others; the Elysian fields, which the votaries of Isis and Serapis still located in

* ἄρχων.

the depths of the earth, were transferred into the ether bathing the fixed stars,[65] and the underworld was thereafter reserved for the wicked who had not been allowed to pass through the celestial gates.

The sublime regions occupied by the purified souls were also the abode of the supreme god.[66] When it transformed the ideas on the destiny of man, astrology also modified those relating to the nature of the divinity. In this matter the Syrian religions were especially original; for even if the Alexandrian mysteries offered man just as comforting prospects of immortality as the eschatology of their rivals, they were backward in building up a commensurate theology. To the Semitic races belongs the honor of having reformed the ancient fetichism most thoroughly. Their base and narrow conceptions of early times to which we can trace their existence, broaden and rise until they form a kind of monotheism.

As we have seen, the Syrian tribes worshiped a god of lightning,[67] like all primitive races. That god opened the reservoirs of the firmament to let the rain fall and split the giant trees of the woods with the double ax that always remained his emblem.[68] When the progress of astronomy removed the constellations to incommensurable distances, the "Baal of the Heavens" (Ba'al šamîn) had to grow in majesty. Undoubtedly at the time of the Achemenides, he was connected with the Ahura-Mazda of the Persians, the ancient god of the vault of heaven, who had become the highest physical and moral power, and this connection helped to transform the old genius of thunder.[69] People continued to worship the material heaven in him; under the Romans he was still simply called

Caelus, as well as "Celestial Jupiter" (*Jupiter Caelestis,* Ζεὺς Οὐράνιος),[70] but it was a heaven studied
by a sacred science that venerated its harmonious
mechanism. The Seleucides represented him on their
coins with a crescent over his forehead and carrying
a sun with seven rays, to symbolize the fact that he
presided over the course of the stars;[71] or else he was
shown with the two Dioscuri at his side, heroes who
enjoyed life and suffered death in turn, according to
the Greek myth, and who had become the symbols
of the two celestial hemispheres. Religious uranography placed the residence of the supreme divinity
in the most elevated region of the world, fixing its
abode in the zone most distant from the earth, above
the planets and the fixed stars. This fact was intended
to be expressed by the term Most-High* applied to
the Syrian Baals as well as to Jehovah.[72] According
to this cosmic religion, the Most High resided in the
immense orb that contained the spheres of all the stars
and embraced the entire universe which was subject
to his domination. The Latins translated the name of
this "Hypsistos" by *Jupiter summus exsuperantissimus*[73] to indicate his preeminence over all divine beings.

As a matter of fact, his power was infinite. The
primary postulate of the Chaldean astrology was that
all phenomena and events of this world were necessarily determined by sidereal influence. The changes
of nature, as well as the dispositions of men, were
controlled according to fate, by the divine energies
that resided in the heavens. In other words, the gods
were almighty; they were the masters of destiny that
governed the universe absolutely. The notion of their

* "Ὕψιστος.

omnipotence resulted from the development of the
ancient autocracy with which the Baals were credited.
As we have stated, they were conceived after the
image of an Asiatic monarch, and the religious terminology was evidently intended to display the humil-
ity of their priests toward them. In Syria we find
nothing analogous to what existed in Egypt, where
the priest thought he could compel the gods to act,
and even dared to threaten them.[74] The distance sepa-
rating the human and the divine always was much
greater with the Semitic tribes, and all that astrology
did was to emphasize the distance more strongly by
giving it a doctrinal foundation and a scientific appearance. In the Latin world the Asiatic religions propagated the conception of the absolute and illimitable
sovereignty of God over the earth. Apuleius calls
the Syrian goddess *omnipotens et omniparens,* "mistress and mother of all things."[75]

The observation of the starry skies, moreover, had
led the Chaldeans to the notion of a divine eternity.
The constancy of the sidereal revolutions inspired the
conclusion as to their perpetuity. The stars follow
their ever uncompleted courses unceasingly; as soon
as the end of their journey is reached, they resume
without stopping the road already covered, and the
cycles of years in which their movements take place
extend from the indefinite past into the indefinite future.[76] Thus a clergy of astronomers necessarily conceived Baal, "Lord of the heavens," as the "Master
of eternity" or "He whose name is praised through all
eternity"[77]—titles which constantly recur in Semitic
inscriptions. The divine stars did not die, like Osiris
or Attis; whenever they seemed to weaken, they were

born to a new life and always remained invincible
(*invicti*).

Together with the mysteries of the Syrian Baals,
this theological notion penetrated into Occidental paganism.[78] Whenever an inscription to a *deus aeternus*
is found in the Latin provinces it refers to a Syrian
sidereal god, and it is a remarkable fact that this
epithet did not enter the ritual before the second century, at the time the worship of the god Heaven
(*Caelus*)[79] was propagated. That the philosophers
had long before placed the first cause beyond the
limits of time was of no consequence, for their theories
had not penetrated into the popular consciousness nor
modified the traditional formulary of the liturgies. To
the people the divinities were beings more beautiful,
more vigorous, and more powerful than man, but born
like him, and exempt only from old age and death, the
immortals of old Homer. The Syrian priests diffused
the idea of a god without beginning and without end
through the Roman world, and thus contributed, along
lines parallel with the Jewish proselytism, to lend the
authority of dogma to what had previously been only
a metaphysical theory.

The Baals were universal as well as eternal, and
their power became limitless in regard to space as it
had been in regard to time. These two principles were
correlative. The title of *"mar῾olam"* which the Baals
bore occasionally may be translated by "Lord of the
universe," or by "Lord of eternity," and efforts certainly have been made to claim the twofold quality
for them.[80] Peopled with divine constellations and
traversed by planets assimilated to the inhabitants of
Olympus, the heavens determined the destinies of the

entire human race by their movements, and the whole earth was subject to the changes produced by their revolutions.[81] Consequently the old *Ba'al šamîn* was necessarily transformed into a universal power. Of course, even under the Cæsars there existed in Syria traces of a period when the local god was the fetich of a clan and could be worshiped by the members of that clan only, a period when strangers were admitted to his altars only after a ceremony of initiation, as brothers, or at least as guests and clients.[82] But from the period when our knowledge of the history of the great divinities of Heliopolis or Hierapolis begins, these divinities were regarded as common to all Syrians, and crowds of pilgrims came from distant countries to obtain grace in the holy cities. As protectors of the entire human race the Baals gained proselytes in the Occident, and their temples witnessed gatherings of devotees of every race and nationality. In this respect the Baals were distinctly different from Jehovah.

The essence of paganism implies that the nature of a divinity broadens as the number of its votaries increases. Everybody credits it with some new quality, and its character becomes more complex. As it gains in power it also has a tendency to dominate its companion gods and to concentrate their functions in itself. To escape this threatening absorption, these gods must be of a very sharply defined personality and of a very original character. The vague Semitic deities, however, were devoid of a well-defined individuality. We fail to find among them a well organized society of immortals, like that of the Greek Olympus where each divinity had its own features and its own particular life full of adventures and experiences, and each followed its special calling to the exclusion of all the others. One was a physician, another a poet, a third a shepherd, hunter or blacksmith. The Greek inscriptions found in Syria are, in this regard, eloquently concise.[83] Usually they have the name of Zeus accompanied by some simple epithet: *kurios** (Lord), *aniketos*† (invincible), *megistos*‡ (greatest). All these Baals seem to have been brothers. They were personalities of indeterminate outline and interchangeable powers and were readily confused.

At the time the Romans came into contact with Syria, it had already passed through a period of syncretism similar to the one we can study with greater precision in the Latin world. The ancient exclusiveness and the national particularism had been overcome. The Baals of the great sanctuaries had enriched themselves with the virtues[84] of their neighbors; then, always following the same process, they had taken certain features from foreign divinities brought over by the Greek conquerors. In that manner their characters had become indefinable, they performed incompatible functions and possessed irreconcilable attributes. An inscription found in Britain[85] assimilates the Syrian goddess to Peace, Virtue, Ceres, Cybele, and even to the sign of the Virgin.

In conformity with the law governing the development of paganism, the Semitic gods tended to become pantheistic because they comprehended all nature and were identified with it. The various deities were nothing but different aspects under which the supreme and infinite being manifested itself. Although Syria re-

---

* κύριος.   † ἀνίκητος.   ‡ μέγιστος.

mained deeply and even coarsely idolatrous in practice, in theory it approached monotheism or, better perhaps, henotheism. By an absurd but curious etymology the name Hadad has been explained as "one, one" ('ad 'ad).[86]

Everywhere the narrow and divided polytheism showed a confused tendency to elevate itself into a superior synthesis, but in Syria astrology lent the firmness of intelligent conviction to notions that were vague elsewhere. The Chaldean cosmology, which deified all elements but ascribed a predominant influence to the stars, ruled the entire Syrian syncretism. It considered the world as a great organism which was kept intact by an intimate solidarity, and whose parts continually influenced each other.

The ancient Semites believed therefore that the divinity could be regarded as embodied in the waters, in the fire of the lightning, in stones or plants. But the most powerful gods were the constellations and the planets that governed the course of time and of all things.

The sun was supreme because it led the starry choir, because it was the king and guide of all the other luminaries and therefore the master of the whole world.[87] The astronomical doctrines of the "Chaldeans" taught that this incandescent globe alternately attracted and repelled the other sidereal bodies, and from this principle the Oriental theologians had concluded that it must determine the entire life of the universe, inasmuch as it regulated the movements of the heavens. As the "intelligent light" it was especially the creator of human reason, and just as it repelled and attracted the planets in turn, it was believed to send out souls, at the time of birth, into the bodies they animated, and to cause them to return to its bosom after death by means of a series of emissions and absorptions.

Later on, when the seat of the Most-High was placed beyond the limits of the universe, the radiant star that gives us light became the visible image of the supreme power, the source of all life and all intelligence, the intermediary between an inaccessible god and mankind, and the one object of special homage from the multitude.[88]

Solar pantheism, which grew up among the Syrians of the Hellenistic period as a result of the influence of Chaldean astrolatry, imposed itself upon the whole Roman world under the empire. Our very rapid sketch of the constitution of that theological system shows incidentally the last form assumed by the pagan idea of God. In this matter Syria was Rome's teacher and predecessor. The last formula reached by the religion of the pagan Semites and in consequence by that of the Romans, was a divinity unique, almighty, eternal, universal and ineffable, that revealed itself throughout nature, but whose most splendid and most energetic manifestation was the sun. To arrive at the Christian monotheism[89] only one final tie had to be broken, that is to say, this supreme being residing in a distant heaven had to be removed beyond the world. So we see once more in this instance, how the propagation of the Oriental cults levelled the roads for Christianity and heralded its triumph. Although astrology was always fought by the church, it had nevertheless prepared the minds for the dogmas the church was to proclaim.

PERSIA.

THE dominant historical fact in western Asia in ancient times was the opposition between the Greco-Roman and Persian civilizations, which was itself only an episode in the great struggle that was constantly in progress between the Orient and the Occident in those countries. In the first enthusiasm of their conquests, the Persians extended their dominion as far as the cities of Ionia and the islands of the Ægean Sea, but their power of expansion was broken at the foot of the Acropolis. One hundred and fifty years later, Alexander destroyed the empire of the Achemenides and carried Hellenic culture to the banks of the Indus. After two and a half centuries the Parthians under the Arsacid dynasty advanced to the borders of Syria, and Mithradates Eupator, an alleged descendant of Darius, penetrated to the heart of Greece at the head of his Persian nobility from Pontus.

After the flood came the ebb. The reconstructed Roman empire of Augustus soon reduced Armenia, Cappadocia and even the kingdom of the Parthians to a kind of vassalage. But after the middle of the third century the Sassanid dynasty restored the power of Persia and revived its ancient pretensions. From that time until the triumph of Islam it was one long duel between the two rival states, in which now one was victorious and now the other, while neither was ever decisively beaten. An ambassador of king Narses to Galerius called these two states "the two eyes of the human race."[1]

The "invincible" star of the Persians might wane and vanish, but only to reappear in greater glory. The political and military strength displayed by this nation through the centuries was the result of its high intellectual and moral qualities. Its original culture was always hostile to such an assimilation as that experienced in different degrees by the Aryans of Phrygia, the Semites of Syria and the Hanites of Egypt. Hellenism and Iranism—if I may use that term— were two equally noble adversaries but differently educated, and they always remained separated by instinctive racial hostility as much as by hereditary opposition of interests.

Nevertheless, when two civilizations are in contact for more than a thousand years, numerous exchanges are bound to occur. The influence exercised by Hellenism as far as the uplands of Central Asia has frequently been pointed out,[2] but the prestige retained by Persia throughout the ages and the extent of area influenced by its energy has not perhaps been shown with as much accuracy. For even if Mazdaism was the highest expression of Persian genius and its influence in consequence mainly religious, yet it was not exclusively so.

After the fall of the Achemenides the memory of their empire long haunted Alexander's successors. Not only did the dynasties which claimed to be descended from Darius, and which ruled over Pontus, Cappa-

docia and Commagene, cultivate political traditions
that brought them nearer to their supposed ancestors,
but those traditions were partly adopted even by the
Seleucides and the Ptolemies, the legitimate heirs of
the ancient masters of Asia. People were fond of recalling the ideals of past grandeur and sought to
realize them in the present. In that manner several
institutions were transmitted to the Roman emperors
through the agency of the Asiatic monarchies. The
institution of the *amici Augusti,* for instance, the appointed friends and intimate counselors of the rulers,
adopted in Italy the forms in use at the court of
the Diadochi, who had themselves imitated the ancient organization of the palace of the Great Kings.[3]

The custom of carrying the sacred fire before the
Cæsars as an emblem of the perpetuity of their power,
dated back to Darius and with other Persian traditions
passed on to the dynasties that divided the empire of
Alexander. There is a striking similarity not only
between the observance of the Cæsars and the practice
of the Oriental monarchs, but also between the beliefs
that they held. The continuity of the political and
religious tradition cannot be doubted.[4] As the court
ceremonial and the internal history of the Hellenistic
kingdoms become better known we shall be able to
outline with greater precision the manner in which the
divided and diminished heritage of the Achemenides,
after generations of rulers, was finally left to those
Occidental sovereigns who called themselves the sacro-
sanct lords of the world as Artaxerxes had done.[5]
It may not be generally known that the habit of wel-
coming friends with a kiss was a ceremony in the

Oriental formulary before it became a familiar custom in Europe.[6]

It is very difficult to trace the hidden paths by which pure ideas travel from one people to another. But certain it is that at the beginning of our era certain Mazdean conceptions had already spread outside of Asia. The extent of the influence of Parseeism upon the beliefs of Israel under the Achemenides cannot be determined, but its existence is undeniable.[7] Some of its doctrines, as for instance those relating to angels and demons, the end of the world and the final resurrection, were propagated everywhere in the basin of the Mediterranean as a consequence of the diffusion of Jewish colonies.

On the other hand, ever since the conquests of Cyrus and Darius, the active attention of the Greeks had been drawn toward the doctrines and religious practices of the new masters of the Orient.[8] A number of legends representing Pythagoras, Democritus and other philosophers as disciples of the magi prove the prestige of that powerful sacerdotal class. The Macedonian conquest, which placed the Greeks in direct relations with numerous votaries of Mazdaism, gave a new impetus to works treating that religion, and the great scientific movement inaugurated by Aristotle caused many scholars to look into the doctrines taught by the Persian subjects of the Seleucides. We know from a reliable source that the works catalogued under the name of Zoroaster in the library of Alexandria contained two million lines. This immense body of sacred literature was bound to attract the attention of scholars and to call forth the reflections of philosophers. The dim and dubious science that reached

even the lower classes under the name of "magic"
was to a considerable extent of Persian origin, as its
name indicates, and along with physician's recipes
and thaumaturgic processes it imparted some theological doctrines in a confused fashion.[9]

This explains why certain institutions and beliefs
of the Persians had found imitators and adepts in the
Greco-Oriental world long before the Romans had
gained a foothold in Asia. Their influence was indirect, secret, frequently indiscernible, but it was certain. The most active agencies in the diffusion of
Mazdaism as of Judaism seem to have been colonies
of believers who had emigrated far from the mother
country. There was a Persian dispersion similar to
that of the Israelites. Communities of magi were
established not only in eastern Asia Minor, but in
Galatia, Phrygia, Lydia and even in Egypt. Everywhere they remained attached to their customs and
beliefs with persistent tenacity.[10]

When Rome extended her conquests into Asia Minor
and Mesopotamia, the influence of Persia became much
more direct. Superficial contact with the Mazdean
populations began with the wars against Mithradates,
but it did not become frequent and lasting until the
first century of our era. During that century the
empire gradually extended its limits to the upper Euphrates, and thereby absorbed all the uplands of Anatolia and Commagene south of the Taurus. The native
dynasties which had fostered the secular isolation of
those distant countries in spite of the state of vassalage
to which they had been reduced disappeared one after
another. The Flavians constructed through those hitherto almost inaccessible regions an immense network

of roads that were as important to Rome as the railways of Turkestan or of Siberia are to modern Russia. At the same time Roman legions camped on the banks of the Euphrates and in the mountains of Armenia. Thus all the little Mazdean centers scattered in Cappadocia and Pontus were forced into constant relation with the Latin world, and on the other hand the disappearance of the buffer states made the Roman and Parthian empires neighboring powers in Trajan's time (98-117 A. D.).

From these conquests and annexations in Asia Minor and Syria dates the sudden propagation of the Persian mysteries of Mithra in the Occident. For even though a congregation of their votaries seems to have existed at Rome under Pompey as early as 67 B. C., the real diffusion of the mysteries began with the Flavians, toward the end of the first century of our era. They became more and more prominent under the Antonines and the Severi, and remained the most important cult of paganism until the end of the fourth century. Through them as a medium the original doctrines of Mazdaism were widely propagated in every Latin province, and in order to appreciate the influence of Persia upon the Roman creeds, we must now give them our careful attention.

However, it must be said that the growing influence of Persia did not manifest itself solely in the religious sphere. After the accession of the Sassanid dynasty (228 A. D.) the country once more became conscious of its originality, again resumed the cultivation of national traditions, reorganized the hierarchy of its official clergy and recovered the political cohesion which had been wanting under the Parthians. It felt and showed its superiority over the neighboring empire that was then torn by factions, thrown upon the mercy of manifestoes, and ruined economically and morally. The studies now being made in the history of that period show more and more that debilitated Rome had become the imitator of Persia.

In the opinion of contemporaries the court of Diocletian, prostrating itself before a master who was regarded as the equal of God, with its complicated hierarchy and crowd of eunuchs that disgraced it, was an imitation of the court of the Sassanides. Galerius declared in unmistakable terms that Persian absolutism must be introduced in his empire,[11] and the ancient Cæsarism founded on the will of the people seemed about to be transformed into a sort of caliphate.

Recent discoveries also throw light upon a powerful artistic school that developed in the Parthian empire and later in that of the Sassanides and which grew up independently of the Greek centers of production. Even if it took certain models from the Hellenic sculpture or architecture, it combined them with Oriental motives into a decoration of exuberant richness. Its field of influence extended far beyond Mesopotamia into the south of Syria where it has left monuments of unequalled splendor. The radiance of that brilliant center undoubtedly illuminated Byzantium, the barbarians of the north, and even China.[12]

The Persian Orient, then, exerted a dominant influence on the political institutions and artistic tastes of the Romans as well as on their ideas and beliefs. The propagation of the religion of Mithra, which always proudly proclaimed its Persian origin, was accompanied by a number of parallel influences of the people from which it had issued. Never, not even during the Mohammedan invasions, had Europe a narrower escape from becoming Asiatic than when Diocletian officially recognized Mithra as the protector of the reconstructed empire.[13] The time when that god seemed to be establishing his authority over the entire civilized world was one of the critical phases in the moral history of antiquity. An irresistible invasion of Semitic and Mazdean conceptions nearly succeeded in permanently overwhelming the Occidental spirit. Even after Mithra had been vanquished and expelled from Christianized Rome, Persia did not disarm. The work of conversion in which Mithraism had failed was taken up by Manicheism, the heir to its cardinal doctrines, and until the Middle Ages Persian dualism continued to cause bloody struggles in the ancient Roman provinces.

* * *

Just as we cannot understand the character of the mysteries of Isis and Serapis without studying the circumstances accompanying their creation by the Ptolemies, so we cannot appreciate the causes of the power attained by the mysteries of Mithra, unless we go far back to their origin.

Here the subject is unfortunately more obscure. The ancient authors tell us almost nothing about the origin of Mithra. One point on which they all agree is that he was a Persian god, but this we should know from the Avesta even if they had not mentioned it. But how did he get to Italy from the Persian uplands?

Two scant lines of Plutarch are the most explicit document we have on the subject. He narrates incidentally that the pirates from Asia Minor vanquished by Pompey in 67 performed strange sacrifices on Olympus, a volcano of Lycia, and practiced occult rites, among others those of Mithra which, he says, "exist to the present day and were first taught by them."[14] Lactantius Placidus, a commentator on Statius and a mediocre authority, also tells us that the cult passed from the Persians to the Phrygians and from the Phrygians to the Romans.[15]

These two authors agree then in fixing in Asia Minor the origin of this Persian religion that later spread over the Occident, and in fact various indications direct us to that country. The frequency of the name Mithradates, for instance, in the dynasties of Pontus, Cappadocia, Armenia and Commagene, connected with the Achemenides by fictitious genealogies, shows the devotion of those kings to Mithra.

As we see, the Mithraism that was revealed to the Romans at the time of Pompey had established itself in the Anatolian monarchies during the preceding period, which was an epoch of intense moral and religious unrest. Unfortunately we have no monuments of that period of its history. The absence of direct testimony on the development of Mazdean sects during the last three centuries before our era prevents us from gaining exact knowledge of the Parseeism of Asia Minor.

None of the temples dedicated to Mithra in that religion have been examined.[16] The inscriptions mentioning his name are as yet few and insignificant, so that it is only by indirect means that we can arrive at conclusions about this primitive cult. The only way to explain its distinguishing features in the Occident is to study the environment in which it originated.

During the domination of the Achemenides eastern

Asia Minor was colonized by the Persians. The uplands of Anatolia resembled those of Persia in climate
and soil, and were especially adapted to the raising of
horses.[17] In Cappadocia and even in Pontus the aristocracy who owned the soil belonged to the conquering
nation. Under the various governments which followed after the death of Alexander, those landlords
remained the real masters of the country, chieftains of
clans governing the canton where they had their domains, and, on the outskirts of Armenia at least, they
retained the hereditary title of satraps through all
political vicissitudes until the time of Justinian, thus
recalling their Persian origin.[18] This military and
feudal aristocracy furnished Mithradates Eupator a
considerable number of the officers who helped him in
his long defiance of Rome, and later it defended the
threatened independence of Armenia against the enterprises of the Cæsars. These warriors worshiped
Mithra as the protecting genius of their arms, and
this is the reason why Mithra always, even in the
Latin world, remained the "invincible" god, the tutelary deity of armies, held in special honor by warriors.

Besides the Persian nobility a Persian clergy had
also become established in the peninsula. It officiated
in famous temples, at Zela in Pontus and Hierocæsarea
in Lydia. Magi, called *magousaioi* or *pyrethes* (fire-
lighters) were scattered over the Levant. Like the
Jews, they retained their national customs and traditional rites with such scrupulous loyalty that Bardesanes of Edessa cited them as an example in his attempt to refute the doctrines of astrology and to show
that a nation can retain the same customs in different
climates.[19] We know their religion sufficiently to be

certain that the Syrian author had good grounds for attributing that conservative spirit to them. The sacrifices of the *pyrethes* which Strabo observed in Cappadocia recall all the peculiarities of the Avestan liturgy. The same prayers were recited before the altar of the fire while the priest held the sacred fasces (*bareçman*) ; the same offerings were made of milk, oil and honey; and the same precautions were taken to prevent the priest's breath from polluting the divine flame. Their gods were practically those of orthodox Mazdaism. They worshiped Ahura Mazda, who had to them remained a divinity of the sky as Zeus and Jupiter had been originally. Below him they venerated deified abstractions (such as Vohumano, "good mind," and Ameretat, "immortality") from which the religion of Zoroaster made its Amshaspends, the archangels surrounding the Most High.[20] Finally they sacrificed to the spirits of nature, the Yazatas: for instance, Anahita or Anaites the goddess of the waters—that made fertile the fields ; Atar, the personification of fire ; and especially Mithra, the pure genius of light.

Thus the basis of the religion of the magi of Asia Minor was Mazdaism, somewhat changed from that of the Avesta, and in certain respects holding closer to the primitive nature worship of the Aryans, but nevertheless a clearly characterized and distinctive Mazdaism, which was to remain the most solid foundation for the greatness of the mysteries of Mithra in the Occident.

Recent discoveries[21] of bilingual inscriptions have succeeded in establishing the fact that the language used, or at least written, by the Persian colonies of Asia Minor was not their ancient Aryan idiom, but

Aramaic, which was a Semitic dialect. Under the Achemenides this was the diplomatic and commercial language of all countries west of the Tigris. In Cappadocia and Armenia it remained the literary and probably also the liturgical language until it was slowly supplanted by Greek during the Hellenistic period. The very name *magousaioi** given to the magi in those countries is an exact transcription of a Semitic plural.[22] This phenomenon, surprising at first sight, is explained by the history of the *magousaioi* who emigrated to Asia Minor. They did not come there directly from Persepolis or Susa, but from Mesopotamia. Their religion had been deeply influenced by the speculations of the powerful clergy officiating in the temples of Babylon. The learned theology of the Chaldeans imposed itself on the primitive Mazdaism, which was a collection of traditions and rites rather than a body of doctrines. The divinities of the two religions became identified, their legends connected, and the Semitic astrology, the result of long continued scientific observations, superimposed itself on the naturalistic myths of the Persians. Ahura Mazda was assimilated to Bel, Anahita to Ishtar, and Mithra to Shamash, the solar god. For that reason Mithra was commonly called *Sol invictus* in the Roman mysteries, and an abstruse and a complicated astronomic symbolism was always part of the teachings revealed to candidates for initiation and manifested itself also in the artistic embellishments of the temple.

In connection with a cult from Commagene we can observe rather closely how the fusion of Parseeism with Semitic and Anatolian creeds took place, because

* μαγουσαῖοι

in those regions the form of religious transformations
was at all times syncretic. On a mountain top in the
vicinity of a town named Doliche, a deity was worshiped who after a number of transformations became
a Jupiter Protector of the Roman armies. Originally
this god, who was believed to have discovered the use
of iron, seems to have been brought to Commagene
by a tribe of blacksmiths, the Chalybes, who had come
from the north.[23] He was represented standing on
a steer and holding in his hand a two-edged ax, an
ancient symbol venerated in Crete during the Myce-
nean age and found also at Labranda in Caria and all
over Asia Minor.[24] The ax symbolized the god's mastery over the lightning which splits asunder the trees
of the forest amidst the din of storms. Once established on Syrian soil, this genius of thunder became
identified with some local Baal and his cult took up
all the Semitic features. After the conquests of Cyrus
and the founding of the Persian domination, this "Lord
of the heavens" was readily confounded with Ahura
Mazda, who was likewise "the full circle of heaven,"
according to a definition of Herodotus,[25] and whom
the Persians also worshiped on mountain tops. When a
half Persian, half Hellenic dynasty succeeded Alexander in Commagene, this Baal became a *Zeus Oro-
masdes** (Ahura Mazda) residing in the sublime ethereal regions. A Greek inscription speaks of the celestial thrones "on which this supreme divinity receives
the souls of its worshipers."[26] In the Latin countries
"Jupiter Caelus" remained at the head of the Mazdean
pantheon,[27] and in all the provinces the temples of

* Ζεῦς 'Ωρομάσδης.

"Jupiter Dolichenus" were erected beside those of Mithra, and the two remained in the closest relations.[28]

The same series of transformations took place elsewhere with a number of other gods.[29] The Mithra worship was thus formed, in the main, by a combination of Persian beliefs with Semitic theology, incidentally including certain elements from the native cults of Asia Minor. The Greeks later translated the names of the Persian divinities into their language and imposed certain forms of their mysteries on the Mazdean cult.[30] Hellenic art lent to the Yazatas that idealized form in which it liked to represent the immortals, and philosophy, especially that of the Stoics, endeavored to discover its own physical and metaphysical theories in the traditions of the magi. But in spite of all these accomodations, adaptations and interpretations, Mithraism always remained in substance a Mazdaism blended with Chaldeanism, that is to say, essentially a barbarian religion. It certainly was far less Hellenized than the Alexandrian cult of Isis and Serapis, or even that of the Great Mother of Pessinus. For that reason it always seemed unacceptable to the Greek world, from which it continued to be almost completely excluded. Even language furnishes a curious proof of that fact. Greek contains a number of theophorous* (god-bearing) names formed from those of Egyptian or Phrygian gods, like Serapion, Metrodoros, Metrophilos—Isidore is in use at the present day—but all known derivations of Mithra are of barbarian formation. The Greeks never admitted the god of their hereditary enemies, and the great centers of Hellenic

* θεοφόρος.

civilization escaped his influence and he theirs.[31] Mithraism passed directly from Asia into the Latin world.

There it spread with lightning rapidity from the time it was first introduced. When the progressive march of the Romans toward the Euphrates enabled them to investigate the sacred trust transmitted by Persia to the magi of Asia Minor, and when they became acquainted with the Mazdean beliefs which had matured in the seclusion of the Anatolian mountains, they adopted them with enthusiasm. The Persian cult was spread by the soldiers along the entire length of the frontiers towards the end of the first century and left numerous traces around the camps of the Danube and the Rhine, near the stations along the wall of Britain, and in the vicinity of the army posts scattered along the borders of the Sahara or in the valleys of the Asturias. At the same time the Asiatic merchants introduced it in the ports of the Mediterranean, along the great waterways and roads, and in all commercial cities. It also possessed missionaries in the Oriental slaves who were to be found everywhere, engaging in every pursuit, employed in the public service as well as in domestic work, in the cultivation of land as well as in financial and mining enterprises, and above all in the imperial service, where they filled the offices.

Soon this foreign god gained the favor of high functionaries and of the sovereign himself. At the end of the second century Commodus was initiated into the mysteries, a conversion that had a tremendous effect. A hundred years later Mithra's power was such that at one time he seemed about to eclipse both Oriental and Occidental rivals and to dominate the entire Roman world. In the year 307 Diocletian, Galerius and Licinius met in a solemn interview at Carnuntum on the Danube and dedicated a sanctuary there to Mithra, "the protector of their empire" (*fautori imperii sui*).[32]

In previous works on the mysteries of Mithra we have endeavored to assign causes for the enthusiasm that attracted humble plebeians and great men of the world to the altars of this barbarian god. We shall not repeat here what any one who has the curiosity may read either in a large or a small book according to his preferences,[33] but we must consider the problem from a different point of view. Of all Oriental religions the Persian cult was the last to reach the Romans. We shall inquire what new principle it contained; to what inherent qualities it owed its superiority; and through what characteristics it remained distinct in the conflux of creeds of all kinds that were struggling for supremacy in the world at that time.

The originality and value of the Persian religion lay not in its doctrines regarding the nature of the celestial gods. Without doubt Parseeism is of all pagan religions the one that comes closest to monotheism, for it elevates Ahura Mazda high above all other celestial spirits. But the doctrines of Mithraism are not those of Zoroaster. What it received from Persia was chiefly its mythology and ritual; its theology, which was thoroughly saturated with Chaldean erudition, probably did not differ noticeably from the Syrian. At the head of the divine hierarchy it placed as first cause an abstraction, deified Time, the Zervan Akarana of the Avesta. This divinity regulated the revolutions of the stars and in consequence was the absolute master of

all things. Ahura Mazda, whose throne was in the
heavens, had become the equivalent of *Ba'al Samin,*
and even before the magi the Semites had introduced
into the Occident the worship of the sun, the source of
all energy and light. Babylonian astrology and astrolatry inspired the theories of the mithreums as well as
of the Semitic temples, a fact that explains the intimate
connection of the two cults. This half religious, half
scientific system which was not peculiarly Persian nor
original to Mithraism was not the reason for the
adoption of that worship by the Roman world.

Neither did the Persian mysteries win the masses
by their liturgy. Undoubtedly their secret ceremonies
performed in mountain caves, or at any rate in the
darkness of the underground crypts, were calculated
to inspire awe. Participation in the liturgical meals
gave rise to moral comfort and stimulation. By submitting to a sort of baptism the votaries hoped to ex-
piate their sins and regain an untroubled conscience.
But the sacred feasts and purifying ablutions connected
with the same spiritual hopes are found in other Oriental cults, and the magnificent suggestive ritual of
the Egyptian clergy certainly was more impressive
than that of the magi. The mythic drama performed
in the grottoes of the Persian god and culminating in
the immolation of a steer who was considered as the
creator and rejuvenator of the earth, must have seemed
less important and affecting than the suffering and
joy of Isis seeking and reviving the mutilated body
of her husband, or than the moaning and jubilation
of Cybele mourning over and reviving her lover Attis.

But Persia introduced dualism as a fundamental
principle in religion. It was this that distinguished

Mithraism from other sects and inspired its dogmatic theology and ethics, giving them a rigor and firmness unknown to Roman paganism. It considered the universe from an entirely new point of view and at the same time provided a new goal in life.

Of course, if we understand by dualism the antithesis of mind and matter, of reason and intuition, it appeared at a considerably earlier period in Greek philosophy,[34] where it was one of the leading ideas of neo-Pythagoreanism and of Philo's system. But the distinguishing feature of the doctrine of the magi is the fact that it deified the evil principle, set it up as a rival to the supreme deity, and taught that both had to be worshiped. This system offered an apparently simple solution to the problem of evil, the stumbling block of theologies, and it attracted the cultured minds as well as the masses, to whom it afforded an explanation of their sufferings. Just as the mysteries of Mithra began to spread Plutarch wrote of them favorably and was inclined himself to adopt them.[35] From that time dates the appearance in literature of the anti-gods,*[36] under the command of the powers of darkness[37] and arrayed against the celestial spirits, messengers or "angels"[38] of divinity. They were Ahriman's *devas* struggling with the Yazatas of Ormuzd.

A curious passage in Porphyry[39] shows that the earliest neo-Platonists had already admitted Persian demonology into their system. Below the incorporeal and indivisible supreme being, below the stars and the planets, there were countless spirits.[40] Some of them, the gods of cities and nations, received special names:

* ἀντίθεοι.

the others comprised a nameless multitude. They were divided into two groups. The first were the benevolent spirits that gave fecundity to plants and animals, serenity to nature, and knowledge to men. They acted as intermediaries between gods and men, bearing up to heaven the homage and prayers of the faithful, and down from heaven portents and warnings. The others were wicked spirits inhabiting regions close to the earth and there was no evil that they did not exert every effort to cause.[41] At the same time both violent and cunning, impetuous and crafty, they were the authors of all the calamities that befell the world, such as pestilence, famine, tempests and earthquakes. They kindled evil passions and illicit desires in the hearts of men and provoked war and sedition. They were clever deceivers rejoicing in lies and impostures. They encouraged the phantasmagoria and mystification of the sorcerers[42] and gloated over the bloody sacrifices which magicians offered to them all, but especially to their chief.

Doctrines very similar to these were certainly taught in the mysteries of Mithra; homage was paid to Ahriman (Arimanius) lord of the somber underworld, and master of the infernal spirits.[43] This cult has continued in the Orient to the present day among the Yezidis, or devil worshipers.

In his treatise against the magi, Theodore of Mopsuestia[44] speaks of Ahriman as Satan.* At first sight there really is a surprising resemblance between the two. Both are heads of a numerous army of demons; both are spirits of error and falsehood, princes of darkness,

* Σατανᾶς.

tempters and corrupters. An almost identical picture of the pair could be drawn, and in fact they are practically the same figure under different names. It is generally admitted that Judaism took the notion of an adversary of God[45] from the Mazdeans along with portions of their dualism. It was therefore natural that Jewish doctrine, of which Christianity is heir, should have been closely allied to the mysteries of Mithra. A considerable part of the more or less orthodox beliefs and visions that gave the Middle Ages their nightmare of hell and the devil thus came from Persia by two channels: on the one hand Judeo-Christian literature, both canonical and apocryphal; and on the other, the remnants of the Mithra cult and the various sects of Manicheism that continued to preach the old Persian doctrines on the antagonism between the two world principles.

But a theoretical adherence of the mind to dogmas that satisfy it, does not suffice to convert it to a new religion. There must be motives of conduct and a basis for hope besides grounds for belief. The Persian dualism was not only a powerful metaphysical conception; it was also the foundation of a very efficacious system of ethics, and this was the chief agent in the success of the mysteries of Mithra during the second and third centuries in the Roman world then animated by unrealized aspirations for more perfect justice and holiness.

A sentence of the Emperor Julian,[46] unfortunately too brief, tells us that Mithra subjected his worshipers to "commandments"* and rewarded faithful observance both in this world and in the next. The impor-

* ἐντολαί.

tance attached by the Persians to their peculiar ethics and the rigor with which they observed its precepts, are perhaps the most striking features of their national character as manifested in history. They were a, race of conquerors subject to a severe discipline, like the Romans, and like them they realized the necessity of discipline in the administration of a vast empire. Certain affinities between the two imperial nations connected them directly without the mediation of the Greek world. Mazdaism brought long awaited satisfaction to the old-time Roman desire for a practical religion that would subject the individual to a rule of conduct and contribute to the welfare of the state.[47] Mithra infused a new vigor into the paganism of the Occident by introducing the imperative ethics of Persia.

Unhappily the text of the Mithraic decalogue has not been preserved and its principal commandments can be restored only by implication.

Mithra, the ancient spirit of light, became the god of truth and justice in the religion of Zoroaster and retained that character in the Occident. He was the Mazdean Apollo, but while Hellenism, with a finer appreciation of beauty, developed the esthetic qualities in Apollo, the Persians, caring more for matters of conscience, emphasized the moral character in Mithra.[48] The Greeks, themselves little scrupulous in that respect, were struck by the abhorrence in which their Oriental neighbors held a lie. The Persians conceived of Ahriman as the embodiment of deceit. Mithra was always the god invoked as the guarantor of faith and protector of the inviolability of contracts. Absolute fidelity to his oath had to be a cardinal virtue in the religion of a soldier, whose first act upon enlistment was to pledge obedience and devotion to the sovereign. This religion exalted loyalty and fidelity and undoubtedly tried to inspire a feeling similar to our modern idea of honor.

In addition to respect for authority it preached fraternity. All the initiates considered themselves as sons of the same father owing to one another a brother's affection. It is a question whether they extended the love of neighbor to that universal charity taught by philosophy and Christianity. Emperor Julian, a devoted mystic, liked to set up such an ideal, and it is probable that the Mithraists of later paganism rose to this conception of duty,[49] but they were not its authors. They seemed to have attached more importance to the virile qualities than to compassion and gentleness. The fraternal spirit of initiates calling themselves soldiers was doubtless more akin to the spirit of comradeship in a regiment that has *esprit de corps,* than to the love of one's neighbor that inspires works of mercy towards all.

All primitive people imagine nature filled with unclean and wicked spirits that corrupt and torture those who disturb their repose; but dualism endowed this universal belief with marvelous power as well as with a dogmatic basis. Mazdaism is governed throughout by ideas of purity and impurity. "No religion on earth has ever been so completely dominated by an ideal of purification."[50] This kind of perfection was the goal of the aspiration and effort of believers. They were obliged to guard with infinite precaution against defiling the divine elements, for instance water or fire, or their own persons, and to wipe out all pollution by repeated lustrations. But, as in the Syrian cults of the imperial period, these Mithraic rites did remain simply formal, mechanical and of the flesh, inspired by the old idea of *tabu*. Mithraic baptism wiped out moral faults; the purity aimed at had become spiritual.

This perfect purity distinguishes the mysteries of Mithra from those of all other Oriental gods. Serapis is the brother and husband of Isis, Attis the lover of Cybele, every Syrian Baal is coupled with a spouse; but Mithra lives alone. Mithra is chaste, Mithra is holy (*sanctus*),[51] and for the worship of fecundity he substitutes a new reverence for continence.

However, although resistance to sensuality is laudable and although the ideal of perfection of this Mazdean sect inclined towards the asceticism to which the Manichean conception of virtue led, yet good does not consist exclusively in abnegation and self-control, but also in action. It is not sufficient for a religion to classify moral values, but in order to be effective it must furnish motives for putting them into practice. Dualism was peculiarly favorable for the development of individual effort and human energy; here its influence was strongest. It taught that the world is the scene of a perpetual struggle between two powers that share the mastery; the goal to be reached is the disappearance of evil and the uncontested dominion, the exclusive reign, of the good. Animals and plants, as well as man, are drawn up in two rival camps perpetually hostile, and all nature participates in the eternal combat of the two opposing principles. The demons created by the infernal spirit emerge constantly from the abyss and roam about the earth; they penetrate everywhere carrying corruption, distress, sickness and death. The celestial spirits and the supporters of piety are compelled constantly to baffle their ever renewed enterprises. The strife continues in the heart and conscience of man, the epitome of the universe, between the divine law of duty and the suggestions of the evil spirits. Life is a merciless war knowing no truce. The task of the true Mazdean consisted in constantly fighting the evil in order to bring about the gradual triumph of Ormuzd in the world. The believer was the assistant of the gods in their work of purification and improvement.

The worshipers of Mithra did not lose themselves in a contemplative mysticism like other sects. Their morality particularly encouraged action, and during a period of laxness, anarchy and confusion, they found stimulation, comfort and support in its precepts. Resistance to the promptings of degrading instincts assumed the glamor and prestige of warlike exploits in their eyes and instilled an active principle of progress into their character. By supplying a new conception of the world, dualism also gave a new meaning to life. This same dualism determined the eschatological beliefs of the Mithraists. The antagonism between heaven and hell was extended into the life hereafter.[52] Mithra, the "invincible" god who assisted the faithful in their struggle against the malignity of the demons, was not only their strong companion in their human trials, but as an antagonist of the infernal powers he insured the welfare of his followers in the future life as well as on earth. When the genius of corruption seizes the corpse after death, the spirits of darkness and the celestial messengers struggle for the possession of the soul that has left its corporeal prison. It stands trial before Mithra, and if its merits outweigh its shortcomings in the divine balance it is defended from Ahriman's agents that seek to drag it into the infernal abyss. Finally it is led into the ethereal regions where Jupiter-Ormuzd reigns in eternal light. The believers in Mithra did not agree with the votaries of Serapis who held that the souls of the just reside in the depths of the earth.[53] To them that somber kingdom was the domain of wrong-doers. The souls of the just live in the boundless light that extends above the stars, and by divesting themselves of all sensuality and all lust in passing through the planetary spheres[54] they become as pure as the gods whose company they enter.

However, when the world came to an end the body also was to share in that happiness because it was believed as in Egypt that the whole person would enjoy eternal life. After time had run its course Mithra would raise all men from the dead, pouring out a marvelous beverage of immortality for the good, but all evil doers would be annihilated by fire together with Ahriman himself.

* * *

Of all the Oriental cults none was so severe as Mithraism, none attained an equal moral elevation, none could have had so strong a hold on mind and heart. In many respects it gave its definite religious formula to the pagan world and the influence of its ideas remained long after the religion itself had come to a violent end. Persian dualism introduced certain principles into Europe that have never ceased to exert an influence. Its whole history proves the thesis with which we began, the power of resistance and of influence possessed by Persian culture and religion. These possessed an originality so independent that after having resisted in the Orient the power of absorption of Hellenism, and after having checked the Christian propaganda, they even withstood the destructive power of Islam. Firdusi (940-1020) glories in the ancient national traditions and the mythical heroes of Mazdaism, and while the idolatry of Egypt, Syria and Asia Minor has long since died out or degenerated, there are votaries of Zoroaster at the present day who piously perform the sacred ceremonies of the Avesta and practise genuine fire worship.

Another witness to the vitality of Mithraic Mazdaism is the fact that it escaped becoming a kind of state religion of the Roman empire during the third century. An oft-quoted sentence of Renan's says:[55] "If Christianity had been checked in its growth by some deadly disease, the world would have become Mithraic." In hazarding that statement he undoubtedly conjured up a picture of what would have been the condition of this poor world in that case. He must have imagined, one of his followers would have us believe,[56] that the morals of the human race would have been but little changed, a little more virile perhaps, a little less charitable, but only a shade different. The erudite theology taught by the mysteries would obviously have shown a laudable respect for science, but as its dogmas were based upon a false physics it would apparently have insured the persistence of an infinity of errors. Astronomy would not be lacking, but astrology would have been unassailable, while the heavens would still be revolving around the earth to accord with its doctrines. The greatest danger, it appears to me, would have been that the Cæsars would have established a theocratic absolutism supported by the Oriental ideas of the divinity of kings. The union of throne and altar would have been inseparable, and Europe would never have known the invigorating struggle between church and state. But on the other hand the discipline of Mithraism, so productive of individual energy, and the democratic organization of its societies in which senators and slaves rubbed elbows, contain a germ of liberty.

We might dwell at some length on these contrasting possibilities, but it is hard to find a mental pastime less profitable than the attempt to remake history and to conjecture on what might have been had events proved otherwise. If the torrent of actions and reactions that carries us along were turned out of its course what imagination could describe the unknown regions through which it would flow?

ASTROLOGY AND MAGIC.

WHEN we consider the absolute authority that astrology exercised under the Roman empire, we find it hard to escape a feeling of surprise. It is difficult to think that people could ever consider astrology as the most valuable of all arts and the queen of sciences,[1] and it is not easy for us to imagine the moral conditions that made such a phenomenon possible, because our state of mind to-day is very different. Little by little the conviction has gained ground that all that can be known about the future, at least the future of man and of human society, is conjecture. The progress of knowledge has taught man to acquiesce in his ignorance.

In former ages it was different: forebodings and predictions found universal credence. The ancient forms of divination, however, had fallen somewhat into disrepute at the beginning of our era, like the rest of the Greco-Roman religion. It was no longer thought that the eagerness or reluctance with which the sacred hens ate their paste, or the direction of the flight of the birds indicated coming success or disaster. Abandoned, the Hellenic oracles were silent. Then appeared astrology, surrounded with all the prestige of an exact science, and based upon the experience of many centuries. It promised to ascertain the occurrences of any one's life with as much precision as the date of an eclipse. The world was drawn towards it by an irresistible attraction. Astrology did away with, and gradually relegated to oblivion, all the ancient methods that had been devised to solve the enigmas of the future. Haruspicy and the augural art were abandoned, and not even the ancient fame of the oracles could save them from falling into irretrievable desuetude. This great chimera changed religion as well as divination, its spirit penetrated everything. And truly, if, as some scholars still hold, the main feature of science is the ability to predict,[2] no branch of learning could compare with this one, nor escape its influence.

The success of astrology was connected with that of the Oriental religions, which lent it their support, as it in turn helped them. We have seen how it forced itself upon Semitic paganism, how it transformed Persian Mazdaism and even subdued the arrogance of the Egyptian sacerdotal caste.[3] Certain mystical treatises ascribed to the old Pharaoh Nechepso and his confidant, the priest Petosiris, nebulous and abstruse works that became, one might say, the Bible of the new belief in the power of the stars, were translated into Greek, undoubtedly in Alexandria, about the year 150 before our era.[4] About the same time the Chaldean genethlialogy began to spread in Italy, with regard to which Berosus, a priest of the god Baal, who came to Babylon from the island of Cos, had previously succeeded in arousing the curiosity of the Greeks. In 139 a prætor expelled the "Chaldaei" from Rome, together with the Jews. But all the adherents of the Syrian goddess, of whom there was quite a number in the Occident, were patrons and defenders of these Oriental prophets, and police measures were no more successful in stopping the diffusion of their doctrines, than in the case of the Asiatic mysteries. In the time of Pompey, the senator Nigidius Figulus, who was an ardent occultist, expounded the barbarian uranography in Latin. But the scholar whose authority contributed most to the final acceptance of sidereal divination was a Syrian philosopher of encyclopedic knowledge, Posidonius of Apamea, the teacher of Cicero.[5] The works of that erudite and religious writer influenced the development of the entire Roman theology more than anything else.

Under the empire, while the Semitic Baals and Mithra were triumphing, astrology manifested its power everywhere. During that period everybody bowed to it. The Cæsars became its fervent devotees, frequently at the expense of the ancient cults. Tiberius neglected the gods because he believed only in fatalism,[6] and Otho, blindly confiding in the Oriental seer, marched against Vitellius in spite of the baneful presages that affrighted his official clergy.[7] The most earnest scholars, Ptolemy under the Antonines for instance, expounded the principles of that pseudo-science, and the very best minds received them. In fact, scarcely anybody made a distinction between astronomy and its illegitimate sister. Literature took up this new and difficult subject, and, as early as the time of Augustus or Tiberius, Manilius, inspired by the sidereal fatalism, endeavored to make poetry of that dry "mathematics," as Lucretius, his forerunner, had done with the Epicurean atomism. Even art looked there for inspiration and depicted the stellar deities. At Rome and in the provinces architects erected sumptuous *septizonia* in the likeness of the seven spheres in which the planets that rule our destinies move.[8] This Asiatic divination was first aristocratic[9]—because the obtaining of an exact horoscope was a complicated matter, and consultations were expensive—but it promptly became popular, especially in the urban centers where Oriental slaves gathered in large numbers. The learned genethlialogers of the observatories had unlicensed colleagues, who told fortunes at street-crossings or in barnyards. Even common epitaphs, which Rossi styles "the scum of inscriptions," have retained traces of that belief. The custom arose of stating in epitaphs the exact length of a life to the very hour, for the moment of birth determined that of death:

Nascentes morimur, finisque ab origine pendet.[10]

Soon neither important nor small matters were undertaken without consulting the astrologer. His previsions were sought not only in regard to great public events like the conduct of a war, the founding of a city, or the accession of a ruler, not only in case of a marriage, a journey, or a change of domicile; but the most trifling acts of every-day life were gravely submitted to his sagacity. People would no longer take a bath, go to the barber, change their clothes or manicure their fingernails, without first awaiting the propitious moment.[11] The collections of "initiatives"* that have come to us contain questions that make us smile: Will a son who is about to be born have a big nose? Will a girl just coming into this world have gallant adventures?[12] And certain precepts sound almost like burlesques: he who gets his hair cut while

* καταρχαί.

the moon is in her increase will become bald—evidently by analogy.[13]

The entire existence of states and individuals, down to the slightest incidents, was thought to depend on the stars. The absolute control they were supposed to exercise over everybody's daily condition, even modified the language in every-day use and left traces in almost all idioms derived from the Latin. If we speak of a martial, or a jovial character, or a lunatic, we are unconsciously admitting the existence, in these heavenly bodies (Mars, Jupiter, Luna) of their ancient qualities.

It must be acknowledged, however, that the Grecian spirit tried to combat the folly that was taking hold of the world, and from the time of its propagation astrology found opponents among the philosophers. The most subtle of these adversaries was the probabilist Carneades, in the second century before our era. The topical arguments which he advanced, were taken up, reproduced, and developed in a thousand ways by later polemicists. For instance, Were all the men that perish together in a battle, born at the same moment, because they had the same fate? Or, on the other hand, do we not observe that twins, born at the same time, have the most unlike characters and the most different fortunes?

But dialectics are an accomplishment in which the Greeks ever excelled, and the defenders of astrology found a reply to every objection. They endeavored especially to establish firmly the truths of observation, upon which rested the entire learned structure of their art: the influence of the stars over the phenomena of nature and the characters of individuals. Can it be denied, they said, that the sun causes vegetation to appear and to perish, and that it puts animals *en rut* or plunges them into lethargic sleep? Does not the movement of the tide depend on the course of the moon? Is not the rising of certain constellations accompanied every year by storms? And are not the physical and moral qualities of the different races manifestly determined by the climate in which they live? The action of the sky on the earth is undeniable, and, the sidereal influences once admitted, all previsions based on them are legitimate. As soon as the first principle is admitted, all corollaries are logically derived from it.

This way of reasoning was universally considered irrefutable. Before the advent of Christianity, which especially opposed it because of its idolatrous character, astrology had scarcely any adversaries except those who denied the possibility of science altogether, namely, the neo-Academicians, who held that man could not attain certainty, and such radical sceptics as Sextus Empiricus. Upheld by the Stoics, however, who with very few exceptions were in favor of astrology, it can be maintained that it emerged triumphant from the first assaults directed against it. The only result of the objections raised to it was to modify some of its theories. Later, the general weakening of the spirit of criticism assured astrology an almost uncontested domination. Its adversaries did not renew their polemics; they limited themselves to the repetition of arguments that had been opposed, if not refuted, a hundred times, and consequently seemed worn out. At the court of the Severi any one who should have denied the influence of the planets upon the events of this world would have been considered more preposterous than he who would admit it to-day.

But, you will say, if the theorists did not succeed in proving the doctrinal falsity of astrology, experience should have shown its worthlessness. Errors must have occurred frequently and must have been followed by cruel disillusionment. Having lost a child at the age of four for whom a brilliant future had been predicted, the parents stigmatized in the epitaph the "lying mathematician whose great renown deluded them."[14] Nobody thought of denying the possibility of such errors. Manuscripts have been preserved, wherein the makers of horoscopes themselves candidly and learnedly explain how they were mistaken in such and such a case, because they had not taken into account some one of the data of the problem.[15] Manilius, in spite of his unlimited confidence in the power of reason, hesitated at the complexity of an immense task that seemed to exceed the capacity of human intelligence,[16] and in the second century, Vettius Valens bitterly denounced the contemptible bunglers who claimed to be prophets, without having had the long training necessary, and who thereby cast odium and ridicule upon astrology, in the name of which they pretended to operate.[17] It must be remembered that astrology, like medicine, was not only a science,* but also an art.†　This comparison, which sounds irreverent to-day, was a flattering one in the eyes of the ancients.[18]　To observe the sky was as delicate a task as to observe the human body; to cast the horoscope of a newly born child, just as perilous as to make a diagnosis, and to interpret the cosmic symptoms just as hard as to inter-

* ἐπιστήμη.　　　　　　　　　† τέχνη.

pret those of our organism. In both instances the
elements were complex and the chances of error infinite. All the examples of patients dying in spite of
the physician, or on account of him, will never keep
a person who is tortured by physical pain from appealing to him for help; and similarly those whose souls
were troubled with ambition or fear turned to the
astrologer for some remedy for the moral fever tormenting them. The calculator, who claimed to determine the moment of death, and the medical practi-
tioner who claimed to avert it received the anxious
patronage of people worried by this formidable issue.
Furthermore, just as marvelous cures were reported,
striking predictions were called to mind or, if need
were, invented. The diviner had, as a rule, only a
restricted number of possibilities to deal with, and the
calculus of probabilities shows that he must have succeeded sometimes. Mathematics, which he invoked,
was in his favor after all, and chance frequently cor-
rected mischance. Moreover, did not the man who
had a well-frequented consulting-office, possess a thousand means, if he was clever, of placing all the chances
on his side, in the hazardous profession he followed,
and of reading in the stars anything he thought ex-
pedient? He observed the earth rather than the sky,
and took care not to fall into a well.

* * *

However, what helped most to make astrology in-
vulnerable to the blows of reason and of common
sense, was the fact that in reality, the apparent rigor
of its calculus and its theorems notwithstanding, it
was not a science but a faith. We mean not only that

it implied belief in postulates that could not be proved
—the same thing might be said of almost all of our
poor human knowledge, and even our systems of physics and cosmology in the last analysis are based upon
hypotheses—but that astrology was born and reared
in the temples of Chaldea and Egypt.[19] Even in the
Occident it never forgot its sacerdotal origin and
never more than half freed itself from religion, whose
offspring it was.   Here lies the connection between
astrology and the Oriental religions, and I wish to
draw the reader's special attention to this point.

The Greek works and treatises on astrology that
have come down to us reveal this essential feature
only very imperfectly.   The Byzantines stripped this
pseudo-science, always regarded suspiciously by the
church, of everything that savored of paganism.   Their
process of purification can, in some instances, be traced
from manuscript to manuscript.[20] If they retained the
name of some god or hero of mythology, the only
way they dared to write it was by cryptography.   They
have especially preserved purely didactic treatises, the
most perfect type of which is Ptolemy's Tetrabiblos
which has been constantly quoted and commented
upon; and they have reproduced almost exclusively
expurgated texts, in which the principles of various
doctrines are drily summarized.   During the classic
age works of a different character were commonly
read.   Many "Chaldeans" interspersed their cosmological calculations and theories with moral consid-
erations and mystical speculations.   In the first part
of a work that he names "Vision,"* Critodemus, in
prophetic language, represents the truths he reveals

*Ὅρασις.

as a secure harbor of refuge from the storms of this world, and he promises his readers to raise them to the rank of immortals.[21] Vettius Valens, a contemporary of Marcus Aurelius, implored them in solemn terms, not to divulge to the ignorant and impious the arcana he was about to acquaint them with.[22] The astrologers liked to assume the appearance of incorruptible and holy priests and to consider their calling a sacerdotal one.[23] In fact, the two ministries sometimes combined: A dignitary of the Mithraic clergy called himself *studiosus astrologiae*[24] in his epitaph, and a member of a prominent family of Phrygian prelates celebrated in verse the science of divination which enabled him to issue a number of infallible predictions.[25]

The sacred character of astrology revealed itself in some passages that escaped the orthodox censure and in the tone some of its followers assumed, but we must go further and show that astrology was religious in its principles as well as in its conclusions, the debt it owed to mathematics and observation notwithstanding.

The fundamental dogma of astrology, as conceived by the Greeks, was that of universal solidarity. The world is a vast organism, all the parts of which are connected through an unceasing exchange of molecules of effluvia. The stars, inexhaustible generators of energy, constantly act upon the earth and man—upon man, the epitome of all nature, a "microcosm" whose every element corresponds to some part of the starry sky. This was, in a few words, the theory formulated by the Stoic disciples of the Chaldeans ;[26] but if we divest it of all the philosophic garments with which it has been adorned, what do we find? The idea of sympathy, a belief as old as human society! The savage peoples also established mysterious relations between all bodies and all the beings that inhabit the earth and the heavens, and which to them were animated with a life of their own endowed with latent power, but we shall speak of this later on, when taking up the subject of magic. Even before the propagation of the Oriental religions, popular superstition in Italy and Greece attributed a number of odd actions to the sun, the moon, and the constellations as well.[27]

The Chaldaei, however, claimed a predominant power for the stars. In fact, they were regarded as gods *par excellence* by the religion of the ancient Chaldeans in its beginnings. The sidereal religion of Babylon concentrated deity, one might say, in the luminous moving bodies at the expense of other natural objects, such as stones, plants, animals, which the primitive Semitic faith considered equally divine. The stars always retained this character, even at Rome. They were not, as to us, infinitely distant bodies moving in space according to the inflexible laws of mechanics, and whose chemical composition may be determined. To the Latins as to the Orientals, they were propitious or baleful deities, whose ever-changing relations determined the events of this world.

The sky, whose unfathomable depth had not yet been perceived, was peopled with heroes and monsters of contrary passions, and the struggle above had an immediate echo upon earth. By what principle have such a quality and so great an influence been attributed to the stars? Is it for reasons derived from their apparent motion and known through observation or experience? Sometimes. Saturn made people apathetic and irresolute, because it moved most slowly of all the planets.[28] But in most instances purely mythological reasons inspired the precepts of astrology. The seven planets were associated with certain deities, Mars, Venus, or Mercury, whose character and history are known to all. It is sufficient simply to pronounce their names to call to mind certain personalities that may be expected to act according to their natures, in every instance. It was natural for Venus to favor lovers, and for Mercury to assure the success of business transactions and dishonest deals. The same applies to the constellations, with which a number of legends are connected: "catasterism" or translation into the stars, became the natural conclusion of a great many tales. The heroes of mythology, or even those of human society, continued to live in the sky in the form of brilliant stars. There Perseus again met Andromeda, and the Centaur Chiron, who is none other than Sagittarius, was on terms of good fellowship with the Dioscuri.

These constellations, then, assumed to a certain extent the good and the bad qualities of the mythical or historical beings that had been transferred upon them. For instance, the serpent, which shines near the northern pole, was the author of medical cures, because it was the animal sacred to Æsculapius.[29]

The religious foundation of the rules of astrology, however, can not always be recognized. Sometimes it is entirely forgotten, and in such cases the rules assume the appearance of axioms, or of laws based upon long observation of celestial phenomena. Here we have a simple aspect of science. The process of assimilation with the gods and catasterism were known in the Orient long before they were practiced in Greece.

The traditional outlines that we reproduce on our celestial maps are the fossil remains of a luxuriant mythological vegetation, and besides our classic sphere the ancients knew another, the "barbarian" sphere, peopled with a world of fantastic persons and animals. These sidereal monsters, to whom powerful qualities were ascribed, were likewise the remnants of a multitude of forgotten beliefs. Zoolatry was abandoned in the temples, but people continued to regard as divine the lion, the bull, the bear, and the fishes, which the Oriental imagination had seen in the starry vault. Old totems of the Semitic tribes or of the Egyptian divisions lived again, transformed into constellations. Heterogeneous elements, taken from all the religions of the Orient, were combined in the uranography of the ancients, and in the power ascribed to the phantoms that it evoked, vibrates in the indistinct echo of ancient devotions that are often completely unknown to us.[30]

Astrology, then, was religious in its origin and in its principles. It was religious also in its close relation to the Oriental religions, especially those of the Syrian Baals and of Mithra; finally, it was religious in the effects that it produced. I do not mean the effects expected from a constellation in any particular instance: as for example the power to evoke the gods that were subject to their domination.[31] But I have in mind the general influence those doctrines exercised upon Roman paganism.

When the Olympian gods were incorporated among the stars, when Saturn and Jupiter became planets and the celestial virgin a sign of the zodiac, they assumed a character very different from the one they had originally possessed. It has been shown[32] how, in Syria, the idea of an infinite repetition of cycles of years according to which the celestial revolutions took place, led to the conception of divine eternity, how the theory of a fatal domination of the stars over the earth brought about that of the omnipotence of the "lord of the heavens," and how the introduction of a universal religion was the necessary result of the belief that the stars exerted an influence upon the peoples of every climate. The logic of all these consequences of the principles of astrology was plain to the Latin as well as to the Semitic races, and caused a rapid transformation of the ancient idolatry. As in Syria, the sun, which the astrologers called the leader of the planetary choir, "who is established as king and leader of the whole world,"[33] necessarily became the highest power of the Roman pantheon.

Astrology also modified theology, by introducing into this pantheon a great number of new gods, some of whom were singularly abstract. Thereafter man worshiped the constellations of the firmament, particutarly the twelve signs of the zodiac, every one of which had its mythologic legend; the sky (*Caelus*) itself, because it was considered the first cause, and was sometimes confused with the supreme being; the four elements, the antithesis and perpetual transmutations of which produced all tangible phenomena, and which were often symbolized by a group of animals ready to devour each other;[34] finally, time and its subdivisions.[35]

The calendars were religious before they were secular; their purpose was not, primarily, to record fleeting

time, but to observe the recurrence of propitious or
inauspicious dates separated by periodic intervals. It
is a matter of experience that the return of certain
moments is associated with the appearance of certain
phenomena; they have, therefore, a special efficacy,
and are endowed with a sacred character. By deter-
mining periods with mathematical exactness, astrology
continued to see in them "a divine power,"[36] to use
Zeno's term. Time, that regulates the course of the
stars and the transubstantiation of the elements, was
conceived of as the master of the gods and the primordial principle, and was likened to destiny. Each part
of its infinite duration brought with it some propitious
or evil movement of the sky that was anxiously observed, and transformed the ever modified universe.
The centuries, the years and the seasons, placed into
relation with the four winds and the four cardinal
points, the twelve months connected with the zodiac,
the day and the night, the twelve hours, all were personified and deified, as the authors of every change
in the universe. The allegorical figures contrived for
these abstractions by astrological paganism did not
even perish with it.[37] The symbolism it had dissemi-
nated outlived it, and until the Middle Ages these
pictures of fallen gods were reproduced indefinitely in
sculpture, mosaics, and in Christian miniatures.[38]

Thus astrology entered into all religious ideas, and
the doctrines of the destiny of the world and of man
harmonized with its teachings. According to Berosus,
who is the interpreter of ancient Chaldean theories,
the existence of the universe consisted of a series of
"big years," each having its summer and its winter.
Their summer took place when all the planets were in

conjunction at the same point of Cancer, and brought
with it a general conflagration. On the other hand,
their winter came when all the planets were joined
in Capricorn, and its result was a universal flood.
Each of these cosmic cycles, the duration of which
was fixed at 432,000 years according to the most probable estimate, was an exact reproduction of those that
had preceded it. In fact, when the stars resumed
exactly the same position, they were forced to act
in identically the same manner as before. This Babylonian theory, an anticipation of that of the "eternal
return of things," which Nietzsche boasts of having
discovered, enjoyed lasting popularity during antiquity,
and in various forms came down to the Renaissance.[39]
The belief that the world would be destroyed by fire,
a theory also spread abroad by the Stoics, found a
new support in these cosmic speculations.

Astrology, however, revealed the future not only
of the universe, but also of man. According to a
Chaldeo-Persian doctrine, accepted by the pagan mystics and previously pointed out by us,[40] a bitter necessity compelled the souls that dwell in great numbers on the celestial heights, to descend upon this
earth and to animate certain bodies that are to hold
them in captivity. In descending to the earth they
travel through the spheres of the planets and receive
some quality from each of these wandering stars, according to its positions. Contrariwise, when death
releases them from their carnal prison, they return
to their first habitation, providing they have led a pious
life, and if as they pass through the doors of the super-
posed heavens they divest themselves of the passions
and inclinations acquired during their first journey,

to ascend finally, as pure essence to the radiant abode of the gods. There they live forever among the eternal stars, freed from the tyranny of destiny and even from the limitations of time.

This alliance of the theorems of astronomy with their old beliefs supplied the Chaldeans with answers to all the questions that men asked concerning the relation of heaven and earth, the nature of God, the existence of the world, and their own destiny. Astrology was really the first scientific theology. Hellenistic logic arranged the Oriental doctrines properly, combined them with the Stoic philosophy and built them up into a system of indiputable grandeur, an ideal reconstruction of the universe, the powerful assurance of which inspired Manilius to sublime language when he was not exhausted by his efforts to master an ill-adapted theme.[41] The vague and irrational notion of "sympathy" is transformed into a deep sense of the relationship between the human soul, an igneous substance, and the divine stars, and this feeling is strengthened by thought.[42] The contemplation of the sky has become a communion. During the splendor of night the mind of man became intoxicated with the light streaming from above; born on the wings of enthusiasm, he ascended into the sacred choir of the stars and took part in their harmonious movements. "He participates in their immortality, and, before his appointed hour, converses with the gods."[43] In spite of the subtle precision the Greeks always maintained in their speculations, the feeling that permeated astrology down to the end of paganism never belied its Oriental and religious origin.

The most essential principle of astrology was that of fatalism. As the poet says:[44]

"Fata regunt orbem, certa stant omnia lege."

The Chaldeans were the first to conceive the idea of an inflexible necessity ruling the universe, instead of gods acting in the world according to their passions, like men in society. They noticed that an immutable law regulated the movements of the celestial bodies, and, in the first enthusiasm of their discovery they extended its effects to all moral and social phenomena. The postulates of astrology imply an absolute determinism. Tyche, or deified fortune, became the irresistible mistress of mortals and immortals alike, and was even worshiped exclusively by some under the empire. Our deliberate will never plays more than a very limited part in our happiness and success, but, among the pronunciamentos and in the anarchy of the third century, blind chance seemed to play with the life of every one according to its fancy, and it can easily be understood that the ephemeral rulers of that period, like the masses, saw in chance the sovereign disposer of their fates.[45]

The power of this fatalist conception during antiquity may be measured by its long persistence, at least in the Orient, where it originated. Starting from Babylonia,[46] it spread over the entire Hellenic world, as early as the Alexandrian period, and towards the end of paganism a considerable part of the efforts of the Christian apologists was directed against it.[47] But it was destined to outlast all attacks, and to impose itself even on Islam.[48] In Latin Europe, in spite of the anathemas of the church, the belief remained confusedly alive all through the Middle Ages that on this earth everything happens somewhat

"Per ovra delle rote magne,
Che drizzan ciascun seme ad alcun fine
Secondo che le stella son campagne."[49]

The weapons used by the ecclesiastic writers in contending against this sidereal fatalism were taken from the arsenal of the old Greek dialectics. In general, they were those that all defenders of free will had used for centuries: determinism destroys responsibility; rewards and punishments are absurd if man acts under a necessity that compels him, if he is born a hero or a criminal. We shall not dwell on these metaphysical discussions,[50] but there is one argument that is more closely connected with our subject, and therefore should be mentioned. If we live under an immutable fate, no supplication can change its decisions; religion is unavailing, it is useless to ask the oracles to reveal the secrets of a future which nothing can change, and prayers, to use one of Seneca's expressions, are nothing but "the solace of diseased minds."[51]

And, doubtless, some adepts of astrology, like the Emperor Tiberius,[52] neglected the practice of religion, because they were convinced that fate governed all things. Following the example set by the Stoics, they made absolute submission to an almighty fate and joyful acceptance of the inevitable a moral duty, and were satisfied to worship the superior power that ruled the universe, without demanding anything in return. They considered themselves at the mercy of even the most capricious fate, and were like the intelligent slave who guesses the desires of his master to satisfy them, and knows how to make the hardest servitude tolerable.[53] The masses, however, never reached that height of resignation. They looked at astrology far more from a religious than from a logical standpoint.[54] The planets and constellations were not only cosmic forces, whose favorable or inauspicious action grew weaker or stronger according to the turnings of a course established for eternity; they were deities who saw and heard, who were glad or sad, who had a voice and sex, who were prolific or sterile, gentle or savage, obsequious or arrogant.[55] Their anger could therefore be soothed and their favor obtained through rites and offerings; even the adverse stars were not unrelenting and could be persuaded through sacrifices and supplications. The narrow and pedantic Firmicus Maternus strongly asserts the omnipotence of fate, but at the same time he invokes the gods and asks for their aid against the influence of the stars. As late as the fourth century the pagans of Rome who were about to marry, or to make a purchase, or to solicit a public office, went to the diviner for his prognostics, at the same time praying to Fate for prosperity in their undertaking.[56] Thus a fundamental antinomy manifested itself all through the development of astrology, which pretended to be an exact science, but always remained a sacerdotal theology.

Of course, the more the idea of fatalism imposed itself and spread, the more the weight of this hopeless theory oppressed the consciousness. Man felt himself dominated and crushed by blind forces that dragged him on as irresistibly as they kept the celestial spheres in motion. His soul tried to escape the oppression of this cosmic mechanism, and to leave the slavery of

Ananke. But he no longer had confidence in the ceremonies of his old religion. The new powers that had taken possession of heaven had to be propitiated by new means. The Oriental religions themselves offered a remedy against the evils they had created, and taught powerful and mysterious processes for conjuring fate.[57] And side by side with astrology we see magic, a more pernicious aberration, gaining gronud.[58]

* * *

If, from the reading of Ptolemy's Tetrabiblos, we pass on to read a magic papyrus, our first impression is that we have stepped from one end of the intellectual world to the other. Here we find no trace of the systematic order or severe method that distinguish the work of the scholar of Alexandria. Of course, the doctrines of astrology are just as chimerical as those of magic, but they are deduced with an amount of logic, entirely wanting in works of sorcery, that compels reasoning intellects to accept them. Recipes borrowed from medicine and popular superstition, primitive practices rejected or abandoned by the sacerdotal rituals, beliefs repudiated by a progressive moral religion, plagiarisms and forgeries of literary or liturgic texts, incantations in. which the gods of all barbarous nations are invoked in unintelligible gibberish, odd and disconcerting ceremonies—all these form a chaos in which the imagination loses itself, a potpourri in which an arbitrary syncretism seems to have attempted to create an inextricable confusion.

However, if we observe more closely how magic operates, we find that it starts out from the same principles and acts along the same line of reasoning

as astrology. Born during the same period in the
primitive civilizations of the Orient, both were based
on a number of common ideas.[59] Magic, like astrology,
proceeded from the principle of universal sympathy,
yet it did not consider the relation existing between
the stars traversing the heavens, and physical or moral
phenomena, but the relation between whatever bodies
there are. It started out from the preconceived idea
that an obscure but constant relation exists between
certain things, certain words, certain persons. This
connection was established without hesitation between
dead material things and living beings, because the
primitive races ascribed a soul and existence similar to those of man, to everything surrounding them.
The distinction between the three kingdoms of nature
was unknown to them; they were "animists." The
life of a person might, therefore, be linked to that of
a thing, a tree, or an animal, in such a manner that one
died if the other did, and that any damage suffered by
one was also sustained by its inseparable associate.
Sometimes the relation was founded on clearly intelligible grounds, like a resemblance between the thing and
the being, as where, to kill an enemy, one pierced a
waxen figure supposed to represent him. Or a contact,
even merely passing by, was believed to have created
indestructible affinities, for instance where the garments
of an absent person were operated upon. Often, also,
these imaginary relations were founded on reasons that
escape us: like the qualities attributed by astrology to
the stars, they may have been derived from old beliefs
the memory of which is lost.

Like astrology, then, magic was a science in some
respects. First, like the predictions of its sister, it

was partly based on observation — observation frequently rudimentary, superficial, hasty, and erroneous, but nevertheless important. It was an experimental discipline. Among the great number of facts noted by the curiosity of the magicians, there were many that received scientific indorsement later on. The attraction of the magnet for iron was utilized by the thaumaturgi before it was interpreted by the natural philosophers. In the vast compilations that circulated under the venerable names of Zoroaster or Hostanes, many fertile remarks were scattered among puerile ideas and absurd teachings, just as in the Greek treatises on alchemy that have come down to us. The idea that knowledge of the power of certain agents enables one to stimulate the hidden forces of the universe into action and to obtain extraordinary results, inspires the researches of physics to-day, just as it inspired the claims of magic. And if astrology was a perverted astronomy, magic was physics gone astray.

Moreover, and again like astrology, magic was a science, because it started from the fundamental conception that order and law exist in nature, and that the same cause always produces the same effect. An occult ceremony, performed with the same care as an experiment in the chemical laboratory, will always have the expected result. To know the mysterious affinities that connect all things is sufficient to set the mechanism of the universe into motion. But the error of the magicians consisted in establishing a connection between phenomena that do not depend on each other at all. The act of exposing to the light for an instant a sensitive plate in a camera, then immersing it, according to given recipes, in appropriate liquids, and of making

the picture of a relative or friend appear thereon, is a
magical operation, but based on real actions and reactions, instead of on arbitrarily assumed sympathies and
antipathies. Magic, therefore, was a science groping
in the dark, and later became "a bastard sister of science," as Frazer puts it.

But, like astrology, magic was religious in origin,
and always remained a bastard sister of religion. Both
grew up together in the temples of the barbarian
Orient. Their practices were, at first, part of the
dubious knowledge of fetichists who claimed to have
control over the spirits that peopled nature and animated everything, and who claimed that they communicated with these spirits by means of rites known
to themselves alone. Magic has been cleverly defined
as 'the strategy of animism."[60] But, just as the growing power ascribed by the Chaldeans to the sidereal
deities transformed the original astrology, so primitive
sorcery assumed a different character when the world
of the gods, conceived after the image of man, separated
itself more and more from the realm of physical forces
and became a realm of its own. This gave the mystic
element which always entered the ceremonies, a new
precision and development. By means of his charms,
talismans, and exorcisms, the magician now communicated with the celestial or infernal "demons" and compelled them to obey him. But these spirits no longer
opposed him with the blind resistance of matter animated by an uncertain kind of life; they were active
and subtle beings having intelligence and will-power.
Sometimes they took revenge for the slavery the magician attempted to impose on them and punished the
audacious operator, who feared them, although in-

voking their aid. Thus the incantation often assumed
the shape of a prayer addressed to a power stronger
than man, and magic became a religion. Its rites developed side by side with the canonical liturgies, and
frequently encroached on them.[61] The only barrier between them was the vague and constantly shifting
borderline that limits the neighboring domains of religion and superstition.

* * *

This half scientific, half religious magic, with its
books and its professional adepts, is of Oriental origin.
The old Grecian and Italian sorcery appears to have
been rather mild. Conjurations to avert hail-storms,
or formulas to draw rain, evil charms to render fields
barren or to kill cattle, love philters and rejuvenating
salves, old women's remedies, talismans against the
evil eye,—all are based on popular superstition and
kept in existence by folk-lore and charlatanism. Even
the witches of Thessaly, whom people credited with the
power of making the moon descend from the sky, were
botanists more than anything else, acquainted with the
marvelous virtues of medicinal plants. The terror
that the necromancers inspired was due, to a considerable extent, to the use they made of the old belief
in ghosts. They exploited the superstitious belief in
ghost-power and slipped metal tablets covered with
execrations into graves, to bring misfortune or death
to some enemy. But neither in Greece nor in Italy is
there any trace of a coherent system of doctrines, of
an occult and learned discipline, nor of any sacerdotal
instruction.

Originally the adepts in this dubious art were despised. As late as the period of Augustus they were generally equivocal beggar-women who plied their miserable trade in the lowest quarters of the slums. But with the invasion of the Oriental religions the magician began to receive more consideration, and his condition improved.[62] He was honored, and feared even more. During the second century scarcely anybody would have doubted his power to call up divine apparitions, converse with the superior spirits and even translate himself bodily into the heavens.[63]

Here the victorious progress of the Oriental religions shows itself. The Egyptian ritual[64] originally was nothing but a collection of magical practices, properly speaking. The religious community imposed its will upon the gods by means of prayers or even threats. The gods were compelled to obey the officiating priest, if the liturgy was correctly performed, and if the incantations and the magic words were pronounced with the right intonation. The well-informed priest had an almost unlimited power over all supernatural beings on land, in the water, in the air, in heaven and in hell. Nowhere was the gulf between things human and things divine smaller, nowhere was the increasing differentiation that separated magic from religion less advanced. Until the end of paganism they remained so closely associated that it is sometimes difficult to distinguish the texts of one from those of the other.

The Chaldeans[65] also were past masters of sorcery, well versed in the knowledge of presages and experts in conjuring the evils which the presages foretold. In Mesopotamia, where they were confidential advisers of the kings, the magicians belonged to the official clergy; they invoked the aid of the state gods in their incantations, and their sacred science was as highly esteemed as haruspicy in Etruria. The immense prestige that continued to surround it, assured its persistence after the fall of Nineveh and Babylon. Its tradition was still alive under the Cæsars, and a number of enchanters rightly or wrongly claimed to possess the ancient wisdom of Chaldea.[66]

And the thaumaturgus, who was supposed to be the heir of the archaic priests, assumed a wholly sacerdotal appearance at Rome. Being an inspired sage who received confidential communications from heavenly spirits, he gave to his life and to his appearance a dignity almost equal to that of the philosopher. The common people soon confused the two,[67] and the Orientalizing philosophy of the last period of paganism actually accepted and justified all the superstitions of magic. Neo-Platonism, which concerned itself to a large extent with demonology, leaned more and more towards theurgy, and was finally completely absorbed by it.

But the ancients expressly distinguished, "magic," which was always under suspicion and disapproved of, from the legitimate and honorable art for which the name "theurgy"[68] was invented. The term "magician,"* which applied to all performers of miracles, properly means the priests of Mazdaism, and a well attested tradition makes the Persians[69] the authors of the real magic, that called "black magic" by the Middle Ages. If they did not invent it—because it is as old as humanity—they were at least the first to place it upon a doctrinal foundation and to assign to it a place

* μάγος.

in a clearly formulated theological system. The Mazdean dualism gave a new power to this pernicious knowledge by conferring upon it the character that will distinguish it henceforth.

Under what influences did the Persian magic come into existence? When and how did it spread? These are questions that are not well elucidated yet. The intimate fusion of the religious doctrines of the Iranian conquerors with those of the native clergy, which took place at Babylon, occurred in this era of belief,[70] and the magicians that were established in Mesopotamia combined their secret traditions with the rites and formulas codified by the Chaldean sorcerers. The universal curiosity of the Greeks soon took note of this marvelous science. Naturalist philosophers like Democritus,[71] the great traveler, seem to have helped themselves more than once from the treasure of observations collected by the Oriental priests. Without a doubt they drew from these incongruous compilations, in which truth was mingled with the absurd and reality with the fantastical, the knowledge of some properties of plants and minerals, or of some experiments of physics. However, the limpid Hellenic genius always turned away from the misty speculations of magic, giving them but slight consideration. But towards the end of the Alexandrine period the books ascribed to the half-mythical masters of the Persian science, Zoroaster, Hostanes and Hystaspes, were translated into Greek, and until the end of paganism those names enjoyed a prodigious authority. At the same time the Jews, who were acquainted with the arcana of the Irano-Chaldean doctrines and proceedings, made some of the recipes known wherever the dispersion brought them.[72] Later, a more immediate influence was exercised upon the Roman world by the Persian colonies of Asia Minor,[73] who retained an obstinate faith in their ancient national beliefs.

The particular importance attributed to magic by the Mazdeans is a necessary consequence of their dualist system, which has been treated by us before.[74] Ormuzd, residing in the heavens of light, is opposed by his irreconcilable adversary, Ahriman, ruler of the underworld. The one stands for light, truth, and goodness, the other for darkness, falsehood, and perversity. The one commands the kind spirits which protect the pious believer, the other is master over demons whose malice causes all the evils that afflict humanity. These opposite principles fight for the domination of the earth, and each creates favorable or noxious animals and plants. Everything on earth is either heavenly or infernal. Ahriman and his demons, who surround man to tempt or hurt him,[75] are evil gods and entirely different from those of which Ormuzd's host consists. The magician sacrifices to them, either to avert evils they threaten, or to direct their ire against enemies of true belief, and the impure spirits rejoice in bloody immolations and delight in the fumes of flesh burning on the altars.[76] Terrible acts and words attended all immolations. Plutarch[77] mentions an example of the dark sacrifices of the Mazdeans. "In a mortar," he says, "they pound a certain herb called wild garlic, at the same time invoking Hades (Ahriman), and the powers of darkness, then stirring this herb in the blood of a slaughtered wolf, they take it away and drop it on a spot never reached by the rays of the sun." A necromantic performance indeed.

We can imagine the new strength which such a conception of the universe must have given to magic. It was no longer an incongruous collection of popular superstitions and scientific observations. It became a reversed religion: its nocturnal rites were the dreadful liturgy of the infernal powers. There was no miracle the experienced magician might not expect to perform with the aid of the demons, providing he know how to master them; he would invent any atrocity in his desire to gain the favor of the evil divinities whom crime gratified and suffering pleased. Hence the number of impious practices performed in the dark, practices the horror of which is equaled only by their absurdity: preparing beverages that disturbed the senses and impaired the intellect; mixing subtle poisons extracted from demoniac plants and corpses already in a state of putridity;[78] immolating children in order to read the future in their quivering entrails or to conjure up ghosts. All the satanic refinement that a perverted imagination in a state of insanity could conceive[79] pleased the malicious evil spirits; the more odious the monstrosity, the more assured was its efficacy. These abominable practices were sternly suppressed by the Roman government. Whereas, in the case of an astrologer who had committed an open transgression, the law was satisfied with expelling him from Rome—whither he generally soon returned,—the magician was put in the same class with murderers and poisoners, and was subjected to the very severest punishment. He was nailed to the cross or thrown to the wild beasts. Not only the practice of the profession, but even the simple fact of possessing works of sorcery made any one subject to prosecution.[80]

However, there are ways of reaching an agreement with the police, and in this case custom was stronger than law. The intermittent rigor of imperial edicts had no more power to destroy an inveterate superstition than the Christian polemics had to cure it. It was a recognition of its strength when state and church united to fight it. Neither reached the root of the evil, for they did not deny the reality of the power wielded by the sorcerers. As long as it was admitted that malicious spirits constantly interfered in human affairs, and that there were secret means enabling the operator to dominate those spirits or to share in their power, magic was indestructible. It appealed to too many human passions to remain unheard. If, on the one hand, the desire of penetrating the mysteries of the future, the fear of unknown misfortunes, and hope, always reviving, led the anxious masses to seek a chimerical certainty in astrology, on the other hand, in the case of magic, the blinding charm of the marvelous, the entreaties of love and ambition, the bitter desire for revenge, the fascination of crime, and the intoxication of bloodshed,—all the instincts that are not avowable and that are satisfied in the dark, took turns in practising their seductions. During the entire life of the Roman empire its existence continued, and the very mystery that it was compelled to hide in increased its prestige and almost gave it the authority of a revelation.

A curious occurrence that took place towards the end of the fifth century at Beirut, in Syria, shows how deeply even the strongest intellects of that period believed in the most atrocious practices of magic. One night some students of the famous law-school of that city attempted to kill a slave in the circus, to aid the master in obtaining the favor of a woman who scorned him. Being reported, they had to deliver up their hidden volumes, of which those of Zoroaster and of Hostanes were found, together with those written by the astrologer Manetho. The whole city was agitated, and searches proved that many young men preferred the study of the illicit science to that of Roman law. By order of the bishop a solemn auto-da-fé was made of all this literature, in the presence of the city officials and the clergy, and the most revolting passages were read in public, "in order to acquaint everybody with the conceited and vain promises of the demons," as the pious writer of the story says.[81]

Thus the ancient traditions of magic continued to live in the Christian Orient after the fall of paganism. They even outlived the domination of the church. The rigorous principles of its monotheism notwithstanding, Islam became infected with those Persian superstitions. In the Occident the evil art resisted persecution and anathemas with the same obstinacy as in the Orient. It remained alive in Rome all through the fifth century,[82] and when scientific astrology in Europe went down with science itself, the old Mazdean dualism continued to manifest itself, during the entire Middle Ages in the ceremonies of the black mass and the worshiping of Satan, until the dawn of the modern era.

* * *

Twin sisters, born of the superstitions of the learned Orient, magic and astrology always remained the hybrid daughters of sacerdotal culture. Their existence was governed by two contrary principles, reason and faith, and they never ceased to fluctuate between these two poles of thought. Both were inspired by a belief in universal sympathy, according to which occult and powerful relations exist between human beings and dead objects, all possessing a mysterious life. The doctrine of sidereal influences, combined with a knowledge of the immutability of the celestial revolutions, caused astrology to formulate the first theory of absolute fatalism, whose decrees might be known beforehand. But, besides this rigorous determinism, it retained its childhood faith in the divine stars, whose favor could be secured and malignity avoided through worship. In astrology the experimental method was reduced to the completing of prognostics based on the supposed character of the stellar gods.

Magic also remained half empirical and half religious. Like our physics, it was based on observation, it proclaimed the constancy of the laws of nature, and sought to conquer the latent energies of the material world in order to bring them under the dominion of man's will. But at the same time it recognized, in the powers that it claimed to conquer, spirits or demons whose protection might be obtained, whose ill-will might be appeased, or whose savage hostility might be unchained by means of immolations and incantations.

All their aberrations notwithstanding, astrology and magic were not entirely fruitless. Their counterfeit learning has been a genuine help to the progress of human knowledge. Because they awakened chimerical hopes and fallacious ambitions in the minds of their adepts, researches were undertaken which undoubtedly would never have been started or persisted in for the sake of a disinterested love of truth. The observations, collected with untiring patience by the Oriental priests, caused the first physical and astronomical discoveries, and, as in the time of the scholastics, the occult sciences led to the exact ones. But when these understood the vanity of the astounding illusions on which astrology and magic had subsisted, they broke up the foundation of the arts to which they owed their birth.

THE TRANSFORMATION OF ROMAN
PAGANISM.

ABOUT the time of the Severi the religion of Europe
must have presented an aspect of surprising variety. Although dethroned, the old native Italian, Celtic
and Iberian divinities were still alive. Though eclipsed
by foreign rivals, they lived on in the devotion of the
lower classes and in the traditions of the rural districts.
For a long time the Roman gods had been established
in every town and had received the homage of an
official clergy according to pontifical rites. Beside
them, however, were installed the representatives of
all the Asiatic pantheons, and these received the most
fervent adoration from the masses. New powers had
arrived from Asia Minor, Egypt, Syria, and the dazzling Oriental sun outshone the stars of Italy's temperate sky. All forms of paganism were simultaneously received and retained while the exclusive monotheism of the Jews kept its adherents, and Christianity
strengthened its churches and fortified its orthodoxy,
at the same time giving birth to the baffling vagaries
of gnosticism. A hundred different currents carried
away hesitating and undecided minds, a hundred contrasting sermons made appeals to the conscience of the
people.

Let us suppose that in modern Europe the faithful

had deserted the Christian churches to worship Allah or Brahma, to follow the precepts of Confucius or Buddha, or to adopt the maxims of the Shinto; let us imagine a great confusion of all the races of the world in which Arabian mullahs, Chinese scholars, Japanese bonzes, Tibetan lamas and Hindu pundits would be preaching fatalism and predestination, ancestor-worship and devotion to a deified sovereign, pessimism and deliverance through annihilation — a confusion in which all those priests would erect temples of exotic architecture in our cities and celebrate their disparate rites therein. Such a dream, which the future may perhaps realize, would offer a pretty accurate picture of the religious chaos in which the ancient world was struggling before the reign of Constantine.

The Oriental religions that successively gained popularity exercised a decisive influence on the transformation of Latin paganism. Asia Minor was the first to have its gods accepted by Italy. Since the end of the Punic wars the black stone symbolizing the Great Mother of Pessinus had been established on the Palatine, but only since the reign of Claudius could the Phrygian cult freely develop in all its splendor and excesses. It introduced a sensual, highly-colored and fanatical worship into the grave and somber religion of the Romans. Officially recognized, it attracted and took under its protection other foreign divinities from Anatolia and assimilated them to Cybele and Attis, who thereafter bore the symbols of several deities together. Cappadocian, Jewish, Persian and even Christian influences modified the old rites of Pessinus and filled them with ideas of spiritual purification and eter-

nal redemption by the bloody baptism of the taurobolium. But the priests did not succeed in eliminating
the basis of coarse naturism which ancient barbaric
tradition had imposed upon them.

Beginning with the second century before our era,
the mysteries of Isis and Serapis spread over Italy
with the Alexandrian culture whose religious expression they were, and in spite of all persecution established themselves at Rome where Caligula gave them
the freedom of the city. They did not bring with them
a very advanced theological system, because Egypt
never produced anything but a chaotic aggregate of
disparate doctrines, nor a very elevated ethics, because
the level of its morality—that of the Alexandrian
Greeks—rose but slowly from a low stage. But they
made Italy, and later the other Latin provinces, familiar with an ancient ritual of incomparable charm
that aroused widely different feelings with its splendid
processions and liturgic dramas. They also gave their
votaries positive assurance of a blissful immortality
after death, when they would be united with Serapis
and, participating body and soul in his divinity, would
live in eternal contemplation of the gods.

At a somewhat later period arrived the numerous
and varied Baals of Syria. The great economic movement starting at the beginning of our era which produced the colonization of the Latin world by Syrian
slaves and merchants, not only modified the material
civilization of Europe, but also its conceptions and
beliefs. The Semitic cults entered into successful competition with those of Asia Minor and Egypt. They
may not have had so stirring a liturgy, nor have been
so thoroughly absorbed in preoccupation with a future

life, although they taught an original eschatology, but they did have an infinitely higher idea of divinity. The Chaldean astrology, of which the Syrian priests were enthusiastic disciples, had furnished them with the elements of a scientific theology. It had led them to the notion of a God residing far from the earth above the zone of the stars, a God almighty, universal and eternal. Everything on earth was determined by the revolutions of the heavens according to infinite cycles of years. It had taught them at the same time the worship of the sun, the radiant source of earthly life and human intelligence.

The learned doctrines of the Babylonians had also imposed themselves upon the Persian mysteries of Mithra which considered time identified with heaven as the supreme cause, and deified the stars; but they had superimposed themselves upon the ancient Mazdean creed without destroying it. Thus the essential principles of the religion of Iran, the secular and often successful rival of Greece, penetrated into the Occident under cover of Chaldean wisdom. The Mithra worship, the last and highest manifestation of ancient paganism, had Persian dualism for its fundamental dogma. The world is the scene and the stake of a contest between good and evil, Ormuzd and Ahriman, gods and demons, and from this primary conception of the universe flowed a strong and pure system of ethics. Life is a combat; soldiers under the command of Mithra, invincible heroes of the faith, must ceaselessly oppose the undertakings of the infernal powers which sow corruption broadcast. This imperative ethics was productive of energy and formed the characteristic feature distinguishing Mithraism from all other Oriental cults.

Thus every one of the Levantine countries—and that is what we meant to show in this brief recapitulation—had enriched Roman paganism with new beliefs that were frequently destined to outlive it. What was the result of this confusion of heterogeneous doctrines whose multiplicity was extreme and whose values were very different? How did the barbaric ideas refine themselves and combine with each other when thrown into the fiery crucible of imperial syncretism? In other words, what shape was assumed by ancient idolatry, so impregnated with exotic theories during the fourth century, when it was finally dethroned? It is this point that we should like to indicate briefly as the conclusion to these studies.

However, can we speak of *one* pagan religion? Did not the blending of the races result in multiplying the variety of disagreements? Had not the confused collision of creeds produced a division into fragments, a communication of churches? Had not a complacent syncretism engendered a multiplication of sects? The "Hellenes," as Themistius told the Emperor Valens, had three hundred ways of conceiving and honoring deity, who takes pleasure in such diversity of homage.[1] In paganism a cult does not die violently, but after long decay. A new doctrine does not necessarily displace an older one. They may co-exist for a long time as contrary possibilities suggested by the intellect or faith, and all opinions, all practices, seem respectable to paganism. It never has any radical or revolutionary transformations. Undoubtedly, the pagan beliefs of the fourth century or earlier did not have the consistency of a metaphysical system nor the rigor of canons formulated by a council. There is always a considerable difference between the faith of the masses and that of cultured minds, and this difference was bound to be great in an aristocratic empire whose social classes were sharply separated. The devotion of the masses was as unchanging as the depths of the sea; it was not stirred up nor heated by the upper currents.[2] The peasants practised their pious rites over anointed stones, sacred springs and blossoming trees, as in the past, and continued celebrating their rustic holidays during seed-time and harvest. They adhered with invincible tenacity to their traditional usages. Degraded and lowered to the rank of superstitions, these were destined to persist for centuries under the Christian orthodoxy without exposing it to serious peril, and while they were no longer marked in the liturgic calendars they were still mentioned occasionally in the collections of folk-lore.

At the other extreme of society the philosophers delighted in veiling religion with the frail and brilliant tissue of their speculations. Like the emperor Julian they improvised bold and incongruous interpretations of the myth of the Great Mother, and these interpretations were received and relished by a restricted circle of scholars. But during the fourth century these vagaries of the individual imagination were nothing but arbitrary applications of uncontested principles. During that century there was much less intellectual anarchy than when Lucian had exposed the sects "for sale at public auction"; a comparative harmony arose among the pagans after they joined the opposition. One single school, that of neo-Platonism, ruled all

minds. This school not only respected positive religion, as ancient stoicism had done, but venerated it,
because it saw there the expression of an old revelation handed down by past generations. It considered
the sacred books divinely inspired—the books of Hermes Trismegistus, Orpheus, the Chaldean oracles, Homer, and especially the esoteric doctrines of the mysteries—and subordinated its theories to their teachings. As there must be no contradiction between all
the disparate traditions of different countries and different periods, because all have emanated from one
divinity, philosophy, the *ancilla theologiae,* attempted
to reconcile them by the aid of allegory. And thus,
by means of compromises between old Oriental ideas
and Greco-Latin thought, an *ensemble* of beliefs slowly
took form, the truth of which seemed to have been
established by common consent. So when the atro-
phied parts of the Roman religion had been removed,
foreign elements had combined to give it a new vigor
and in it themselves became modified. This hidden
work of internal decomposition and reconstruction had
unconsciously produced a religion very different from
the one Augustus had attempted to restore.

However, we would be tempted to believe that there
had been no change in the Roman faith, were we to
read certain authors that fought idolatry in those days.
Saint Augustine, for instance, in his *City of God,*
pleasantly pokes fun at the multitude of Italian gods
that presided over the paltriest acts of life.[3] But the
useless, ridiculous deities of the old pontifical litanies
no longer existed outside of the books of antiquaries.
As a matter of fact, the Christian polemicist's authority in this instance was Varro. The defenders of the

church sought weapons against idolatry even in Xe-
nophanes, the first philosopher to oppose Greek polytheism. It has frequently been shown that apologists
find it difficult to follow the progress of the doctrines
which they oppose, and often their blows fall upon
dead men. Moreover, it is a fault common to all
scholars, to all imbued with book learning, that they
are better acquainted with the opinions of ancient
authors than with the sentiments of their contemporaries, and that they prefer to live in the past rather
than in the world surrounding them. It was easier to
reproduce the objections of the Epicureans and the
skeptics against abolished beliefs, than to study the
defects of an active organism with a view to criticizing
it. In those times the merely formal culture of the
schools caused many of the best minds to lose their
sense of reality.

The Christian polemics therefore frequently give us
an inadequate idea of paganism in its decline. When
they complacently insisted upon the immorality of the
sacred legends they ignored the fact that the gods and
heroes of mythology had no longer any but a purely
literary existence.[4] The writers of that period, like
those of the Renaissance, regarded the fictions of
mythology as details necessary to poetical composition. They were ornaments of style, rhetorical devices,
but not the expression of a sincere faith. Those old
myths had fallen to the lowest degree of disrepute
in the theater. The actors of mimes ridiculing Jupiter's
gallant adventures did not believe in their reality any
more than the author of Faust believed in the compact
with Mephistopheles.

So we must not be deceived by the oratorical effects

of a rhetorician like Arnobius or by the Ciceronian
periods of a Lactantius. In order to ascertain the
real status of the beliefs we must refer to Christian
authors who were men of letters less than they were
men of action, who lived the life of the people and
breathed the air of the streets, and who spoke from
experience rather than from the treatises of myth-
mongers. They were high functionaries like Prudentius;[5] like the man to whom the name "Ambrosiaster"[6]
has been given since the time of Erasmus; like the
converted pagan Firmicus Maternus,[7] who had written a treatise on astrology before opposing "The Error
of the Profane Religions"; like certain priests brought
into contact with the last adherents of idolatry through
their pastoral duties, as for instance the author of the
homilies ascribed to St. Maximus of Turin;[8] finally like
the writers of anonymous pamphlets, works prepared
for the particular occasion and breathing the ardor
of all the passions of the movement.[9] If this inquiry
is based on the obscure indications in regard to their
religious convictions left by members of the Roman
aristocracy who remained true to the faith of their
ancestors, like Macrobius or Symmachus; if it is particularly guided by the exceptionally numerous inscriptions that seem to be the public expression of the
last will of expiring paganism, we shall be able to gain
a sufficiently precise idea of the condition of the
Roman religion at the time of its extinction.

One fact becomes immediately clear from an ex-
amination of those documents. The old national religion of Rome was dead.[10] The great dignitaries
still adorned themselves with the titles of augur and
quindecimvir, or of consul and tribune, but those ar-

chaic prelacies were as devoid of all real influence upon religion as the republican magistracies were powerless in the state. Their fall had been made complete on the day when Aurelian established the pontiffs of the Invincible Sun, the protector of his empire, beside and above the ancient high priests. The only cults still alive were those of the Orient, and against them were directed the efforts of the Christian polemics, who grew more and more bitter in speaking of them. The barbarian gods had taken the place of the defunct immortals in the devotion of the pagans. They alone still had empire over the soul.

With all the other "profane religions," Firmicus Maternus fought those of the four Oriental nations. He connected them with the four elements. The Egyptians were the worshipers of water— the water of the Nile fertilizing their country; the Phrygians of the earth, which was to them the Great Mother of everything; the Syrians and Carthaginians of the air, which they adored under the name of celestial Juno;[11] the Persians of fire, to which they attributed pre-eminence over the other three principles. This system certainly was borrowed from the pagan theologians. In the common peril threatening them, those cults, formerly rivals, had become reconciled and regarded themselves as divisions and, so to speak, congregations, of the same church. Each one of them was especially consecrated to one of the elements which in combination form the universe. Their union constituted the pantheistic religion of the deified world.

All the Oriental religions assumed the form of mysteries.[12] Their dignitaries were at the same time pontiffs of the Invincible Sun, fathers of Mithra, cele-

brants of the taurobolium of the Great Mother, prophets of Isis; in short, they had all titles imaginable.
In their initiation they received the revelation of an
esoteric doctrine strengthened by their fervor.[13] What
was the theology they learned?   Here also a certain
dogmatic homogeneity has established itself.

All writers agree with Firmicus that the pagans
worshiped the *elementa*.[14]   Under this term were included not only the four simple substances which by
their opposition and blending caused all phenomena
of the visible world,[15] but also the stars and in general
the elements of all celestial and earthly bodies.[16]

We therefore may in a certain sense speak of the
return of paganism to nature worship; but must this
transformation be regarded as a retrogression toward
a barbarous past, as a relapse to the level of primitive
animism? If so, we should be deceived by appearances.
Religions do not fall back into infancy as they grow
old.   The pagans of the fourth century no longer
naively considered their gods as capricious genii, as
the disordered powers of a confused natural philosophy; they conceived them as cosmic energies whose
providential action was regulated in a harmonious system.   Faith was no longer instinctive and impulsive,
for erudition and reflection had reconstructed the entire theology.   In a certain sense it might be said that
theology had passed from the fictitious to the metaphysical state, according to the formula of Comte. It
was intimately connected with the knowledge of the
day, which was cherished by its last votaries with love
and pride, as faithful heirs of the ancient wisdom of
the Orient and Greece.[17]   In many instances it was
nothing but a religious form of the cosmology of the

period. This constituted both its strength and its weakness. The rigorous principles of astrology determined its conception of heaven and earth.

The universe was an organism animated by a God, unique, eternal and almighty. Sometimes this God was identified with the destiny that ruled all things, with infinite time that regulated all visible phenomena, and he was worshiped in each subdivision of that endless duration, especially in the months and the seasons.[18] Sometimes, however, he was compared with a king; he was thought of as a sovereign governing an empire, and the various gods then were the princes and dignitaries interceding with the rulers on behalf of his subjects whom they led in some manner into his presence. This heavenly court had its messengers or "angels" conveying to men the will of the master and reporting again the vows and petitions of his subjects. It was an aristocratic monarchy in heaven as on earth.[19] A more philosophic conception made the divinity an infinite power impregnating all nature with its overflowing forces. "There is only one God, sole and supreme," wrote Maximus of Madaura about 390, "without beginning or parentage, whose energies, diffused through the world, we invoke under various names, because we are ignorant of his real name. By successively addressing our supplications to his different members we intend to honor him in his entirety. Through the mediation of the subordinate gods the common father both of themselves and of all men is honored in a thousand different ways by mortals who are thus in accord in spite of their discord."[20]

However, this ineffable God, who comprehensively embraces everything, manifests himself especially in the resplendent brightness of the ethereal sky.[21] He reveals his power in water and in fire, in the earth, the sea and the blowing of the winds; but his purest, most radiant and most active epiphany is in the stars whose revolutions determine every event and all our actions. Above all he manifests himself in the sun, the motive power of the celestial spheres, the inexhaustible seat of light and life, the creator of all intelligence on earth. Certain philosophers like the senator Praetextatus, one of the *dramatis personae* of Macrobius, confounded all the ancient divinities of paganism with the sun in a thorough-going syncretism.[22]

Just as a superficial observation might lead to the belief that the theology of the last pagans had reverted to its origin, so at first sight the transformation of the ritual might appear like a return to savagery. With the adoption of the Oriental mysteries barbarous, cruel and obscene practices were undoubtedly spread, as for instance the masquerading in the guise of animals in the Mithraic initiations, the bloody dances of the *galli* of the Great Mother and the mutilations of the Syrian priests. Nature worship was originally as "amoral" as nature itself. But an ethereal spiritualism ideally transfigured the coarseness of those primitive customs. Just as the doctrine had become completely impregnated with philosophy and erudition, so the liturgy had become saturated with ethical ideas.

The taurobolium, a disgusting shower-bath of lukewarm blood, had become a means of obtaining a new and eternal life; the ritualistic ablutions were no longer external and material acts, but were supposed to cleanse the soul of its impurities and to restore its original innocence; the sacred repasts imparted an intimate virtue to the soul and furnished sustenance to the spiritual life. While efforts were made to maintain the continuity of tradition, its content had slowly been transformed. The most shocking and licentious fables were metamorphosed into edifying narratives by convenient and subtle interpretations which were a joy to the learned mythographers. Paganism had become a school of morality, the priest a doctor and director of the conscience.[23]

The purity and holiness imparted by the practice of sacred ceremonies were the indispensable condition for obtaining eternal life.[24] The mysteries promised a blessed immortality to their initiates, and claimed to reveal to them infallible means of effecting their salvation. According to a generally accepted symbol, the spirit animating man was a spark, detached from the fires shining in the ether; it partook of their divinity and so, it was believed, had descended to the earth to undergo a trial. It could literally be said that

"Man is a fallen god who still remembers heaven."

After having left their corporeal prisons, the pious souls reascended towards the celestial regions of the divine stars, to live forever in endless brightness beyond the starry spheres.[25]

But at the other extremity of the world, facing this luminous realm, extended the somber kingdom of evil spirits. They were irreconcilable adversaries of the gods and men of good will, and constantly left the infernal regions to roam about the earth and scatter evil. With the aid of the celestial spirits, the faithful had to struggle forever against their designs and seek to avert their anger by means of bloody sacrifices.

But, with the help of occult and terrible processes, the magician could subject them to his power and compel them to serve his purposes. This demonology, the monstrous offspring of Persian dualism, favored the rise of every superstition.[26]

However, the reign of the evil powers was not to last forever. According to common opinion the universe would be destroyed by fire[27] after the times had been fulfilled. All the wicked would perish, but the just would be revived and establish the reign of universal happiness in the regenerated world.[28]

The foregoing is a rapid sketch of the theology of paganism after three centuries of Oriental influence. From coarse fetichism and savage superstitions the learned priests of the Asiatic cults had gradually produced a complete system of metaphysics and eschatology, as the Brahmins built up the spiritualistic monism of the Vedanta beside the monstrous idolatry of Hinduism, or, to confine our comparisons to the Latin world, as the jurists drew from the traditional customs of primitive tribes the abstract principles of a legal system that governs the most cultivated societies. This religion was no longer like that of ancient Rome, a mere collection of propitiatory and expiatory rites performed by the citizen for the good of the state; it now pretended to offer to all men a world-conception which gave rise to a rule of conduct and placed the end of existence in the future life. It was more unlike the worship that Augustus had attempted to restore than the Christianity that fought it. The two opposed creeds moved in the same intellectual and moral sphere,[29] and one could actually pass from one to the other without shock or interruption. Sometimes when reading the long works of the last Latin writers, like Ammianus Marcellinus or Boëthius, or the panegyrics of the official orators,[30] scholars could well ask whether their authors were pagan or Christian. In the time of Symmachus and Praetextatus, the members of the Roman aristocracy who had remained faithful to the gods of their ancestors did not have a mentality or morality very different from that of adherents of the new faith who sat with them in the senate. The religious and mystical spirit of the Orient had slowly overcome the whole social organism and had prepared all nations to unite in the bosom of a universal church.

NOTES.

PREFACE.

1. We are indebted for more than one useful suggestion to our colleagues Messrs. Charles Michel and Joseph Bidez, who were kind enough to read the proofs of the French edition.

2. An outline of the present state of the subject will be found in a recent volume by Gruppe, *Griechische Mythologie,* 1906, pp. 1606 ff., whose views are sharply opposed to the negative conclusions formulated, with certain reservations, by Harnack, *Ausbreitung des Christentums,* II, pp. 274 ff. Among the latest studies intended for the general reader that have appeared on this subject, may be mentioned in Germany those of Geffcken (*Aus der Werdezeit des Christentums,* Leipsic, 1904, pp. 114 ff.), and in England those of Cheyne (*Bible Problems,* 1904), who expresses his opinion in these terms: "The Christian religion is a synthesis, and only those who have dim eyes can assert that the intellectual empires of Babylonia and Persia have fallen."—Very useful is the new book of Clemen, *Religionsgeschichtliche Erklärung des Neuen Testaments,* Giessen, 1909.

3. *Mon. myst. Mithra,* I, p. 342, n. 4; see the new texts commented on by Usener, *Rhein. Museum,* LX, 1905, pp. 466 ff.; 489 ff., and my paper "Natalis Invicti," *C. R. Acad. des inscr.,* 1911.

4. See page 70. Compare also *Mon. myst. Mithra,* I, p. 341. The imitation of the church is plain in the pagan reform attempted by the emperor Julian.

5. See Harnack, *Militia Christi,* 1905.

6. I have collected a number of texts on the religious "militias" in *Mon. myst. Mithra,* I, p. 317, n. 1. Others could certainly be discovered: Apuleius, *Metam.,* XI, 14: *E cohorte re-*

ligionis unus (in connection with a mystic of Isis) ;—Vettius Valens (V, 2, p. 220, 27, Kroll ed.) : Στρατιῶται τῆς εἱμαρμένης; (VII, 3, p. 271, 28) Συστρατεύεσθαι τοῖς καιροῖς γενναίως. See Minucius Felix, 36, § 7: *Quod patimur non est poena, militia est.*—We might also mention the commonplace term *militia Veneris,* which was popular with the Augustan poets (Propertius, IV, 1, 137; see I, 6, 30; Horace, *Od.,* III, 26, and especially the parallel developed by Ovid, *Amor.,* I, 9, 1 ff., and *Ars amat.,* III, 233 ff).—Socrates, in Plato's *Apologia* (p. 28 E), incidentally likens the philosophic mission imposed on him by the divinity to the campaigns he waged under the orders of the archons, but the comparison of God with a "strategus" was developed especially by the Stoics; see Capelle, "Schrift von der Welt," *Neue Jahrb. für das klass. Altert.,* XV, 1905, p. 558, n. 6, and Seneca, *Epist.,* 107, 9: *Optimum est Deum sine murmuratione comitari, malus miles est qui imperatorem gemens sequitur.*—See now also Reitzenstein, *Hellenistische Mysterienreligion,* 1910, p. 66.

7. See *Rev. des études grecques,* XIV, 1901, pp. 43 ff.

8. This has been clearly shown by Wendland in connection with the idea of the σωτηρία, *Zeitschrift für neutest. Wiss.,* V, 1904, pp. 355 ff. More recently he has thrown light on the general influence of Hellenistic civilization on Christianity (*Die hellenistisch-römische Kultur in ihren Beziehungen zum Judentum und Christentum,* Tübingen, 1908). A first attempt to determine the character of Hellenistic mysteries is to be found in Reitzenstein's *Hellenistische Mysterienreligion,* 1910.

I. ROME AND THE ORIENT.

1. Renan, *L'Antéchrist,* p. 130.

2. M. Krumbacher (*Byzant. Zeitschr.,* XVI, 1907, p. 710) notes, in connection with the idea that I am defending here: "In ähnlicher Weise war dieser Gedanke (der Ueberflügelung des Abendlandes durch die auf allen Kulturgebieten vordringende Regsamkeit der Orientalen) kurz vorher in meiner Skizze der byzantinischen Literatur (*Kultur der Gegenwart,* I, 8 [1907], pp. 246-253) auseinandergelegt worden; es ist ein erfreulicher und bei dem Wirrsal widerstreitender Doctrinen tröstlicher Beweis für den Fortschritt der Erkenntniss, dass

zwei von ganz verschiedenen Richtungen ausgehende Diener der Wissenschaft sich in so wichtigen allgemeinen Fragen so nahe kommen."

3. Cf. Kornemann, "Aegyptische Einflüsse im römischen Kaiserreich" (*Neue Jahrb. für das klass. Altertum*, II, 1898, p. 118 ff.) and Otto Hirschfeld, *Die kaiserl. Verwaltungsbeamten*, 2d. ed., p. 469.

4. See Cicero's statement regarding the ancient Roman dominion (*De off.*, II, 8): "Illud patrocinium orbis terrae verius quam imperium poterat nominari."

5. O. Hirschfeld, *op. cit.*, pp. 53, 91, 93, etc.; cf. Mitteis, *Reichsrecht und Volksrecht*, p. 9, n. 2, etc. Thus have various institutions been transmitted from the ancient Persians to the Romans; see Ch. VI, n. 5.

6. Rostovtzew, "Der Ursprung des Kolonats" (*Beiträge zur alten Gesch.*, I, 1901, p. 295); Haussoullier, *Histoire de Milet et du Didymeion*, 1902, p. 106.

7. Mitteis, *Reichsrecht und Volksrecht in den östlichen Provinzen*, 1891, pp. 8 ff.

8. Mommsen, *Gesammelte Schriften*, II, 1905, p. 366: "Seit Diocletian übernimmt der östliche Reichsteil, die *partes Orientis*, auf allen Gebieten die Führung. Dieser späte Sieg des Hellenismus über die Lateiner ist vielleicht nirgends auffälliger als auf dem Gebiet der juristischen Schriftstellerei."

9. De Vogüe and Duthoit, *L'Architecture civile et religieuse de la Syrie centrale*, Paris, 1866-1877.

10. This result is especially due to the researches of M. Strzygowski, but we cannot enter here into the controversies aroused by his publications: *Orient oder Rom*, 1911; *Hellas in des Orients Umarmung*, Munich, 1902, and especially *Kleinasien, ein Neuland der Kunstgeschichte*, Leipsic, 1903; [cf. the reports of Ch. Diehl, *Journal des Savants*, 1904, pp. 236 ff. = *Etudes byzantines*, 1905, pp. 336 ff.; Gabriel Millet, *Revue archéolog.*, 1905, I, pp. 93 ff.; Marcel Laurent, *Revue de l'Instr. publ. en Belgique*, 1905, pp. 145 ff.]; *Mschatta*, 1904, [cf. *infra*, Ch. VI, n. 12].—M. Bréhier, "Orient ou Byzance?" (*Rev. archéol.*, 1907, II, pp. 396 ff.), gives a substantial summary of the question.—In his last volume, *Amida* (1910), M. Strzy-

gowski tries to find the source of medieval art in Mesopotamia. For this controversy see Diehl's *Manuel d'art byzantin,* 1910.

11. See also Pliny, *Epist. Traian.,* 40: "Architecti tibi [in Bithynia] deesse non possunt....cum ex Graecia etiam ad nos [at Rome] venire soliti sint."—Among the names of architects mentioned in Latin inscriptions there are a great many revealing Greek or Oriental origin (see Ruggiero, *Dizion. epigr.,* s. v. "Architectus"), in spite of the consideration which their eminently useful profession always enjoyed at Rome..

12. The question of the artistic and industrial influences exercised by the Orient over Gaul during the Roman period, has been broached frequently—among others by Courajod (*Leçons du Louvre,* I, 1899, pp. 115, 327.ff.)—but it has never been seriously studied in its entirety. Michaëlis has recently devoted a suggestive article to this subject in connection with a statue from the museum of Metz executed in the style of the school of Pergamum (*Jahrb. der Gesellsch. für lothring. Geschichte,* XVII, 1905, pp. 203 ff.). By the influence of Marseilles in Gaul, and the ancient connection of that city with the towns of Hellenic Asia, he explains the great difference between the works of sculpture discovered along the upper Rhine, which had been civilized by the Italian legions, and those unearthed on the other side of the Vosges. This is a very important discovery rich in results. We believe, however, that Michaëlis ascribes too much importance to the early Marseilles traders traveling along the old "tin road" towards Brittany and the "amber road" towards Germany. The Asiatic merchants and artisans did not set out from one point only. There were many emigrants all over the valley of the Rhone. Lyons was a half-Hellenized city, and the relations of Arles with Syria, of Nimes with Egypt, etc., are well known. We shall speak of them in connection with the religions of those countries.

13. Even in the bosom of the church the Latin Occident of the fourth century was still subordinate to the Greek Orient, which imposed its doctrinal problems upon it (Harnack, *Mission und Ausbreitung,* II, p. 283, n. 1).

14. The sacred formulas have been collected by Alb. Dieterich, *Eine Mithrasliturgie,* pp. 212 ff. He adds Δοίη σοὶ "Οσιρις

τὸ ψυχρὸν ὕδωρ, *Archiv für Religionswiss.*, VIII, 1905, p. 504, n. 1. [Cf. *infra*, ch. IV, n. 90.] Among the hymns of greatest importance for the Oriental cults we must cite those in honor of Isis, discovered in the island of Andros (Kaibel, *Epigr.*, 4028) and elsewhere (seè ch. IV, n. 6). Fragments of hymns in honor of Attis have been preserved by Hippolytus (*Philosoph.*, V, 9. pp. 168 ff.) The so-called orphic hymns (Abel, *Orphica*, 1883), which date back to a rather remote period, do not seem to contain many Oriental elements (see Maas, *Orpheus*, 1895, pp. 173 ff.), but this does not apply to the gnostic hymns of which we possess very instructive fragments.—Cf. *Mon. myst. de Mithra*, I, p. 313, n. 1.

15. Regarding the imitations of the stage, see Adami, *De poetis scen. Graecis hymnorum sacrorum imitatoribus*, 1901. Wünsch has shown the liturgic character of a prayer to Asklepios, inserted by Herondas into his mimiambi (*Archiv für Religionswiss.*, VII, 1904, pp. 95 ff.) Dieterich believes he has found an extensive extract from the Mithraic liturgy in a magic papyrus of Paris (see *infra*, ch. VI, Bibliography). But all these discoveries amount to very little if we think of the enormous number of liturgic texts that have been lost, and even in the case of ancient Greece we know little regarding this sacred literature. See Ausfeld, *De Graecorum precationibus*, Leipsic, 1903; Ziegler, *De precationum apud Graecos formis quaestiones selectae*, Breslau, 1905; H. Schmidt, *Veteres philosophi quomodo iudicaverint de precibus*, Giessen, 1907.

16. For instance, the hymn "which the magi sung" about the steeds of the supreme god; its contents are given by Dion Chrysostom, *Orat.*, XXXVI, 39 (see *Mon. myst. Mithra*, I. p. 298; II, p. 60).

17. I have in mind the hymns of Cleanthes (Von Arnim, *Stoic. fragm.*, I, Nos. 527, 537), also Demetrius's act of renunciation in Seneca, *De Provid.*, V, 5, which bears a surprising resemblance to one of the most famous Christian prayers, the *Suscipe* of Saint Ignatius which concludes the book of Spiritual Exercises (Delehaye, *Les légendes hagiographiques*, 1905, p. 170, n. 1).—In this connection we ought to mention the prayer translated in the *Asclepius*, the Greek text

of which has recently been found on a papyrus (Reitzenstein, *Archiv für Religionswiss.*, VII, 1904, p. 395). On pagan prayers introduced into the Christian liturgy see Reitzenstein and Wendland, *Nachrichten Ges. Wiss.*, Göttingen, 1910, pp. 325 ff.

18. This point has been studied more in detail in our *Monuments relatifs aux mystères de Mithra,* from which we have taken parts of the following observations (I, pp. 21 ff.).

19. Lucian's authorship of the treatise Περὶ τῆς Συρίης θεοῦ has been questioned but wrongly; see Maurice Croiset, *Essai sur Lucien,* 1882, pp. 63, 204. I am glad to be able to cite the high authority of Nöldeke in favor of its authenticity. Nöldeke writes me on this subject: "Ich habe jeden Zweifel daran schon lange aufgegeben.... Ich habe lange den Plan gehabt, einen Commentar zu diesem immerhin recht lehrreichen Stück zu schreiben und viel Material dazu gesammelt. Aus der Annahme der Echtheit dieser Schrift ergiebt sich mir, dass auch das Περὶ ἀστρονομίας echt ist.

20. Cf. Frisch, *De compositione libri Plutarchei qui inscribitur,* Περὶ ῎Ισιδος, Leipsic, 1906, and the observations of Neustadt, *Berl. Philol. Wochenschr.,* 1907, p. 1117.—One of Plutarch's sources is the Ἰουδαϊκά by Apion.—See also Scott Moncrieff, *Journ. of Hell. Studies,* XIX, 1909, p. 81.

21. See ch. VII, pp. 202-203.

22. Cf. *Mon myst. Mithra,* I, p. 75, p. 219.—For Egypt see Georges Foucart, "L'art et la religion dans l'ancienne Egypte," *Revue des idées,* Nov. 15, 1908,

23. The narrative and symbolic sculpture of the Oriental cults was a preparation for that of the Middle Ages, and many remarks in Mâle's beautiful book *L'Art du XIIIᵉ siècle en France,* can be applied to the art of dying paganism.

II. WHY THE ORIENTAL RELIGIONS SPREAD.

BIBLIOGRAPHY: Boissier, *La religion romaine d'Auguste aux Antonins,* especially Bk. II, ch. II.—Jean Réville, *La religion à Rome sous les Sévères,* Paris, 1886.—Wissowa, *Religion und Cultus der Römer,* Munich, 1902, pp. 71 ff., 289 ff.—Samuel Dill, *Roman Society from Nero to Marcus Aurelius,* London, 1905.—Bigg, *The Church's Task Under the Roman Empire,*

Oxford, 1905.—Cf. also Gruppe, *Griech. Mythologie und Religionsgeschichte,* 1906, pp. 1519 ff.—Wendland, *Die hellenistisch-römische Kultur in ihren Beziehungen zum Judentum und zum Christentum,* Tübingen, 1907, pp. 54 f.—The monographs will be cited in connection with the different cults which they treat.

1. *Mélanges Fredericq,* Brussels, 1904, pp. 63 ff. (*Pourquoi le latin fut la seule langue liturgique de l'Occident*); cf. the observations of Lejay, *Rev. d'hist. et litt. relig.,* XI, 1906, p. 370.

2. Holl, *Volkssprache in Kleinasien* (*Hermes,* 1908, pp. 250 ff.).

3. The volume of Hahn, *Rom und Romanismus im griechisch-römischen Osten bis auf die Zeit Hadrians* (Leipsic, 1906) discusses a period for the most part prior to the one that interests us. On the period following we have nothing but a provisional sketch by the same author, *Romanismus und Hellenismus bis auf die Zeit Justinians* (*Philologus,* Suppl. X), 1907.

4. Cf. Tacitus, *Annales,* XIV, 44: "*Nationes in familiis habemus quibus diversi ritus, externa sacra aut nulla sunt.*"

5. S. Reinach, *Epona* (Extr. *Rev. archéol.*). 1895.

6. The theory of the degeneration of races has been set forth in particular by Stewart Chamberlain, *Die Grundlagen des XIX. Jahrhunderts,* 3d. ed., Munich, 1901, pp. 296 ff.—The idea of selection by retrogression, of the *Ausrottung der Besten,* has been defended, as is well known, by Seeck in his *Geschichte des Untergangs der antiken Welt,* which outlines the religious consequence (II, p. 344). His system is developed in the third volume which appeared in 1909.

7. Apuleius, *Metam.,* XI, 14 ff. See Preface. Manilius said of the divine stars (IV, 910; cf. II, 125),
"*Ipse vocat nostros animos ad sidera mundus.*"

8. Hepding, *Attis,* pp. 178 ff., 187.

9. The intimate connection between the juridical and religious ideas of the Romans has left numerous traces even in their language. One of the most curious is the double meaning of the term *supplicium,* which stands at the same time for a supplication addressed to the gods and a punishment de-

manded by custom, and later by law. In regard to the development of this twofold meaning, see the recent note by Richard Heinze, *Archiv für lateinische Lexicographie*, XV, pp. 90 ff. Sematology is often synonymous with the study of customs.
10. Réville, *op. cit.*, p. 144.

11. On ecstasy in the mysteries in general, cf. Rohde, *Psyche*, 2d ed., pp. 315-319; in the Oriental religions cf. De Jong, *De Apuleio Isiacorum mysteriorum teste*, 1900, p. 100; De Jong, *Das antike Mysterienwesen*, Leyden, 1909. *Mon, myst. Mithra*, I, p. 323.

12. Firmicus Maternus mentioned this in *De errore prof. relig.*, c. 8.

13. For Babylonia, cf. Strab., XVI, 1, § 6, and *infra*, ch. V, n. 51; for Egypt, *id.*, XVII, 21, § 46. From the very interesting account Otto has written of the science of the Egyptian priests during the Hellenistic period (*Priester und Tempel*, II, pp. 211 ff.; 234), it appears that it remained quite worthy of consideration although progress had ceased.

14. **Strabo**, *loc. cit.*: ᾿Ανατιθέασι δὲ τῷ ῾Ερμῇ πᾶσαν τὴν τοιαύτην σοφίαν; Pliny, *Hist. nat.*, VI, 26, § 121: "(Belus) *inventor fuit sideralis scientiae*"; cf. Solinus, 56, § 3; Achilles, *Isag.*, I (Maass, *Comm. in Arat.*, p. 27): Βήλῳ τὴν εὕρεσιν ἀναθέντες. Let us remember that Hammurabi's code was represented as the work of Marduk.—In a general way, the gods are the authors of all inventions useful to humanity; cf. Reitzenstein, *Poimandres*, 1904, p. 123; Deissmann, *Licht von Osten*, 91 ff. Likewise in the Occident: *CIL*, VII, 759 = Bücheler, *Carm. epigr.*, 24: "(Dea Syria) ex quis muneribus nosse contigit deos," etc., cf. Plut., *Crass.*, 17. — "Religion im Sinne des Orients ist die Erklärung alles dessen was ist, also eine Weltauffassung" (Winckler, *Himmelsbild der Babylonier*, 1903, p. 9).

15. *Mon. myst. Mithra*, I, p. 312. — Manicheism likewise brought a complete cosmological system from Babylonia. Saint Augustine criticizes the book of that sect for containing long dissertations and absurd stories about matters that have nothing at all to do with salvation; see my *Recherches sur le manichéisme*, 1908, p. 53.

16. Cf. Porphyry, *Epist. Aneb.*, 11; Jambl., *De myst.*, II, 11.

17. This upright character of the Roman religion has been thoroughly expounded by G. Boissier (*op. cit.*, I, 30 ff, 373 ff). See also the remarks by Bailey, *Religion of Ancient Rome*, London, 1907, pp. 103 ff.

18. Varro in Augustine *De civ. Dei*, IV, 27; VI, 5; cf. Varro, *Antiq. rerum divin.*, ed. Aghad, pp. 145 ff. The same distinction between the religion of the poets, of the legislators and of the philosophers has been made by Plutarch, *Amatorius*, 18, p. 763 C. The author of this division is Posidonius of Apamea. See Diels, *Doxographi Graeci*, p. 295, 10, and Wendland, *Archiv für Gesch. der Philos.*, I, pp. 200 ff.

19. Luterbacher, *Der Prodigienglaube der Römer*, Burgdorf, 1904.

20. Juvenal, II, 149; cf. Diodorus, I, 93, § 3. Cf. Plutarch also in speaking of future punishment (*Non posse suaviter vivi*, c. 26, p. 1104 C-E: *Quo modo poetas aud.*, c. 2, p. 17 C-E; *Consol. ad Apollon.*, c. 10, p. 106 F), "nous laisse entendre que pour la plupart de ses contemporains ce sont là des contes de nourrice qui ne peuvent effrayer que des enfants" (Decharme, *Traditions religieuses chez les Grecs*, 1904, p. 442).

21. Aug., *Civ. Dei*, VI, 2; Varro, *Antiqu.*, ed. Aghad, 141; "Se timere ne (dii) pereant non incursu hostili sed civium neglegentia."

22. I have developed this point in my *Mon. myst. Mithra.* I, pp. 279 ff.

23. In Greece the Oriental cults expanded much less than in any other religion, because the Hellenic mysteries, especially those of Eleusis, taught similar doctrines and satisfied the religious needs.

24. The development of the "ritual of purification" has been broadly expounded in its entirety, by Farnell in *The Evolution of Religion*, 1905, pp. 88 ff.

25. We shall mention this subject again when speaking of the taurobolium in ch. III, pp. 67 ff.

26. We cannot dwell here upon the various forms assumed by that purifying rite of the Oriental mysteries. Often these forms remained quite primitive, and the idea that inspired them is still clear, as where Juvenal (VI, 521 f.) pictures the

worshiper of the *Magna Mater* divesting himself of his beautiful garments and giving them to the *archigallus* to wipe out all the misdeeds of the year (*ut totum semel expiet annum*). The idea of a mechanical transfer of the pollution by relinquishing the clothes is frequent among savages; see Farnell, *op. cit.*, p. 117; also Frazer, *Golden Bough*, I², p. 60.

27. Dieterich, *Eine Mithrasliturgie*, pp. 157 ff.; Hepding, *Attis*, pp. 194 ff.—Cf. Frazer, *Golden Bough*, III² pp. 424 ff

28. Cf. Augustine *Civit. Dei*, X, 28: "Confiteris tamen (sc. Porphyrius) etiam spiritalem animam sine theurgicis artibus et sine teletis quibus frustra discendis elaborasti, posse continentiae virtute purgari," cf. *ibid.*, X, 23 and *infra*, ch. VIII, n. 24.

29. Here we can only touch upon a subject of very great interest. Porphyry's treatise *De abstinentia* offers a fuller treatment than is often possible in this kind of studies.—See Farnell, *op. cit.*, pp. 154 ff.

30. On ἐξομολόγησις in the religions of Asia Minor, cf. Ramsay, *Cities*, I, p. 134, p. 152, and Chapot, *La province romaine d'Asie*, 1904, pp. 509 ff. See also Crusius, "Paroemiographica," *Sitzungsb. Bayr. Akad.*, 1910, p. 111.

31. Menander in Porphyry *De abstin.*, II, 15; cf. Plutarch, *De Superstit.*, 7, p. 168 D.; Tertullian, *De Paenit.*, c. 9.—Regarding the sacred fishes of Atargatis, see *infra*, ch. V.—In Apuleius (*Met.* VIII, 28) the *gallus* of the goddess loudly accuses himself of his crime and punishes himself by flagellation. See Gruppe, *Griech. Myth.*, p. 1545; Farnell, *Evol. of Religion*, p. 55.—As a matter of fact, the confession of sin is an old religious tradition dating back to the Babylonians; cf. Lagrange, *Religions sémit.*, p. 225 ff. Schrank, *Babylonische Sühnriten*, 1909, p. 46.

32. Juvenal, VI, 523 ff., 537 ff.; cf. Seneca, *Vit. beat.*, XXVI, 8.

33. On liturgic feasts in the religion of Cybele: *infra*, ch. II; in the mysteries of Mithra: *Mon. myst. Mithra*, I. p. 320; in the Syrian cults: ch. V, n. 37. See in general, Hepding, *Attis*, pp. 185 ff.

34. We know according to Herbert Spencer that the pro-

gressive differentiation of the ecclestiastic and lay functions is one of the characteristics of religious evolution. In this regard Rome was far behind the Orient.

35. An essential result of the researches of Otto (*op. cit.*) is the proof of the opposition existing in Egypt since the Ptolemies between the hierarchic organization of the Egyptian clergy and the almost anarchical autonomy of the Greek priests. See our remarks on the clergy of Isis and the Galli. On the Mithraic hierarchy see our *Mysteries of Mithra*, Chicago, 1903, p. 165.

36. The development of the conceptions of "salvation" and "saviour" after the Hellenistic period has been studied by Wendland, Σωτήρ (*Zeitschrift für neutestam. Wissensch.*, V, 1904, pp. 335 ff.). See also Lietzmann, *Der Weltheiland,* Bonn, 1909. W. Otto, "Augustus Σωτήρ," *Hermes,* XLV, 1910, pp. 448 ff.

37. Later on we shall expound the two principal doctrines, that of the Egyptian religions (identification with Osiris, god of the dead), and that of the Syrian and Persian religions (ascension into heaven).

38. At that time man's fate after death was the one great interest. An interesting example of the power of this idea is furnished by Arnobius. He became converted to Christianity because, according to his peculiar psychology, he feared that his soul might die, and believed that Christ alone could protect him against final annihilation (cf. Bardenhewer, *Gesch. der altkirchlichen Literatur,* II, 1903, p. 470.

39. Lucretius had expressed this conviction (II, 1170 ff.). It spread to the end of the empire as disasters multiplied; cf. *Rev. de philologie,* 1897, p. 152.

40. Boissier, *Rel. rom.,* I³, p. 359; Friedländer, *Sittengesch.,* I⁶, pp. 500 ff.

III. ASIA MINOR.

BIBLIOGRAPHY: Jean Réville, *La religion à Rome sous les Sévères,* pp. 62 ff.—Drexler in Roscher, *Lexikon der Mythol.,* s. v. *"Meter,"* II, 2932.—Wissowa, *Religion und Cultus der Römer,* pp. 263 ff., where the earlier bibliography will be found,

p. 271.—Showerman, "The Great Mother of the Gods" (*Bulletin of the University of Wisconsin*, No. 43), Madison, 1901.— Hepding, *Attis, seine Mythen und sein Kult*, Giessen, 1903.— Dill, *Roman Society from Nero to Marcus Aurelius*, London, 1905, pp. 547 ff.—Gruppe, *Griech. Mythologie*, 1906, pp. 1521 ff. Eisele, "Die phrygischen Kulte," *Neue Jahrb. für das klass. Altertum*, XXIII, 1909, pp. 620 ff.

For a number of years Henri Graillot has been collecting the monuments of the religion of Cybele with a view to publishing them in their entirety.—Numerous remarks on the Phrygian religion will be found in the works and articles of Ramsay, especially in *Cities and Bishoprics of Phrygia*, 1895, and *Studies in the Eastern Roman Provinces*, 1906.

1. Arrien, fr. 30 (*FGH*, III, p. 592). Cf. our *Studia Pontica*, 1905, pp. 172 ff., and Statius, *Achill.*, II, 345: "Phrygas lucos.... vetitasque solo, procumbere pinus"; Virg., *Aen.*, IX, 85.

2. Lion; cf. S. Reinach, *Mythes, cultes*, I, p. 293. The lion, represented in Asia Minor at a very remote period as devouring a bull or other animals, might possibly represent the sacred animal of Lydia or Phrygia vanquishing the protecting *totem* of the tribes of Cappadocia or the neighboring countries (I am using the term *totem* in its broadest meaning). This at least is the interpretation given to similar groups in Egypt. Cf. Foucart, *La méthode comparat. et l'histoire des religions*, 1909, p. 49, p. 70.

3. Πότνια θηρῶν. On this title, cf. Radet, *Revue des études anciennes*, X, 1908, pp. 110 ff. The most ancient type of the goddess, a winged figure leading lions, is known from monuments dating back to the period of the Mermnadi (687-546 B. C.),

4. Cf. Ramsay, *Cities and Bishoprics of Phrygia*, I, p. 7, p. 94.

5. Foucart, *Le culte de Dionysos en Attique* (Extract from the *Mém. Acad. Inscr.*, XXXVII), 1904, pp. 22 ff.—The Thracians also seem to have spread, in Asia Minor, the cult of the "riding god" which existed until the beginning of the Roman period; cf. Remy, *Le Musée belge*, XI, 1907, pp. 136 ff.

6. Catullus, LXIII.

7. The development of these mysteries has been well expounded by Hepding, pp. 177 ff. (see Gruppe, *Gr. Myth.*, p. 1544).—Ramsay has recently commented upon inscriptions of Phrygian mystics, united by the knowledge of certain secret signs (τέκμωρ); cf. *Studies in the Eastern Roman Provinces*, 1906, pp. 346 ff.

8. Dig., XLVIII, 8, 4, 2: "Nemo liberum servumve invitum sinentemve castrare debet." Cf. Mommsen, *Strafrecht*, p. 637.

9. Diodorus, XXXVI, 6; cf. Plutarch, *Marius*, 17.

10. Cf. Hepding, *op. cit.*, p. 142.

11. Cf. chap. VI.

12. Wissowa, *op. cit.*, p. 291.

13. Hepding, *op. cit.*, pp. 145 ff. Cf. Pauly-Wissowa, *Realenc.*, s. v. "Dendrophori," V, col. 216 and Suppl., col, 225, s. v. "Attis."

14. Cf. Tacitus, *Annales*, XI, 15.

15. This opinion has recently been defended by Showerman, *Classical Journal*, II, 1906, p. 29.

16. Frazer, *The Golden Bough*, II², pp. 130 ff.

17. Hepding, pp. 160 ff. Cf. the texts of Ambrosiaster cited in *Rev. hist. et litt. relig.*, VIII, 1903, p. 423, n. 1,

18. Hepding, p. 193. Cf. Gruppe, p. 1541.

19. On this diffusion, cf. Drexler in Roscher, *Lexikon*, s. v. "Meter," col. 918.

20. Gregory of Tours, *De glor. confess.*, c. 76. Cf. *Passio S. Symphoriani* in Ruinart, *Acta sinc.*, ed. of 1859, p. 125. The *carpentum* mentioned in these texts is found in Africa; cf. *CIL*, VIII, 8457, and Graillot, *Rev. archéol.*, 1904, I, p. 353; Hepding, *op. cit.*, p. 173, n. 7.

21. Θαρρεῖτε μύσται τοῦ θεοῦ σεσωσμένου | ἔσται γὰρ ὑμῖν ἐκ πόνων σωτηρία; cf. Hepding, *op. cit.*, p. 167.—Attis has become a god through his death (see Reitzenstein, *Poimandres*, p. 93), and in the same way were his votaries to become the equals of the divinity through death. The Phrygian epitaphs frequently have the character of dedications, and it appears that the graves were grouped about the temple, see Ramsay, *Studies*, pp. 65 ff., 271 ff., *passim*.

22. Perdrizet, *Bull. corr. hell.*, XIX, 1905, p. 534 ff.

23. We know of those beliefs of the Sabaziasts from the frescoes in the catacombs of Praetextatus; the *Mercurius nuntius*, who leads the dead, is found beside Attis under the Greek name of Hermes (see Hepding, p. 263).—Maybe the inscription *CIL*, VI, 509 = *Inscr. graec.*, XIV, 1018, should be completed: 'Ρείῃ ['Ερμῇ] τε γενέθλῳ; cf. *CIL*, VI, 499. Hermes appears beside the Mother of the gods on a bas-relief by Ouchak published by Michon, *Rev. des études anciennes*, 1906, p. 185, pl. II. See also Mendel, "Musée de Brousse," *Bull. corr. hell.*, 1909, p. 255.—The Thracian Hermes is mentioned in Herodotus, see Maury, *Rel. de la Grèce*, III, p. 136.

24. Besides Bellona-Ma, subordinate to Cybele and Sabazius, who was as much Jewish as Phrygian, there was only one god of Asia Minor, the Zeus Bronton (the Thunderer) of Phrygia, prominently mentioned in Roman epigraphy. See Pauly-Wissowa, *Realenc.*, s. v. and Suppl. I, col. 258.

25. Cf. *CIL*, VI, 499: "Attidi menotyranno invicto." "Invictus" is the characteristic epithet of the solar divinities.

26. P. Perdrizet, "Mèn" (*Bull. corr. hell.*, XX), 1896; Drexler in Roscher, *Lexikon*, s. v., II, col. 2687.

27. *CIL*, VI, 50 = *Inscr. graec.*, XIV, 1018.

28. Schürer, *Sitzungsb. Akad. Berlin*, XIII, 1897, p. 200 f. and our *Hypsistos* (Suppl. *Revue instr. publ. en Belgique*), 1897.

29. The term is taken from the terminology of the mysteries: the inscription cited dates back to 370 A. D. In 364, in connection with Eleusis, Agorius Praetextatus spoke of συνέχοντα τὸ ἀνθρώπειον γένος ἁγιώτατα μυστήρια (Zozimus, IV, 3, 2). Earlier the "Chaldean oracles" applied to the intelligible god the term μήτρα συνέχουσα τὰ πάντα (Kroll, *De orac. Chaldeïcis*, p. 19).

30. Henri Graillot, *Les dieux Tout-Puissants, Cybèle et Attis* (*Revue archéol.*, 1904, I), pp.. 331 ff.—Graillot is rather inclined to admit a Christian influence, but *omnipotentes* was used as a liturgic epithet in 288 A. D., and at about the same date Arnobius (VII, 32) made use of the periphrasis *omnipotentia numina* to designate the Phrygian gods, and he cer-

tainly was understood by all. This proves that the use of that periphrasis was general, and that it must have dated back to a much earlier period. As a matter of fact a dedication has been found at Delos, reading Διὶ τῷ πάντων κρατοῦντι καὶ Μητρὶ μεγάληι τῆι πάντων κρατούσῃ (*Bull. corr. hellén.*, 1882, p. 502, No. 25), that reminds the reader of the παντοκράτωρ of the Septugint; and Graillot (*loc. cit.*, p. 328, n. 7) justly observes, in this connection, that on certain bas-reliefs Cybele was united with the Theos Hypsistos, that is to say, the god of Israel; see Perdrizet, *Bull. corr. hell.*, XXIII, 1899, p. 598. On the influence of Judaism on the cult of Men cf. Sam. Wide, *Archiv für Religionsw.*, 1909, p. 227.—On the omnipotence of the Syrian gods, see ch. V, pp. 128 ff.

31. We are here giving the substance of a short essay on "Les mystères de Sabazius et le judaïsme," published in the *Comptes Rendus Acad. Inscr.*, Febr. 9, 1906, pp. 63 ff. Cf. "A propos de Sabazius," *Musée belge*, XIV, 1910, pp. 56 ff.

32. Cf. *Monuments myst. de Mithra*, I, p. 333 f. The very early assimilation of Cybele and Anahita justifies to a certain extent the unwarranted practice of calling Cybele the Persian Artemis. See Radet, *Revue des études anciennes*, X, 1908, p. 157. The pagan theologians often considered Attis as the primeval man whose death brought about the creation, and so they likened him to the Mazdean Gayomart, see Bousset, *Hauptprobleme der Gnosis*, 1907, pp. 184 ff.

33. Prudentius, *Peristeph.*, X, 1011 f.

34. Their meaning has been revealed through an inscription at Pergamum published by Schröder, *Athen. Mitt.*, 1904, pp. 152 ff.; cf. *Revue archéologique*, 1905, I, pp. 29 ff.—The ideas on the development of that ceremony, which we are summarizing here, have been expounded by us more fully in the *Revue archéologique*, 1888, II, pp. 132ff.; *Mon. myst. de Mithra*, I, pp. 334 ff.; *Revue d'histoire et de litt. relig.*, VI, 1901, p. 97.— Although the conclusions of the last article have been contested by Hepding (*op. cit.*, 70 f.), it cannot be doubted that the taurobolium was already practised in Asia Minor, in the cult of the Ma-Bellona. Moore (*American Journal of Archeology*, 1905, p. 71) justly refers to the text of Steph. Byz., in this connection: Μάσταυρα· ἐκαλεῖτο δὲ καὶ ἡ 'Ρέα Μᾶ καὶ ταῦρος αὐτῃ

ἐθύετο παρὰ Λύδοις.   The relation between the cult of Ma and that of Mithra is shown in the epithet of Ἀνείκητος, given to the goddess as well as to the god; see *Athen. Mitt.*, XXIX, 1904, p. 169, and Keil und von Premerstein, "Reise in Lydien," *Denkschr. Akad. Wien,* 1908, p. 28 (inscription of the Hyrkanis plain).

35. Prudentius, Peristeph., 1027: *Pectus sacrato dividunt venabulo."* The *harpé* shown on the taurobolic altars, is perhaps in reality a boar-spear having a kind of hilt (*mora*; cf. Grattius, *Cyneg.,* 110) to prevent the blade from entering too far.

36. Hepding, pp. 196 ff.; cf. *supra,* n. 21.

37. *CIL,* VI, 510, = Dessau, *Inscr. sel.,* 4152.   Cf. Gruppe, *Griech. Myth.,* p. 1541, n. 7.

38. Hepding, pp. 186 ff.

39. *CIL,* VI, 499: "Dii animae mentisque custodes."   Cf. 512: "Diis magnis et tutatoribus suis," and *CIL,* XII, 1277, where Bel is called *mentis magister.*

40. Hippolytus, *Refut. haeres.,* V, 9.

41. Julien, *Or.,* V; cf. Paul Allard, *Julien l'Apostat,* II, pp. 246 ff.; Mau, *Die Religionsphilosophie Kaiser Julians,* 1908, pp. 90 ff.   Proclus also devoted a philosophic commentary to the Cybele myth (Marinus, *Vita Procli,* 34).

42. Regarding all this see *Revue d'histoire et de littérat. relig.,* VIII, 1903, pp. 423, ff.—Frazer (*Osiris, Attis, Adonis,* 1907, pp. 256 ff.) has recently defended the position that the commemoration of the death of Christ was placed by a great many churches upon March 25th to replace the celebration of Attis's death on the same date, just as Christmas has been substituted for the *Natalis Invicti.*   The text of Ambrosiaster cited in our article (Pseudo Augustin, *Quaest, veter. Test,* LXXXIV, 3, p. 145, 13, Souter ed.) shows that this was asserted even in antiquity.

IV. EGYPT.

BIBLIOGRAPHY: Lafaye, *Histoire du culte des divinités d'Alexandrie hors de l'Egypte,* Paris, 1884, and article "Isis" in Daremberg and Saglio, *Dictionn. des antiquités,* III, 1899,

where may be found (p. 586) an index of the earlier works.—
Drexler, art. "Isis" in Roscher, *Lexikon der Mythol.*, II, p.
373-548.—Réville, *op. cit.*, pp. 54 ff.—Wissowa, *op. cit.*, pp.
292 ff.—Dill, *op. cit.*, pp. 560 ff.—Gruppe, *Griechische Mythologie und Religionsgesch.*, pp. 1563-1581 (published after the
revision of this chapter).—The study of the Roman cult of
the Alexandrian gods is inseparable from that of the Egyptian
religion. It would be impossible to furnish a bibliography of
the latter here. We shall only refer the reader to the general
works of Maspero, *Etudes de Mythologie*, 4 vols., Paris, 1893,
and *Histoire ancienne des peuples de l'Orient*, 1895 (*passim*).
—Wiedemann, *Religion of the Ancient Egyptians*, London,
1897 [cf. Hastings, *Dictionary of the Bible*, "Religion of
Egypt," V, pp. 177-197].—Erman, *Die ägyptische Religion*,
Berlin, 1910.—Naville, *La religion des anciens Egyptiens* (six
lectures delivered at the Collège de France), 1906.—W. Otto,
Priester und Tempel im hellenistischen Aegypten, 2 vols., 1905,
1908.—The publication of a *Bulletin critique des religions de
l'Egypte* by Jean Capart, begun in the *Rev. de l'hist. des religions* (LI, 1905, pp. 192 ff.; LIII, 1906, pp. 307 ff.; 1909, pp.
162 ff.).

1. Cf. on this controversy Bouché-Leclercq, *Histoire des
Lagides*, I, p. 102; S. Reinach, *Cultes, Mythes et Religions*, II,
pp. 347 f.; Lehmann, *Beiträge zur alten Geschichte*, IV, 1904,
pp. 396 ff.; Wilcken, *Archiv f. Papyrusforschung*, III, 1904,
pp. 249 ff.; Otto, *Priester und Tempel*, I, 1905, pp. 11 ff.;
Gruppe, *loc. cit.*, pp. 1578 ff.; Petersen, *Die Serapislegende*,
1910, pp. 47 ff.; Schmidt, *Kultübertragungen*, 1910, pp. 47 ff.

2. Herodotus, II, 42, 171.—Cf. n. 4.

3. Ælius Aristides, VIII, 56 (I, p. 96, ed. Dindorf). Cf.
Plut., *De Iside et Osiride*, ed. Parthey, p. 216.

4. Plut., *De Is. et Osir.*, 28; cf. Otto, *Priester und Tempel*,
II, pp. 215 ff.—This Timotheus is undoubtedly the same
one that wrote about the Phrygian mysteries; see *infra*, n.
79.—The question, to what extent the Hellenistic cult had the
form ascribed to it by Plutarch and Apuleius immediately
after its creation, is still unsettled; see Otto, *Priester und
Tempel*, II, p. 222. We do not appear to have any direct
proof of the existence of "mysteries" of Isis and Serapis

prior to the Empire, but all probabilities are in favor of a more ancient origin, and the mysteries were undoubtedly connected with the ancient Egyptian esoterism.—See *infra*, n. 78.

5. Diogenes Laertius, V, 5, § 76: "Ὅθεν καὶ τοὺς παιᾶνας ποιῆσαι τοὺς μέχρι νῦν ᾀδομένους. The μέχρι νῦν Diogenes took undoubtedly from his source, Didymus. See Artemidorus, *Onirocr.*, II, 44 (p. 143, 25 Hercher).—This information is explicitly confirmed by an inscription which mentions ἡ ἱερὰ τάξις τῶν παιανιστῶν (*Inscr. Graec.*, XIV, 1034).

6. Kaibel, *Epigr.* 1028 = Abel, *Orphica*, p. 295, etc.—See *supra*, ch. I, n. 14.—According to recent opinion, M. de Wilamowitz was good enough to write me, the date of the Andros hymn cannot have been later than the period of Cicero, and it is very probably contemporary with Sulla.—See *supra*, ch. I, n. 14.—On other similar texts, see Gruppe, *Griech. Mythol.*, p. 1563.

7. Amelung, *Le Sérapis de Bryaxis* (*Revue archéol*, 1903, II), p. 178.

8. P. Foucart, *Le culte de Dionysos en Attique* (*Mém. Acad. des Inscr.*, XXXVII), 1904. On the Isis cult in ancient Greece, we can now refer to Gruppe, *Griech. Myth.*, pp. 1565 ff.; Ruhl, *De Sarapide et Iside in Graecia cultis* (Diss. Berlin) 1906, has made careful use of the epigraphic texts dating back to the time before the Roman period.

9. The only exception is the Zeus Ammon, who was only half Egyptian and owed his very early adoption to the Greek colonies of Cyrene; see Gruppe, *Griech. Myth.*, p. 1558. The addition of other goddesses, like Nephtis or Bubastis to Isis is exceptional.

10. Concerning the impression which Egypt made on travelers, see Friedländer, *Sittengesch.*, II⁶, 144 ff.; Otto, *Priester und Tempel*, II, p. 210.

11. Juvenal, XV, 10, and the notes of Friedländer on these passages.—The Athenian comic writers frequently made fun of the Egyptian zoolatry (Lafaye, *op. cit.*, p. 32). Philo of Alexandria considered the Egyptians as the most idolatrous heathens and he attacked their animal worship, in particular

(*De Decal.*, 16, II, p. 193 M., and *passim*). The pagan writers were no less scandalized (Cicero, *Nat. deor.*, III, 15, etc.) except where they preferred to apply their ingenuity to justify it. See Dill, *loc. cit.*, p. 571.—The features of this cult in ancient Egypt have been recently studied by George Foucart, *Revue des idées*, Nov. 15, 1908, and *La méthode comparative et l'histoire des religions*, 1909, pp. 43 ff.

12. Macrobius, *Sat.*, I, 20, § 16.

13. Holm, *Gesch. Siziliens*, I, p. 81.

14. Libanius, *Or.*, XI, 114 (I, p. 473 Förster). Cf. Drexler in Roscher, *op. cit.*, col. 378.

15. Pausan., I, 18, 4: Σαράπιδος ὃν παρὰ Πτολεμαίου θεὸν εἰσηγάγοντο. Ruhl (*op. cit.*, p. 4) attaches no historic value to this text, but, as he points out himself, we have proof that an official Isis cult existed at Athens under Ptolemy Soter, and that Serapis was worshiped in that city at the beginning of the third century.

16. Dittenberger, *Or. gr. inscr. sel.*, No. 16.

17. Apul., *Metam.*, XI, 17.

18. Thus it is found to be the case from the first half of the third century at Thera, a naval station of the Ptolemies (Hiller von Gärtringen, *Thera*, III, pp. 85 ff.; cf. Ruhl, *op. cit.*, p. 59), and also at Rhodes (*Rev. archéol.*, 1905, I, p. 341). Cult of Serapis at Delos, cf. *Comptes rendus Acad. inscr.*, 1910, pp. 294 ff.

19. A number of proofs of its diffusion have been collected by Drexler, *loc. cit.*, p. 379. See Lafaye, "Isis" (cf. *supra*), p. 577; and Ruhl, *De Sarapide et Iside in Graecia cultis*, 1906.

20. This interpretation has already been proposed by Ravaisson (*Gazette archéologique*, I, pp. 55 ff.), and I believe it to be correct, see *Comptes Rendus Acad. Inscr.*, 1906, p. 75, n. 1.

21. The power of the Egyptian cult in the Oriental half of the empire has been clearly shown by von Domaszewski (*Röm. Mitt.*, XVII, 1902, pp. 333 ff.), but perhaps with some exaggeration. All will endorse the restrictions formulated by Harnack, *Ausbreitung des Christentums*, II, p. 274.

22. The very early spread of Orphic doctrines in Magna Graecia, evidenced by the tablets of Sybaris and Petilia (Diels,

Vorsokratiker, II², p. 480) must have prepared the way for it. These tablets possess many points in common with the eschatological beliefs of Egypt, but, as their latest commentator justly remarks (Harrison, *Prolegomena to the Study of Greek Religion,* p. 624), these new ideas are fairly overwhelmed in the old mythology. The mysteries of Isis and Serapis seemed to offer a revelation that had been a presentiment for a long time, and the affirmation of a truth foreshadowed by early symbols.

23. *CIL,* X, 1781, I, 15-6.

24. Apul., *Metam.,* XI, 30.

25. Wissowa, *op. cit.,* p. 292-3; cf. Seeck, *Hermes,* XLIII, 1908, p. 642.

26. Manicheism was later persecuted on a similar pretext, see *Collat. Mos. et Rom. leg.,* 15, 3, § 4: "De Persica adversaria nobis gente progressa."

27. A full list of the inscriptions and monuments discovered in the various cities is given by Drexler in Roscher, *Lexikon,* s. v. "Isis," II, col. 409 ff.

28. Hirschfeld, *CIL,* XII, p. 382, and *Wiener Studien,* V, 1883, pp. 319-322.

29. Cf. Wissowa, *op. cit.,* pp. 294 ff.

30. Minuc. Fel., *Octav.* 22, 2: "Haec Ægyptia quondam nunc et sacra Romana sunt."

31. *Carmen contra paganos (Anthol. lat.,* ed. Riese, I, 20 ff.) v. 91, 95 ff.; cf. Ps. Aug., *Quaest. Vet. Test.,* CXIV, 11 (p. 308, 10 Souter), and *Rev. hist. litt. relig.,* VIII, 1903, p. 422, n. 1.

32. Rufin, II, 24: *"Caput ipsum idolatriae."* A miniature from an Alexandrian chronicle shows the patriarch Theophilus, crowned with a halo, stamping the Serapeum under foot, see Bauer and Strzygowski, *Eine alexandrinische Weltchronik (Denkschr. Akad. Wien,* LI), 1905, to the year 391, pp. 70 ff., 122, and pl. VI.

33. Cf. Drexler in Roscher, s. v. "Isis," II, p. 425; Harnack, *Ausbreitung des Christentums,* II, pp. 147 ff.—Some curious details showing the persistence of the Isis cult among the professors and students of Alexandria during the last years of the

fifth century are given in the life of Severus of Antioch by Zachariah the Scholastic (*Patrol. orient.*, I, ed. Kugener), pp. 17 ff., 27 ff.

34. Ps.-Apul., 34. Compare with a similar prophecy in the Sibylline oracles, V, 184 f. (p. 127, Geffcken ed.).

35. Iseum of Beneventum; cf. *Notizie debgli scavi di ant.*, 1904, pp. 107 ff. Iseum of the Campus Martius: see Lanciani, *Bollet. communale di Roma*, 1883, pp. 33 ff.; Marucchi, *ibid.*, 1890, pp. 307 f.—The *signa Memphitica* (made of Memphian marble), are mentioned in an inscription (Dessau, *Inscr. sel.*, 4367-8).—The term used in connection with Caracalla: "Sacra Isidis Romam deportavit," which Spartianus (*Carac.*, 9; cf. Aur. Vict., *Cæs.*, 21, 4) no longer understood, also seems to refer to a transfer of sacred Egyptian monuments. At Delos a statue of a singer taken from some grave of the Saïs period had been placed in the temple. Everything Egyptian was looked upon as sacred. (Ruhl, *op. cit.*, p. 53).

36. Gregorovius, *Gesch. des Kaisers Hadrian*, pp. 222 ff.; cf. Drexler, *loc. cit.*, p. 410.

37. The term is Wiedemann's.

38. Naville, *op. cit.*, pp. 89 ff.

39. On the ἱερογραμματεύς Cheremon, see Otto, *Priester und Tempel* II, p. 216; Schwartz in Pauly-Wissowa, *Realenc.*, III, col. 2025 ff.

40. Doctrines of Plutarch: cf. Decharme, *Traditions religieuses chez les Grecs*, pp. 486 ff. and *supra*, ch. I, n. 20.

41. I did not mention Hermetism, made prominent by the researches of Reitzenstein, because I believe its influence in the Occident to have been purely literary. To my knowledge there is no trace in the Latin world of an Hermetic sect with a clergy and following. The *Heliognostae* or *Deinvictiaci* who, in Gaul, attempted to assimilate the native Mercury with the Egyptian Thoth, (*Mon. myst. Mithra*, I, p. 49, n. 2; cf. 359), were Christian gnostics. I believe that Reitzenstein misunderstood the facts when he stated (*Wundererzählungen*, 1906, p. 128): "Die hermetische Literatur ist im zweiten und dritten Jahrhundert für alle religiös-interessierten der allgemeine Ausdruck der Frömmigkeit geworden." I believe that Her-

metism, which is used as a label for doctrines of very different origin, was influenced by "the universal spirit of devotion," and was not its creator. It was the result of a long continued effort to reconcile the Egyptian traditions first with Chaldean astrology, then with Greek philosophy, and it became transformed simultaneously with the philosophy. But this subject would demand extended development. It is admitted by Otto, the second volume of whose book has been published since the writing of these lines, that not even during the Hellenistic period was there enough theological activity of the Egyptian clergy to influence the religion of the times. (*Priester und Tempel*, II, pp. 218-220).

42. Plut., *De Isid.*, 9.

43. Apul., *Metam.*, XI, 5.

44. *CIL*, X, 3800 = Dessau, *Inscr. sel.*, 4362.

45. See the opening pages of this chapter.

46. Plut,. *De Iside et Osir.*, 52; cf. Hermes Trismegistus, "Ὅροι Ἀσκληπίου, c. 16; and Reitzenstein, *Poimandres*, p. 197.

47. Cf. Naville, *op. cit.*, pp. 170 ff.

48. Juv., VI, 489: "Isiacae sacraria lenae"; cf. Friedländer, *Sittengeschichte*, I⁶, p. 502.

49. In a recent book Farnell has brilliantly outlined the history of the ritual of purification and that of the conception of purity throughout antiquity (*Evolution of Religion*, London, 1905, pp. 88-192), but unfortunately he has not taken Egypt into account where the primitive forms have been maintained with perhaps the fewest alterations.

50. Juv., VI, 522 ff.

51. Friedländer, *Sittengeschichte*, I⁶, p. 510.—On this transformation of the Isis cult, cf. Réville, *op. cit.*, p. 56.

52. Plut., *De Iside*, c. 2; cf. Apul., *Met.*, XI, 6, end.

53. Ælius Arist., *In Sarap.*, 25 (II, p. 359, Keil ed.); see Diodorus, I, 93, and Apuleius, XI, 6, end.—On future rewards and punishments in Hermetism, see Ps.-Apul., *Asclepius*, c. 28; Lydus, *De mensib.*, IV, 32 and 149, Wünsch ed.

54. Porph., *Epist. ad Aneb.*, 29. The answer of the Ps.-Iamblichus (*de Myst.*, VI, 5-7) is characteristic. He main-

tained that these threats were addressed to demons; however, he was well aware that the Egyptians did not distinguish clearly between incantations and prayers (VI, 7, 5).

55. Cf. G. Hock, *Griechische Weihegebräuche,* 1905, pp. 65 ff. Ps.-Apul., *Asclep.,* 23: "Homo fictor est deorum qui in templis sunt et non solum inluminatur, verum etiam inluminat"; c. 37: "Proavi invenerunt artem qua efficerent deos." Cf. George Foucart, *loc. cit.* [n. 61]: "La statuaire égyptienne a, avant tout autre, le caractère de créer des êtres vivants."

56. Maspero, *Sur la toute-puissance de la parole* (*Recueil de travaux,* XXIV), 1902, pp. 163-175; cf. my *Récherches sur le manichéisme,* p. 24, n. 2.—The parallelism between the divine and the sacerdotal influence is established in Ps.-Apul., *Asclepius, 23.*

57. Iamblichus, *Myst.,* VI, 6; cf. G. Foucart, *La méthode comparative et l'histoire des religions,* 1909, p. 131, 141, 149 ff. and *infra,* n. 66. The Egyptians prided themselves on having been the first "to know the sacred names and to use the sacred speech" (Luc., *De Dea Syr.,* 1).

58. This has been proven by Otto, *Priester und Tempel,* I, pp. 114 ff. Cf. *supra,* chap. II, n. 35. Certain busts have recently inspired Mr. Dennison to give his attention to the tonsure of the votaries of Isis (*American Journ. of Archeology,* V, 1905, p. 341). The Pompeian frescoes representing priests and ceremonies of the Isis cult are particularly important for our knowledge of the liturgy (Guimet, *C. R. Acad. des Inscr.,* 1896, pls. VII-IX. Cf. von Bissing, *Transact. congr. relig. Oxford,* 1908, I, pp. 225 ff.).

59. *CIL,* XII, 3061: "Ornatrix fani."

60. Cf. Kan, *De Iove Dolicheno,* 1901, p. 33.

61. Cf. Moret, *Le rituel du culte divin journalier en Egypte,* Paris, 1902. Just as the ritual of consecration brought the statue to life (*supra,* n. 55), the repeated sacrifices sustained life and made it *longa durare per tempora* (Ps.-Apul., *Asclep.,* 38). The epithet of ἀείζωος, given to several divinities (*CIG,* 4598; *Griech. Urkunden* of Berlin, I, No. 124), expresses it exactly. All this is in conformity with the old ideas prevailing in the valley of the Nile (see George Foucart, *Revue des*

idées, Nov. 15, 1908).—When compared with the Egyptian ceremonial, the brief data scattered through the Greek and Latin authors become wonderfully clear and coherent.

62. Apul., XI, 22: "Rituque sollemni apertionis celebrato ministerio." Cf. XI, 20: "Matutinas apertiones templi."

63. Jusephus, *Ant. Jud.,* XVIII, 3, 5, § 174.

64. Servius ad Verg., *Aen.,* IV, 512: "In templo Isidis aqua sparsa de Nilo esse dicebatur"; cf. II, 116. When, by pouring water taken from the river, reality took the place of this fiction, the act was much more effective; see Juv. VII, 527.

65. This passage, together with a chapter from Apuleius (XI, 20), is the principal text we mave in connection with the ritual of those Isis matins. (*De Abstin.,* IV, 9):

''Ὡς που ἔτι καὶ νῦν ἐν τῇ ἀνοίξει τοῦ ἁγίου Σαράπιδος ἡ θεραπεία διὰ πυρὸς καὶ ὕδατος γίνεται, λείβοντος τοῦ ὑμνῳδοῦ τὸ ὕδωρ καὶ τὸ πῦρ φαίνοντος, ὁπηνίκα ἑστὼς ἐπὶ τοῦ οὐδοῦ τῇ πατρίῳ τῶν Αἰγυπτίων φωνῇ ἐγείρει τὸν θεόν.

Arnobius (VII, 32) alludes to the same belief of the votaries of Isis: "Quid sibi volunt excitationes illae quas canitis matutini conlatis ad tibiam vocibus? Obdormiscunt enim superi remeare ut ad vigilias debeant? Quid dormitiones illae quibus ut bene valeant auspicabili salutatione mandatis?"

66. On the power of "barbarian names" see my *Mon. myst. Mithra,* I, p. 313, n. 4; Dieterich, *Mithrasliturgie,* pp. 111 ff. Cf. Charles Michel, *Note sur un passage de Jamblique* (Mélanges, Louis Havet), 1909, p. 279.—On the persistence of the same idea among the Christians, cf. Harnack, *Ausbreitung des Christ.,* I, pp. 124 ff.; Heitmüller, *Im Namen Jesu,* Göttingen, 1903 (rich material).

67. Apul., *Met.,* XI, 9.

68. *CIL,* II, 3386 = Dessau, *Inscr. sel.,* 442; cf. 4423.

69. Apul., XI, 24; cf. Lafaye, pp. 118 ff. Porphyry (*De Abstin.,* IV, 6) dwells at length on this contemplative character of the Egyptian devotion: The priests ἀπέδοσαν ὅλον τὸν βίον τῇ τῶν θεῶν θεωρίᾳ καὶ θεάσει.

70. In the Pharaonic ritual the closing ceremony seems to have taken place during the morning, but in the Occident the sacred images were exposed for contemplation, and the an-

cient Egyptian service must, therefore, have been divided into two ceremonies.

71. Herodotus, II, 37.

72. Cf. Maspero, *Rev. critique,* 1905, II, p. 361 ff.

73. Apul., *Metam.,* XI, 7 ff.—This festival seems to have persisted at Catana in the worship of Saint Agatha; cf. *Analecta Bollandiana,* XXV, 1906, p. 509.

74. Similar masquerades are found in a number of pagan cults (*Mon. myst. Mithra,* I, p. 315), and from very early times they were seen in Egypt; see von Bissing, *loc. cit.,* n. 58, p. 228.

75. The *pausarii* are mentioned in the inscriptions; cf. Dessau, *Inscr. sel.,* 4353, 4445.

76. Schäfer, *Die Mysterien des Osiris in Abydos unter Sesostris III,* Leipsic, 1904; cf. Capart, *Rev. hist. relig.,* LI, 1905, p. 229, and Wiedemann, *Mélanges Nicole,* pp. 574 ff. Junker, "Die Stundenwachen in den Osirismysterien" (*Denkschrift Akad. Wien,* LIV) 1910.

77. In the Abydos mysteries, the god Thoth set out in a boat to seek the body of Osiris. Elsewhere it was Isis who sailed out in quest of it. We do not know whether this scene was played at Rome; but it certainly was played at Gallipoli where make-believe fishermen handled the nets in a make-believe Nile; cf. P. Foucart, *Rech. sur les myst. d'Eleusis (Mém. Acad. Inscr.,* XXXV), p. 37.

78. Cheremon in Porphyry, *Epist. ad Aneb.,* 31:

Καὶ τὰ κρυπτὰ τῆς Ἰσιδος ἐπαινεῖ καὶ τὸ ἐν Ἀβύδῳ ἀπόρρητον δείξει.

Cf. Iamblichus, *De myster.,* VI, 5-7.—On the "mysteries" of Isis in Egypt, cf. Foucart, *loc. cit.,* p. 19 f.; De Jong, *De Apuleio Isiacorum mysteriorum teste,* Leyden, 1900, pp. 79 f., and *Das antike Mysterienwesen,* Leyden, 1909.

79. Cf. *supra.*—De Jong, *op. cit.,* pp. 40 ff.; Gruppe, *Griech. Mythol.,* p. 1574.

80. *La Cité antique,* I, ch. II, end.

81. Cf. Erman, *op. cit.,* pp. 96-97.

82. Sufficient proof is contained in the bas-reliefs cited above (n. 20), where apotheosized death assumes the shape of Sera-

pis. Compare Kaibel, *Inscr. gr.*, XIV, 2098: Εὐψύχι μετὰ τοῦ Ὀσείριδος. This material conception of immortality could be easily reconciled with the old Italian ideas, which had persisted in a dormant state in the minds of the people, see Friedländer, *Sittengeschichte*, III,[6] p. 758.

83. Reitzenstein, *Archiv für Religionswiss.*, VII, 1904, 406 ff. These are perhaps the most striking pages written on the meaning of the ceremony; it is an ἀπαθανατισμός. Cf. also Reitzenstein, *Hellenistische Wundererzählungen*, p. 116.

84. Apul., *Metam.*, 23.—De Jong, the latest commentator on this passage, seems inclined to take it as a mere ecstatic vision, but the vision was certainly caused by a dramatic scene in the course of which hell and heaven were shown in the dark. —The Egyptians represented them even on the stage; see Suetonius, *Calig.*, 8: "Parabatur et in mortem spectaculum quo argumenta inferorum per Aegyptios et Aethiopas explicarentur."

85. Apul., *Met.*, XI, 6 end.

86. *Ibid.*, c. 24: "Inexplicabili voluptate <aspectu> divini simulacri perfruebar."

87. Plut., *De Isid.*, 78, p. 383 A:

Ὡς ἂν ἐξηρτημέναις (ταῖς ψυχαῖς) ἀπ᾽ αὐτοῦ (τοῦ Ὀσίριδος) καὶ θεωμέναις ἀπλήστως καὶ ποθούσαις τὸ μὴ φατὸν μηδὲ ῥητὸν ἀνθρώποις κάλλος.

88. Cf., *supra*, n. 22.

89. We find similar wishes on the Egyptian monuments, frequently at least since the Middle Empire. "Donnez-moi de l'eau courante à boire.... Mettez-moi la face au vent du nord sur le bord de l'eau et que sa fraîcheur calme mon cœur" (Maspero, *Etudes égyptiennes*, I, 1881, p. 189). "Oh, si j'avais de l'eau courante à boire et si mon visage était tourné vers le vent du nord" (Naville, *op. cit.*, p. 174). On a funerary stele in the Brussels museum (Capart, *Guide*, 1905, p. 71) is inscribed, "Que les dieux accordent de boire l'eau des sources, de respirer les doux vents du nord."—The very material origin of this wish appears in the funeral texts, where the soul is shown crossing the desert, threatened with hunger and thirst, and obtaining refreshment by the aid of the gods (Maspero, *Etudes de mythol. et d'archéol. égypt.*, 1883, I, pp.

366 ff.).—On a tablet at Petilia (see *supra*, n. 22), the soul of the deceased is required to drink the fresh water (ψυχρὸν ὕδωρ) flowing from the lake of Memory in order to reign with the heroes. There is nothing to prevent our admitting with Foucart ("Myst. d'Eleusis," *Mém. Acad. des Inscr.*, XXXV, 2, p. 67), that the Egyptian ideas may have permeated the Orphic worship of southern Italy after the fourth or third century, since they are found expressed a hundred years earlier at Carpentras (*infra*, n. 90).

90. Δοίη σοι ὁ "Οσιρις τὸ ψυχρὸν ὕδωρ, at Rome: Kaibel, *Inscr. gr.* XIV, 1488, 1705, 1782, 1842; cf. 658 and *CIL*, VI, 3, 20616.—Σοὶ δὲ ᾽Οσείριδος ἁγνὸν ὕδωρ Εἶσις χαρίσαιτο, *Rev. archéol.*, 1887, p. 199, cf. 201.—Ψυχῇ διψώσῃ ψυχρὸν ὕδωρ μετάδος, *CIG*, 6267=Kaibel, 1890. It is particularly interesting to note that almost the same wish appears on the Aramaic stele of Carpentras (*C. I. Sem.*, II, 141), which dates back to the fourth or fifth century B. C.: "Blessed be thou, take water from in front of Osiris."—A passage in the book of Enoch manifestly inspired by Egyptian conceptions, mentions the "spring of water," the "spring of life," in the realm of the dead (Enoch, xxii. 2, 9. Cf. Martin, *Le livre d'Hénoch*, 1906, p. 58, n. 1, and Bousset, *Relig. des Judentums*, 1903, p 271). From Judaism the expression has passed into Christianity. Cf. Rev. vii. 17; xxi. 6.

91. The Egyptian origin of the Christian expression has frequently been pointed out and cannot be doubted; see Lafaye, *op. cit.*, p. 96, n. 1; Rohde, *Psyche*, II, p. 391; Kraus, *Realencycl. der christl. Alt.*, s. v. "Refrigerium"; and especially Dieterich, *Nekyia*, pp. 95 ff. Cf. Perdrizet, *Rev. des études anc.*, 1905, p. 32; Audollent, *Mélanges Louis Havet*, 1909, p. 575.—The *refrigerii sedes*, which the Catholic Church petitions for the deceased in the anniversary masses, appears in the oldest Latin liturgies, and the Greeks, who do not believe in purgatory, have always expressed themselves along the same lines. For instance, Nubian inscriptions which are in perfect agreement with the euchology of Constantinople hope the soul will rest ἐν τόπῳ χλοερῷ, ἐν τόπῳ ἀναψύξεως (G. Lefebvre, *Inscr. gr. chrét. d'Eg.*, No. 636, 664 ff., and introd., p. xxx; cf. Dumont, *Mélanges*, Homolle ed., pp. 585 ff.). The detail is not without significance because it furnishes a valu-

able indication as to the Egyptian origin of prayer for the dead; this is unknown to Graeco-Roman paganism which prayed to the deified dead but never *for* the dead as such. The Church took this custom from the Synagogue, but the Jews themselves seem to have taken it from the Egyptians during the Hellenistic period, undoubtedly in the course of the second century (S. Reinach, *Cultes, mythes,* I, p. 325), just as they were indebted to the Egyptians for the idea of the "spring of life" (*supra,* n. 90). The formula in the Christian inscriptions cited,

ἀνάπαυσον τὴν ψυχὴν ἐν κόλποις ᾿Αβραὰμ καὶ ᾿Ισαὰκ καὶ ᾿Ιακώβ,

appears to indicate a transposition of the doctrine of identification with Osiris. In this way we can explain the persistence in the Christian formulary of expressions, like *requies aeterna,* corresponding to the most primitive pagan conceptions of the life of the dead, who were not to be disturbed in their graves.—A name for the grave, which appears frequently in Latin epitaphs, viz., *domus aeterna* (or *aeternalis*) is undoubtedly also of Egyptian importation. In Egypt, "la tombe est la maison du mort, sa maison d'éternité, comme disent les textes" (Capart, *Guide du musée de Bruxelles,* 1905, p. 32). The Greeks were struck by this expression which appears in innumerable instances. Diodorus of Sicily (I, 51, § 2) was aware that the Egyptians

τοὺς τῶν τετελευτηκότων τάφους ἀϊδίους οἴκους προσαγορεύουσιν, ὡς ἐν ῞Αιδου διατελούντων τὸν ἄπειρον αἰῶνα (cf. I, 93, § 1, εἰς τὴν αἰώνιον οἴκησιν).—

It is probable that this appellation of the tomb passed from Egypt into Palestine and Syria. It appears already in Ecclesiastes, xii. 7 (*beth 'olam* = "house of eternity"), and it is found in Syrian epigraphy (for instance in inscriptions of the third century (*Comptes Rendus Acad. Inscr.,* 1906, p. 123), also in the epigraphy of Palmyra. (Chabot, *Journal asiatique,* 1900, p. 266, No. 47).—Possibly the hope for consolation, Εὐψύχει, οὐδεὶς ἀθάνατος, frequently found engraved upon tombs even in Latin countries was also derived from the Egyptian religion, but this is more doubtful. Εὐψύχει is found in the epitaphs of initiates in the Alexandrian mysteries. Kaibel, *Inscr. gr.,* XIV, 1488, 1782 (Εὐψυχεῖ κυρία καὶ δοίη σοι ὁ ῎Οσιρις τὸ ψυχρὸν ὕδωρ), 2098 (cf. *supra,* n. 90). Possibly the twofold meaning of εὔψυχος which stands both for *animosus* and *frigidus* (see Dieterich, *Nekyia, loc. cit.*) has been played upon. But on the other hand, the idea contained in the formula "Be cheerful, nobody is immortal," also inspired the "Song of the Harpist," a canonical hymn that was sung in Egypt on the day of the funeral. It invited the listener to "make his heart glad" before the sadness of inevitable death (Maspero, *Etudes égyptiennes*, I, 1881, pp. 171 ff.; cf. Naville, *op. cit.*, p. 171).

V. SYRIA.

BIBLIOGRAPHY: The Syrian religions have been studied with especial attention to their relation with Judaism: Baudissin, *Studien zur semitischen Religionsgeschichte,* 2 vols., Leipsic, 1876. The same author has published veritable monographs on certain divinities (Astarte, Baal, Sonne, etc.) in the *Realencyclopädie für prot. Theol.,* of Herzog-Hauck, 3d ed.—Bäthgen, *Beiträge zur semitischen Religionsgeschichte,* Berlin, 1888. —W. Robertson Smith, *The Religion of the Semites,* 2d ed., London, 1894.—Lagrange, *Etudes sur les religions sémitiques,* 2d ed., Paris, 1905. The results of the excavations in Palestine, which are important in regard to the funeral customs and the oldest idolatry, have been summarized by Father Hugues Vincent, *Canaan d'après l'exploration récente,* 1907.—On the propagation of the Syrian religions in the Occident, see Réville, *op. cit.,* pp. 70 *et passim*; Wissowa, *Religion der Römer,* pp. 299 ff.; Gruppe, *Griech. Mythol.,* pp. 1582 f.—Important obsei vations will be found in Clermont-Ganneau, *Recueil d'archéologie orientale,* 8 vols., 1888, and in Dussaud, *Notes de mythologie syrienne,* Paris, 1903. We have published a series of articles on particular divinities in the *Realencyclopädie* of Pauly-Wissowa (Baal, Balsamem, Dea Syria, Dolichenus, Gad, etc.). Other monographs are cited below.

1. Lucian, *Lucius,* 53 ff.; Apul., *Metam.,* VIII, 24 ff. The description by these authors has recently been confirmed by the discovery of an inscription at Kefr-Hauar in Syria: a slave of the Syrian goddess "sent by her mistress (κυρία)," boasts of having brought back "seventy sacks" from each of her trips (Fossey, *Bull. corr. hell.,* XXI, 1897, p. 60; on the

meaning of πήρα, "sack," see Deissmann, *Licht von Osten,*
1908, p. 73).

2. Cf. Riess in Pauly-Wissowa, s. v. *Astrologie,* col. 1816.

3. Cato, *De agric.,* V, 4.

4. On dedication of Romans to Atargatis, see *Bull. corr.
hell.,* VI, 1882, p. 497, No. 15; p. 498, No. 17.

5. Since the year 187 we find the Syrian musicians (*sambucistriae*) mentioned also at Rome. Their number grew
steadily (Livy, XXXIX, 6; see Friedländer, *Sittengesch.,* III⁸,
p. 346.

6. Florus, II, 7 (III, 9); cf. Diodorus Sic., fr. 34, 2, 5.

7. Plut., *Vit. Marii,* 17.

8. Juvenal, VI, 351; Martial, IV, 53, 10; IX, 2, 11, IX, 22, 9

9. *CIL,* VI, 399; cf. Wissowa, *op. cit.,* p. 201.—Suetonius,
Nero, 56.

10. A temple of the Syrian gods at Rome, located at the
foot of the Janiculum, has been excavated very recently. Cf.
Gauckler, *Bolletino communale di Roma,* 1907, pp. 5 ff. (Cf.
Hülsen, *Mitt. Inst. Rom,* XXII, 1907, pp. 225 ff.); *Comptes
Rendus Acad. Inscr.,* 1907, pp. 135 ff.; 1908, pp. 510 ff.; 1909,
pp. 424 ff., pp. 617 ff.; Nicole and Darier, *Le sanctuaire des
dieux orientaux au Janicule,* Rome, 1909 (Extr. des "Mél.
Ecole franç. de Rome," XXIX). In it have been found dedications to Hadad of the Lebanon, to the Hadad ἀκροφείτης,
and to Maleciabrudus (in regard to the latter see Clermont-Ganneau, *Rec. d'archéol. or.,* VIII, 1907, p. 52). Cf. my article
"Syria Dea" in Daremberg-Saglio-Pottier, *Diction. des antiquités gr. et rom.,* 1911.

11. I have said a few words on this colonization in my *Mon.
rel. aux myst. de Mithra,* I, p. 262. Courajod has considered
it in regard to artistic influences, *Leçons du Louvre,* I, 1899,
pp. 115, 327 ff. For the Merovingian period see Bréhier, *"Les
colonies d'orientaux en Occident au commencement du moyen
âge (Byzant. Zeitschr.,* XII), 1903, pp. 1 ff.

12. Kaibel, *Inscr. gr.,* XIV, 2540.

13. *Comptes Rendus Acad. Inscr.,* 1899, p. 353 = Waltzing,
Corporations professionelles, II, No. 1961 = *CIL, III S.,*

14165[8].—Inscription of Thaïm of Canatha: Kaibel, *Inscr. gr.*, XIV, 2532.

14. Gregory of Tours, *Hist. Fr.*, VIII, 1.—On the diffusion of the Syrians in Gaul, see Bréhier, *loc. cit.*, p. 16 ff

15. Cf. Bréhier, *Les origines du crucifix dans l'art religieux*, Paris, 1904.

16. Adonis: Wissowa, p. 300, n. 1.—Balmarcodès: Pauly-Wissowa, *Realenc.*, s. v.; Jalabert, *Mél. fac. orient. Beyrouth*, I, p. 182.—Marnas: The existence at Ostia of a "Marneum" can be deduced from the dedication *CIG*, 5892 (cf. Drexler in Roscher, *Lexikon*, s. v., col. 2382).—On Maleciabrudus, cf. *supra*, n. 10.—The Maiuma festival was probably introduced with the cult of the god of Gaza, Lydus, *De Mensib.*, IV, 80 (p. 133, Wünsch ed.) = Suidas s. v. Μαιουμᾶς and Drexler, *loc. cit.*, col. 2287. Cf. Clermont-Ganneau, *Rec. d'archéol. orient.*, IV, p. 339.

17. Cf. Pauly-Wissowa, s. v. "Damascenus, Dusares."

18. Malalas, XI, p. 280, 12 (Bonn).—The temple has recently been excavated by a German mission; cf. Puchstein, *Führer in Baalbek*, Berlin, 1905.—On the Hadad at Rome, cf. *supra*, n. 10.

19. *CIL*, X, 1634: "Cultores Iovis Heliopolitani Berytenses qui Puteolis consistunt"; cf. Wissowa, *loc. cit.*, p. 504, n. 3; Ch. Dubois, *Pouzzoles antique*, Paris, 1906, p. 156.

20. A list of the known military societies has been made by Cichorius in Pauly-Wissowa, *Realencycl.*, s. v. "Ala" and "Cohors."

21. *CIL*, VII, 759 = Buecheler, *Carmina epigr.*, 24. Two inscriptions dedicated to the Syrian Hercules (Melkarth) and to Astarte have been discovered at Corbridge, near Newcastle (*Inscr. gr.*, XIV, 2553). It is possible that Tyrian archers were cantoned there.

22. Baltis: Pauly-Wissowa, *Realencyclop.*, s. v.

23. Pauly-Wissowa, *Realenc.*, s. v. "Aziz"; cf. Wissowa, *op. cit.*, p. 303, n. 7.

24. On the etymology of Malakbel, see Dussaud, *Notes*, 24 ff. On the religion in the Occident see Edu. Meyer in Roscher, *Lexikon*, s. v.

25. Kan, *De Iovis Dolicheni cultu,* Groningen, 1901; cf. Pauly-Wissowa, *Realencycl.,* s. v. "Dolichenus."

26. Réville, *Relig. sous les Sévères,* pp. 237 ff.; Wissowa, *op. cit.,* p. 305; cf. Pauly-Wissowa, s. v. "Elagabal."—In a recent article (*Die politische Bedeutung der Religion von Emesa* [*Archiv für Religionsw.,* XI], 1908, pp. 223 ff.) M. von Domaszewski justly lays stress on the religious value of the solar monotheism that arose in the temples of Syria, but he attributes too important a part in its formation to the clergy of Emesa (see *infra,* n. 88). The preponderant influence seems to have been exercised by Palmyra (see *infra,* n. 59).

27. Cf. *infra,* n. 59.

28. Cf. Curtiss, *Primitive Semitic Religion To-day,* Chicago, 1902; Jaussen, *Coutumes des Arabes du pays de Moab,* Paris, 1908, pp. 297 ff.

29. Cf. Robertson Smith, *passim*; Lagrange, pp. 158-216; Vincent, *op. cit.,* pp. 102-123; 144 f.—The power of this Semitic litholatry equaled its persistence. Philo of Byblus defined the bethels as λίθοι ἔμψυχοι (2, § 20, FHG, III, p. 563): Hippolytus also tells us (V, 1, p. 145, Cruice), that in the Syrian mysteries ('Ασσυρίων τελεταί) it was taught that the stones were animated (οἱ λίθοι εἰσὶν ἔμψυχοι· ἔχουσι γὰρ τὸ αὐξητικόν), and the same doctrine perpetuated itself in Manicheism. (Titus of Bostra, II, 60, p. 60, 25, de Lagarde ed.:

Οὐκ αἰσχύνεται δὲ καὶ τοὺς λίθους ἐψυχῶσθαι λέγων καὶ τὰ πάντα ἔμψυχα εἰσηγούμενος).

During the last years of paganism the neo-Platonists developed a superstitious worship of the bethels; see Conybeare, *Transactions of the Congress of Hist. of Rel.,* Oxford, 1908, p. 177.

30. Luc., *De dea Syria,* c. 41. Cf. the inscription of Narnaka with the note of Clermont-Ganneau, *Etudes d'arch. orient.,* II, p. 163.—For bull worship in Syria cf. Ronzevalle, *Mélanges fac. orient. Beyrouth,* I, 1906, pp. 225, 238; Vincent, *op. cit.,* p. 169.

31. Philo Alex., *De provid.,* II, c. 107 (II, 646 M.); cf. Lucian, *De dea Syria,* 54.

32. For instance on Mount Eryx in Sicily (Ael., *Nat. Anim.,*

IV, 2).—Cf. Pauly-Wissowa, *Realenc.*, s. v. "Dea Syria," col. 2242.

33. Tibullus, I, 7, 17.

34. Lucian, *De dea Syria*, 14; 54. Cf. Diodorus, II, 4, 2; Ovid, *Met.*, IV, 46; V, 331.

35. Pauly-Wissowa, *loc. cit.*, col. 2241; W. Robertson Smith, p. 175.

36. The ancient authors frequently alluded to this superstition of the Syrians (the texts have been collected by Selden, *De dis Syris*, II, C. 3, pp. 268 ff., ed. of 1672). W. Robertson Smith (*loc. cit.*, p. 449), is right in connecting it with certain ideas of savages. Like many primitive beliefs, this one has continued to the present day. It has been pointed out to me that at Sam-Keuï, a little west of Doliché, there is a pond fed by a spring and well stocked with fish, which one is forbidden to take. Near the mosque of Edessa is a large pond where catching fish is prohibited. They are considered sacred, and the people believe that any one who would eat them would die instantly. (Sachau, *Reise in Syrien*, 1883, pp. 196 ff. Cf. Lord Warkworth, *Diary in Asiatic Turkey*, London, 1898, p. 242). The same is the case at the mosque of Tripoli and elsewhere (Lammens, *Au pays des Nosaïris* [*Revue de l'Orient chrétien*], 1908, p. 2). Even in Asia Minor this superstition is found. At Tavshanli, north of Aezani on the upper Rhyndacus, there is to-day a square cistern filled with sacred fish which no one is allowed to take (on the authority of Munro). Travelers in Turkey have frequently observed that the people do not eat fish, even when there is a scarcity of food (Sachau, *loc. cit.*, p. 196) and the general belief that their flesh is unhealthful and can cause sickness is not entirely unfounded. Here is what Ramsay has to say on the subject (*Impressions of Turkey*, London, 1897, p. 288): "Fish are rarely found and when found are usually bad: the natives have a prejudice against fish, and my own experience has been unfavorable.... In the clear sparkling mountain stream that flows through the Taurus by Bozanti-Khan, a small kind of fish is caught; I had a most violent attack of sickness in 1891 after eating some of them, and so had all who partook." Captain Wilson, who spent a number of years in

Asia Minor, asserts (*Handbook of Asia-Minor*, p. 19), that "the natives do not eat fish to any extent." The "totemic" prohibition in this instance really seems to have a hygienic origin. People abstained from all kinds of fish because some species were dangerous, that is to say, inhabited by evil spirits, and the tumors sent by the Syrian goddess were merely the edemas caused by the poisoning.

37. On the Ἰχθύs symbolism I will merely refer to Usener, *Sintflutsagen,* 1899, pp. 223 ff. Cf. S. Reinach, *Cultes, mythes,* III, 1908, pp. 43 ff. An exhaustive book on this subject has recently appeared: Dölger, ΙΧΘΥΣ, *das Fischsymbol in früh-christlicher Zeit,* I, Rome, 1910.

On sacred repasts where fish was eaten see Mnaseas, fragment 32 (*Fragm. histor. graec.,* III, 115); cf. Dittenberger, *Sylloge,* 584: Ἐὰν δέ τις τῶν ἰχθύων ἀποθάνῃ, καρπούσθω αὐθημερὸν ἐπὶ τοῦ βωμοῦ, and Diog. Laert., VIII, 34. There were also sacred repasts in the Occident in the various Syrian cults: *Cenatorium et triclinium* in the temples of Jupiter Dolichenus (*CIL,* III, 4789; VI, 30931; XI, 696, cf. *Mon. myst. Mithra,* II, p. 501); *promulsidaria et mantelium* offered to the Venus Caelestis (*CIL,* X, 1590); construction of a temple to Malachbel with a *culina* (*CIL,* III, 7954). Mention is made of a δειπνοκρίτης, δείπνοις κρείνας πολλὰ μετ᾽ εὐφροσύνης, in the temple of the Janiculum (Gauckler, *C. R. Acad. Inscr.,* 1907, p. 142; *Bolletino communale,* 1907, pp. 15 ff.). Cf. Lagrange, *Religions sémitiques,* II, p. 609, and Pauly-Wissowa, *Realenc.,* s. v. "Gad."

38. W. Robertson Smith, pp. 292 ff.

39. An inscription discovered at Kefr-Hauar (Fossey, *Bull. corr: hell.,* 1897, p. 60) is very characteristic in this respect. A "slave" of the Syrian goddess in that inscription offers his homage to his "mistress" (κυρία).

40. Notably at Aphaca where they were not suppressed until the time of Constantine (Eusebius, *Vit. Const.,* III, 55; cf. Sozom., II, 5).

41. Much has been written about the sacred prostitutions in paganism, and it is well known that Voltaire ridiculed the scholars who were credulous enough to believe in the tales of Herodotus. But this practice has been proven by irre-

futable testimony. Strabo, for instance, whose great-uncle was arch-priest of Comana, mentions it in connection with that city, (XII, 3, 36, p. 559 C), and he manifests no surprise. The history of religion teaches many stranger facts; this one, however, is disconcerting. The attempt has been made to see in it a relic of the primitive promiscuity or polyandry, or a persistence of "sexual hospitality," ("No custom is more widely spread than the providing for a guest a female companion, who is usually a wife or daughter of the host," says Wake, *Serpent Worship*, 1888, p. 158); or the substitution of union with a man for union with the god (Gruppe, *Griech. Mythol.*, p. 915). But these hypotheses do not explain the peculiarities of the religious custom as it is described by more reliable authors. They insist upon the fact that the girls were dedicated to the temple service while *virgins,* and that after having had *strangers* for lovers, they married in their own country. Thus Strabo (XI, 14, § 16, p. 532 C.) narrates in connection with the temple of Anaïtis in Acilisena, that θυγατέρας οἱ ἐπιφανέστατοι τοῦ ἔθνους ἀνιεροῦσι παρθένους, αἷς νόμος ἐστὶ καταπορνευθείσαις πολὺν χρόνον παρὰ τῇ θεῷ μετὰ ταῦτα δίδοσθαι πρὸς γάμον, οὐκ ἀπαξιοῦντος τῇ τοιαύτῃ συνοικεῖν οὐδενός. Herodotus (I, 93), who relates about the same thing of the Lydian women, adds that they acquired a dowry in that manner; an inscription at Tralles (*Bull. corr. hell.*, VII, 1885, p. 276) actually mentions a descendant of a sacred prostitute (ἐκ προγόνων παλλακί-δων) who had temporarily filled the same office (παλλακεύσασα κατὰ χρησμὸν Διί). Even at Thebes in Egypt there existed a similar custom with striking local peculiarities in the time of Strabo (XVII, 1, § 46), and traces of it seem to have been found in Greece among the Locrians (Vurtheim, *De Aiacis origine,* Leyden, 1907). Every Algerian traveler knows how the girls of the Ouled-Naïl earn their dowry in the *ksours* and the cities, before they go back to their tribes to marry, and Doutté (*Notes sur l'Islam maghrébien, les Marabouts,* Extr. *Rev. hist. des relig.,* XL-XLI, Paris, 1900), has connected these usages with the old Semitic prostitution, but his thesis has been attacked and the historical circumstances of the arrival of the Ouled-Naïl in Algeria in the eleventh century render it very doubtful (Note by Basset).—It seems certain (I do not know whether this explanation has ever been offered) that this strange practice is a modified utilitarian form of an ancient exogamy. Besides it had certain favorable results, since it protected the girl against the brutality of her kindred until she was of marriageable age, and this fact must have insured its persistence; but the idea that inspired it at first was different. "La première union sexuelle impliquant une effusion de sang, a été interdite, lorsque ce sang était celui d'une fille du clan versé par le fait d'un homme du clan" (Salomon Reinach, *Mythes, cultes,* I, 1905, p. 79. Cf. Lang, *The Secret of the Totem,* London, 1905.) Thence rose the obligation on virgins to yield to a stranger first. Only then were they permitted to marry a man of their own race. Furthermore, various means were resorted to in order to save the husband from the defilement which might result from that act (see for inst., Reinach, *Mythes, cultes,* I, p. 118).—The opinion expressed in this note was attacked, almost immediately after its publication, by Frazer (*Adonis, Attis, Osiris,* 1907, pp. 50 ff.) who preferred to see in the sacred prostitutions a relic of primitive communism. But at least one of the arguments which he uses against our views is incorrect. Not the women, but the men, received presents in Acilisena (Strabo, *loc. cit.*) and the communistic theory does not seem to account for the details of the custom prevailing in the temple of Thebes. There the horror of blood clearly appears. On the discovery of a skull (having served at a rite of consecration) in the temple of the Janiculum, see the article cited above, "Dea Syria," in *Dict. des antiquités.*

42. Porphyry, *De Abstin.,* II, 56; Tertull., *Apol.,* 9. Cf. Lagrange, *op. cit.,* p. 445.

43. Even in the regions where the cities developed, the Baal and the Baalat always remained the divinities πολιοῦχοι, the protectors of the city which they were supposed to have founded.

44. Le Bas-Waddington, 2196.—Suidas, s. v. Φυλάρχης (II, 2, col. 1568, Bernhardy). Cf. Marquardt, *Staatsverwaltung,* I, p. 405, 409.

45. Hippolytus, *Adv. Haeres.,* V, 11, § 7: Ἀσσυρίων τελεταί; § 18: Ἀσσυρίων μυστήρια (pp. 145, 148, ed. by Cruice). Cf. Origen, *Contra Celsum,* I, 12. Pognon (*Inscrip. sémitiques,*

1907, No. 48) has recently published a Syrian epitaph that is unfortunately mutilated, but which seems to be that of an adept of the pagan mysteries; see Nöldeke, *Zeitschrift für Assyr.*, XXI, 1907, p. 155.

46. On the Semitic notion of purity, W. Robertson Smith has written admirably and convincingly (pp. 446 ff. and *passim*). The question has been taken up from a different point of view by Lagrange, pp. 141 ff.—The development of the notion of purity in the ancient religions has been recently expounded by Farnell, *The Evolution of Religion*, 1905, pp. 88 ff., especially pp. 124 ff. Cf. also *supra*, p. 91 f. An example of the prohibitions and purifications is found in the Occident in an inscription, unfortunately mutilated, discovered at Rome and dedicated to Beellefarus (*CIL*, VI, 30934, 31168; cf. Lafaye, *Rev. hist. relig.*, XVII, 1888, pp. 218 ff.; Dessau, *Inscr. sel.*, 4343). If I have understood the text correctly it commands those who have eaten pork to purify themselves by means of honey.—On penances in the Syrian religions see ch. II, n. 31.

47. M. Clermont-Ganneau (*Etudes d'archéologie orientale*, II, 1896, p. 104) states that the epithet ἅγιος is extremely rare in pagan Hellenism, and almost always betrays a Semitic influence. In such cases it corresponds to קדש, which to the Semites is the epithet *par excellence* of the divinity. Thus Eshmon is קדש; cf. Lidzbarski, *Ephemer. für semit. Epigraph.*, II, p. 155; Clermont-Ganneau, *Recueil d'archéol. orient.*, III, p. 330; V, p. 322.—In Greek Le Bas-Waddington, 2720, has: Οἱ κάτοχοι ἁγίου οὐρανίου Διός. Dittenberger, *Orientis inscript.*, 620, Ζεὺς ἅγιος Βεελ βωσῶρος. Some time ago I copied at a dealer's, a dedication engraved upon a lamp: Θεῷ ἁγίῳ 'Αρελσέλῳ, in Latin: J. Dolichenus *sanctus*, *CIL*, VI, 413, X, 7949. —J. Heliopolitanus *sanctissimus*, *CIL*, VIII, 2627.—"Caelestis *sancta*," VIII, 8433, etc.—The African Saturn (= Baal) is often called *sanctus*.—*Hera sancta* beside Jupiter Dolichenus, VI, 413.—Malakbel is translated by *Sol sanctissimus*, in the bilingual inscription of the Capitol, VI, 710 = Dessau, 4337. Cf. *deus sanctus aeternus*, V, 1058, 3761, and *Comptes Rendus Acad. Inscr.*, 1906, p. 69.—See in general Delehaye, *Analecta Bollandiana*, 1909, pp. 157 ff.

48. As curious examples of Greco-Syrian syncretism we may mention the bas-relief of Ed-Douwaïr in the Louvre, which has been analyzed in detail by Dussaud (*Notes*, pp. 89 ff.), and especially that of Homs in the Brussels museum (*ibid.*, 104 ff.).

49. Macrobius, I, 23, § 11: "Ritu Assyrio magis quam Aegyptio colitur"; cf. Lucian, *De dea Syria*, 5.—"Hermetic" theories penetrated even to the Sabians of Osrhoene (Reitzenstein, *Poimandres*, 166 ff.), although their influence seems to have been merely superficial (Bousset, *Göttingische gelehrt. Anzeigen*, 1905, 704 ff.—The existence of κάτοχοι at Baetocécé and elsewhere appears to be due to Egyptian influence (Jalabert, *Mélanges de la fac. orient. de Beyrouth*, II, 1907, pp. 308 ff.). The meaning of κάτοχος which has been interpreted in different ways, is established, I think, by the passages collected by Kroll, *Cat. codd. astrol. graec.*, V, pars 2, p. 146; cf. Otto, *Priester und Tempel*, I, p. 119; Bouché-Leclercq, *Hist. des Lagides*, IV, p. 335. It refers to the poor, the sick and even the "illumined" living within the temple enclosures and undoubtedly supported by the clergy, as were the refugees of the Christian period who availed themselves of the right of sanctuary in the churches (cf. *Comptes Rendus Acad. Inscr.*, 1907, p. 454).

50. Cf. *infra*, n. 59.

51. Strabo, XVI, 1, 6. Cf. Pliny, *H. N.*, VI, 6: "Durat adhuc ibi Iovis Beli templum.". . Cf. my *Mon. myst. Mithra*, I, pp. 35 ff.; Chapot, *Mém. soc. antiq. de France*, 1902, pp. 239 ff.; Gruppe, *Griech. Mythol.*, p. 1608, n. 1.

52. Lucian, *De dea Syria*, c. 10.

53. Harnack, *Dogmengeschichte*, I, pp. 233 ff. and *passim*.

54. On the worship of Bel in Syria cf. *Comptes Rendus Acad. Inscr.*, 1907, pp. 447 ff.—Cf. *infra*, n. 59.

55. On the Heliopolitan triad and the addition of Mercury to the original couple see Perdrizet, *Rev. études anc.*, III, 1901, p. 258; Dussaud, *Notes*, p. 24; Jalabert, *Mélanges fac. orient. de Bayrouth*, I, 1906, pp. 175 ff.—Triad of Hierapolis: Lucian, *De dea Syria*, c. 33. According to Dussaud, the three divinities came from Babylon together, *Notes*, p. 115.—The existence of a Phœnician triad (Baal, Astarte, Eshmoun or Mel-

karth), and of a Palmyrian triad has been conjectured but without sufficient reason (*ibid.,* 170, 172 ff.); the existence of Carthaginian triads is more probable (cf. Polybius, VII, 9, 11, and von Baudissin, *Iolaos* [*Philothesia für Paul Kleinert*], 1907, pp. 5 ff.—See in general Usener, *Dreiheit* (Extr. *Rhein. Museum,* LVIII), 1903, p. 32. The triads continued in the theology of the "Chaldaic Oracles" (Kroll, *De orac. Chald.,* 13 ff.) and a threefold division of the world and the soul was taught in the "Assyrian mysteries" (*Archiv für Religionswiss.,* IX, 1906, p. 331, n. 1).

56. Boll, *Sphaera,* p. 372.—The introduction of astrology into Egypt seems to date back no further than the time of the Ptolemies.

57. The Seleucides, like the Roman emperors later, believed in Chaldean astrology (Appian., *Syr.,* 28; Diodorus, II, 31, 2; cf. Riess in Pauly-Wissowa, *Realenc.,* s. v. "Astrologie," col. 1814), and the kings of Commagene, as well as of a great number of Syrian cities, had the signs of the zodiac as emblems on their coins. It is even certain that this pseudo-science penetrated into those regions long before the Hellenistic period. Traces of it are found in the Old Testament (Schiaparelli; translation by Lüdke, *Die Astron. im Alten Testament,* 1904, p. 46). It modified the entire Semitic paganism. The only cult which we know in any detail, that of the Sabians, assigned the highest importance to it; but in the myths and doctrines of the others its influence is no less apparent (Pauly-Wissowa, *Realencycl.,* s. v. "Dea Syria," IV, col. 2241, and s. v. "Gad"; cf. Baudissin, *Realencycl. für prot. Theol.,* s. v., "Sonne," pp. 510-520). To what extent, for instance, the clergy of Emesa had been subjected to its ascendency is shown by the novel of Heliodorus, written by a priest of that city (Rohde, *Griech. Roman²,* p. 464 [436]), and by the horoscope that put Julia Domna upon the throne (*Vita Severi,* 3, 8; cf. A. von Domaszewski, *Archiv für Religionsw.,* XI, 1908, p. 223). The irresistible influence extended even to the Arabian paganism (Nöldeke in Hastings, *Encyclop. of Religion,* s. v. "Arabs," I, p. 661; compare, *Orac. Sibyll.,* XIII, 64 ff., on Bostra). The sidereal character which has been attributed to the Syrian gods, was borrowed, but none the less real. From very early times the Semites worshiped the sun,

the moon, and the stars (see Deut. iv. 19; Job xxxi. 25), especially the planet Venus, but this cult was of secondary importance only (see W. Robertson Smith, *op. cit.*, p. 135, n. 1), although it grew in proportion as the Babylonian influence became stronger. The polemics of the Fathers of the Syrian Church show how considerable its prestige was in the Christian era (cf. Ephrem, *Opera Syriaca*, Rome, 1740, II, pp. 447 ff.; the "Assyrian" Tatian, c. 9 ff., etc.).

58. Humann and Puchstein, *Reise in Klein-Asien und Nord-Syrien*, 1890, pl. XL; *Mon. myst. Mithra*, I, p. 188, fig. 8; Bouché-Leclercq, *Astrol. gr.*, p. 439.

59. Cf. Wissowa, *op. cit.*, p. 306-7.—On the temple of Bel at Palmyra, cf. Sobernheim, *Palmyrenische Inschriften* (*Mitt. der vorderasiat. Gesellsch.*, X), 1905, pp. 319 ff.; Lidzbarski, *Ephemeris*, I, pp. 255 ff., II, p. 280.—Priests of Bel: Clermont-Ganneau, *Recueil d'arch. orient.*, VII, p. 12, 24, 364. Cf. *supra*, n. 54. The power of Palmyra under Zenobia, who ruled from the Tigris to the Nile, must have had as a corollary the establishment of an official worship that was necessarily syncretic. Hence its special importance for the history of paganism. Although the Babylonian astrology was a powerful factor in this worship, Judaism seems to have had just as great an influence in its formation. There was at Palmyra a large Jewish colony, which the writers of the Talmud considered only tolerably orthodox (Chaps, *Gli Ebrei di Palmira* [*Rivista Israelitica*, I], Florence, 1904, pp. 171 ff., 238 f. Cf. "Palmyra" in the *Jewish Encycl.*; Jewish insc. of Palmyra; Euting, *Sitzb. Berl. Acad.*, 1885, p. 669; Landauer, *ibid.*, 1884, pp. 933 ff.). This colony seems to have made compromises with the idolaters. On the other hand we see Zenobia herself rebuilding a synagogue in Egypt (*Revue archéologique*, XXX, 1875, p. 111; *Zeitschrift für Numismatik*, V, p. 229; Dittenberger, *Orientis inscript.*, 729). This influence of Judaism seems to explain the development at Palmyra of the cult of Ζεὺς ὕψιστος καὶ ἐπήκοος, "he whose name is blessed in eternity." The name of Hypsistos has been applied everywhere to Jehovah and to the pagan Zeus (*supra*, p. 62, 128) at the same time. The text of Zosimus (I, 61), according to which Aurelian brought from Palmyra to Rome the statues of Ἡλίου τε καὶ Βήλου (this has been wrongly changed to read τοῦ καὶ Βήλου), proves that the

astrological religion of the great desert city recognized a supreme god residing in the highest heavens, and a solar god, his visible image and agent, according to the Semitic theology of the last period of paganism (*supra*, p. 134).

60. I have spoken of this solar eschatology in the memorial cited *infra*, n. 88.

61. This opinion is that of Posidonius (see Wendland, *Philos Schrift über die Vorsehung*, Berlin, 1892, p. 68, n. 1; 70, n. 2). It is shared by the ancient astrologers.

62. This old pagan and gnostic idea has continued to the present day in Syria among the Hosaïris; cf. Dussaud, *Histoire et religion des Nosaïris*, 1900, p. 125.

63. The belief that pious souls are guided to heaven by a psychopompus, is found not only in the mysteries of Mithra (*Mon. myst. Mithra*, I, p. 310), but also in the Syrian cults where that rôle was often assigned to the solar god, see Isid. Lévy, *Cultes syriens dans le Talmud* (*Revue des études juives*, XLIII), 1901, p. 5, and Dussaud, *Notes*, p. 27; cf. the Le Bas-Waddington inscription, 2442:

"Βασιλεῦ δέσποτα (= the sun), ἵλαθι καὶ δίδου πᾶσιν ἡμῖν ὑγίην καθαράν, πρῆξις ἀγαθὰς καὶ βίου τέλος ἐσθλόν."—

The same idea is found in inscriptions in the Occident; as for instance in the peculiar epitaph of a sailor who died at Marseilles (Kaibel, *Inscr. gr.*, XIV, 2462 = *Epigr.*, 650):

"'Εν δέ [τε] τεθνειῶισιν ὁμηγύρι[ές] γε πέλουσιν
δοιαί · τῶν ἑτέρη μὲν ἐπιχθονίη πεφόρηται,
ἡ δ' ἑτέρη τείρεσσι σὺν αἰθερίοισι χορεύει,
ἧς στρατιῆς εἰς εἰμί, λαχὼν θεὸν ἡγεμονῆα."

It is the same term that Julian used (*Césars*, p. 336 C) in speaking of Mithra, the guide of souls: ἡγεμόνα θεόν. Cf. also *infra*, n. 66 and ch. VIII, n. 24.

64. The Babylonian origin of the doctrine that the souls returned to heaven by crossing the seven planetary spheres, has been maintained by Anz (*Zur Frage nach dem Ursprung des Gnostizismus*, 1897; cf. *Mon. myst. Mithra*, I. pp. 38 ff., p. 309; Bousset, *Die Himmelsreise der Seele* [*Archiv für Religionsw.*, IV], 1901, pp. 160 ff.) and "Gnosis" in Pauly-Wissowa, *Realencyclopädie*, col. 1520. It has since been denied by Reitzenstein (*Poimandres*, p. 79; cf. Kroll, *Berl. philol. Wochensch.*,

1906, p. 486). But although it may have been given its precise shape and been transformed by the Greeks and even by the Egyptians, I persist in believing that it is of Chaldean and religious origin. I heartily agree with the conclusions recently formulated by Bousset, (*Göttingische gelehrte Anzeigen*, 1905, pp. 707 ff.). We can go farther: Whatever roots it may have had in the speculations of ancient Greece (Aristoph., *Pax*, 832, Plato, *Tim.*, 42B, cf. Haussoullier, *Rev. de philol.*, 1909, pp. 1 ff.), whatever traces of it may be found in other nations (Dieterich, *Mithrasliturgie*, pp. 182 ff.; *Nekyia*, p. 24, note; Rohde, *Psyche*, II, p. 131, n. 3), the idea itself of the soul rising to the divine stars after death certainly developed under the influence of the sidereal worship of the Semites to a point where it dominated all other eschatological theories. The belief in the eternity of souls is the corollary to the belief in the eternity of the celestial gods (p. 129). We cannot give the history of this conception here, and we shall limit ourselves to brief observations. The first account of this system ever given at Rome is found in "Scipio's Dream" (c. 3); it probably dates back to Posidonius of Apamea (cf. Wendland, *Die hellenistisch-römische Kultur*, p. 85, 166, n. 3, 168, n. 1), and is completely impregnated with mysticism and astrolatry. The same idea is found a little later in the astrologer Manilius (I, 758; IV, 404, etc.). The shape which it assumed in Josephus (*Bell. Judaic.*, V, 1, 5, § 47) is also much more religious than philosophical and is strikingly similar to a dogma of Islam (happiness in store for those dying in battle; a Syrian [*ibid.*, § 54] risks his life that his soul may go to heaven). This recalls the inscription of Antiochus of Commagene (Michel, *Recueil*, No. 735, l. 40):

Σῶμα πρὸς οὐρανίους Διὸς Ὠρομάσδου θρόνους θεοφιλῆ ψυχὴν προπέμψαν εἰς τὸν ἄπειρον αἰῶνα κοιμήσεται.

It must be said that this sidereal immortality was not originally common to all men; it was reserved "omnibus qui patriam conservaverint adiuverint, auxerint" (*Somn. Scip.* c. 3, c. 8; cf. *Manil.*, I, 758; Lucan, *Phars.*, IX, 1 ff.; Wendland, *op. cit.*, p. 85 n. 2), and this also is in conformity with the oldest Oriental traditions. The rites first used to assure immortality to kings and to make them the equals of the gods were extended little by little as a kind of privilege, to the important persons of the state, and only very much later were they applied to all who died.

Regarding the diffusion of this belief from the beginning of the first century of our era, see Diels, *Elementum*, 1899, p. 73, cf. 78; Badstübner, *Beiträge zur Erklärung Senecas*, Hamburg, pp. 2 ff.—It is expressed in many inscriptions (Friedländer, *Sitteng.*, III, pp. 749 ff.; Rohde, *Psyche*, p. 673, cf. 610; epitaph of Vezir-Keupru, *Studia Pontica*, No. 85; *CIL*. III (Salone), 6384; *supra*, n. 63, etc.) It gained access into Judaism and paganism simultaneously (cf. Bousset, *Die Religion des Judentums im neutest. Zeitalter*, 1903, p. 271, and, for Philo of Alexandria, Zeller, *Philos. der Griechen*, V, p. 397 and p. 297). —During the third century it was expounded by Cornelius Labeo, the source of Arnobius and Servius (Nieggetiet, *De Cornelio Labeone* [Diss. Munster], 1908, pp. 77-86). It was generally accepted towards the end of the empire; see *infra*, n. 25.—I hope soon to have the opportunity of setting forth the development of this sidereal eschatology with greater precision in my lectures on "Astrology and Religion in Antiquity" which will appear in 1912 (chap. VI).

65. According to the doctrine of the Egyptian mysteries the Elysian Fields were in the under-world (Apul., *Metam.*, XI, 6).—According to the astrological theory, the Elysian Fields were in the sphere of the fixed stars (Macrobius, *Comm. somn. Scip.*, I, 11, § 8; cf. *infra*, chap. VIII, n. 25). Others placed them in the moon (Servius, *Ad Aen.*, VI, 887; cf. Norden, *Vergils Buch* VI, p. 23; Rohde, *Psyche*, pp. 609 ff.). Iamblichus placed them between the moon and the sun (Lydus, *De mens.*, IV, 149, p. 167, 23, Wünsch).

66. The relation between the two ideas is apparent in the alleged account of the Pythagorean doctrine which Diogenes Laertius took from Alexander Polyhistor, and which is in reality an apocryphal composition of the first century of our era. It was said that Hermes guided the pure souls, after their separation from the body, εἰς τὸν "Ὕψιστον (Diog. Laert., VIII, § 31; cf. Zeller, *Philos. der Griechen*, V, p. 106, n. 2). —On the meaning of Hypsistos, cf. *supra*, p. 128. It appears very plainly in the passage of Isaiah, xiv, 13, as rendered by the Septuagint:

Εἰς τὸν οὐρανὸν ἀναβήσομαι, ἐπάνω τῶν ἀστέρων θήσω τὸν θρόνον μου...
ἔσομαι ὅμοιος τῷ Ὑψίστῳ.

67. Originally he was the thunder-god, in Greek Κεραυνός.
Under this name he appeared for instance on the bas-relief
preserved in the museum of Brussels (Dussaud, *Notes,* p. 105).
Later, by a familiar process, the influence of a particular god
becomes the attribute of a greater divinity, and we speak of
a Ζεὺς Κεραύνιος (cf. Usener, *Keraunos,* Rhein. Museum, N. F.,
LX, 1901).—This Zeus Keraunios appears in many inscriptions
of Syria (*CIG,* 4501, 4520; Le Bas-Waddington, 2195, 2557 *a,*
2631, 2739; cf. Roscher, *Lexikon Myth.,* s. v. "Keraunos").
He is the god to whom Seleucus sacrificed when founding
Seleucia (Malalas, p. 199), and a dedication to the same god
has been found recently in the temple of the Syrian divinities
at Rome (*supra,* n. 10).—An equivalent of the Zeus Keraunios is the Zeus Καταιβάτης—"he who descends in the lightning"—worshiped at Cyrrhus (Wroth, *Greek Coins in the
British Museum*: "Galatia, Syria," p. 52 and LII; Roscher,
Lexikon, s. v.)

68. For instance the double ax was carried by Jupiter Dolichenus (cf. *supra,* p. 147). On its significance, cf. Usener,
loc. cit., p. 20.

69. Cf. Lidzbarski, *Balsamem, Ephem. semit. Epigr.,* I, p.
251.—Ba'al Samaïn is mentioned as early as the ninth century
B. C. in the inscription of Ben Hadad (Pognon, *Inscr. sémit.,*
1907, pp. 165 ff.; cf. Dussaud, *Rev. archéol.,* 1908, I, p. 235).
In Aramaic papyri preserved at Berlin, the Jews of Elephan-
tine call Jehovah "the god of heaven" in an address to a
Persian governor, and the same name was used in the alleged
edicts of Cyrus and his successors, which were inserted in
the book of Esdras (i. 1; vi. 9, etc.)—If there were the
slightest doubt as to the identity of the god of thunder with
Baalsamin, it would be dispelled by the inscription of Et-
Tayibé, where this Semitic name is translated into Greek as
Ζεὺς μέγιστος κεραύνιος; cf. Lidzbarski, *Handbuch,* p. 477, and
Lagrange, *op. cit.,* p. 508.

70. On the worship of Baalsamin, confused with Ahura-
Mazda and transformed into *Caelus,* see *Mon. myst. Mithra,*
p. 87.—The texts attesting the existence of a real cult of

heaven among the Semites are very numerous. Besides the ones I have gathered (*loc. cit.*, n. 5); see Conybeare, *Philo about the Contemplative Life*, p. 33, n. 16; Kayser, *Das Buch der Erkenntniss der Wahrheit*, 1893, p. 337, and *infra*, n. 75. Zeus Οὐράνιος: Le Bas-Waddington, 2720 a (Baal of Bétocécé); Renan, *Mission de Phénicie*, p. 103.—Cf. *Archiv für Religionswissenschaft*, IX, 1906, p. 333.

71. Coins of Antiochus VIII Grypus (125-96 B. C.); Babelon, *Rois de Syrie, d'Arménie*, 1890, p. CLIV, pp. 178 ff.

72. All these qualities ascribed to the Baals by astrological paganism (ὕψιστος, παντοκράτωρ, etc.), are also the attributes which, according to the doctrine of Alexandrian Judaism, characterized Jehovah (see *supra*, n. 66). If he was originally a god of thunder, as has been maintained, the evolution of the Jewish theology was parallel to that of the pagan conceptions (see *supra*, n. 69).

73. On this subject cf. *Jupiter summus exsuperantissimus* (*Archiv f. Religionsw.*, IX), 1906, pp. 326 ff.

74. Ps.-Iamblichus, *De mysteriis*, VI, 7 (cf. Porph., *Epist. Aneb.*, c. 29), notes this difference between the two religions.

75. Apul., *Met.*, VIII, 25. Cf. *CIL*, III, 1090; XII, 1227 (= Dessau, 2998, 4333); Macrobius, *Comm. somn. Scipionis*, I, 14, § 2: "Nihil aliud esse deum nisi caelum ipsum et caelestia ipsa quae cernimus, ideo ut summi omnipotentiam dei ostenderet posse vix intellegi."—Ἥλιος παντοκράτως: Macrob., I, 23, 21.

76. Diodorus, II, 30: Χαλδαῖοι τὴν τοῦ κόσμου φύσιν ἀίδιόν φασιν εἶναι κ. τ. λ; cf. Cicero, *Nat. deor.*, II, 20, § 52 ff.; Pliny, *H. N.*, II, 8, § 30. The notion of eternity was correlative with that of εἱμαρμένη; cf. Ps.-Apul., *Asclep.*, 40; Apul., *De deo Socratis*, c. 2: "(The planets) quae in deflexo cursu....meatus aeternos divinis vicibus efficiunt."—This subject will be more fully treated in my lectures on "Astrology and Religion" (chaps. IV-V).

77. At Palmyra: De Vogüé, *Inscr. sem.*, pp. 53 ff., etc.—On the first title, see *infra*, n. 80.

78. Note especially *CIL*, VI, 406 = 30758, where Jupiter Dolichenus is called *Aeternus conservator totius poli.* The

relation to heaven here remained apparent. See *Somn. Scip.*, III, 4; IV, 3.

79. Cf. *Rev. archéol.*, 1888, I, pp. 184 ff.; Pauly-Wissowa, s. v. "Aeternus," and *Festschrift für Otto Benndorf*, 1898, p. 291.—The idea of the eternity of the gods also appeared very early in Egypt, but it does not seem that the mysteries of Isis—in which the death of Osiris was commemorated— made it prominent, and it certainly was spread in the Occident only by the sidereal cults.

80. The question has been raised whether the epithet מרא עלמא means "lord of the world" or "lord of eternity" (cf. Lidz- barski, *Ephemeris*, I, 258; II, 297; Lagrange, p. 508), but in our opinion the controversy is to no purpose, since in the spirit of the Syrian priests the two ideas are inseparable and one expression in itself embraces both, the world being con- ceived as eternal (*supra*, n. 76). See for Egypt, Horapoll., *Hieroglyph.*, I (serpent as symbol of the αἰών and κόσμος). At Palmyra, too, the title "lord of all" is found, מרא כל (Lidz- barski, *loc. cit.*); cf. Julian, *Or.*, IV, p. 203, 5 (Hertlein) : ʾΟ βασιλεὺς τῶν ὅλων Ἥλιος, and *infra*, n. 81; n. 87. Already at Babylon the title "lord of the universe" was given to Shamash and Hadad; see Jastrow, *Religion Babyloniens*, I, p. 254, n. 10. Nöldeke has been good enough to write me as follows on this subject: "Daran kan kein Zweifel sein, dass עלם zunächst (lange Zeit) Ewigkeit heisst, und dass die Bedeutung 'Welt' secundär ist. Ich halte es daher für so gut wie gewiss dass das palmyrenische מרא עלמא, wenn es ein alter Name ist, den 'ewigen' Herrn bedeutet, wie ohne Zweifel אל עולם, Gen., xxi. 33. Das biblische Hebräisch kennt die Bedeutung 'Welt' noch nicht, abgesehen wohl von der späten Stelle, Eccl. iii. 11. Und, so viel ich sehe, ist im Palmyrenischen sonst עלמא immer 'Ewigkeit,' z. B. in der häufigen Redensart לבריך שמה לעלמא. Aber das daneben vorkommende palmyr. מרא כל führt aller- dings darauf, dass die palmyrenische Inschrift auch in מרא עלמא den 'Herrn der Welt' sah. Ja der syrische Uebersetzer sieht auch in jenem hebräischen אל עולם 'den Gott der Welt.' Das Syrische hat nämlich einen formalen Unterschied festgestellt zwischen 'ălăm, dem Status absolutus, 'Ewigkeit,' und 'ălmā [ălᵉmā] dem Status emphaticus 'Welt.'—Sollte übrigens die

Bedeutung Welt diesem Worte erst durch Einfluss griechischer Speculation zu Teil geworden sein? In der Zingirli-Inschrift bedeuted בצלם noch bloss 'in seiner Zeit.'"

81. Cf. *CIL*, III, 1090 = Dessau, *Inscr.*, 2998: "Divinarum humanarumque rerum rectori." Compare *ibid.*, 2999 and Cagnet, *Année épigr.*, 1905, No. 235: "I. O. M., id est universitatis principi." Cf. the article of the *Archiv* cited, n. 73. The *Asclepius* says (c. 39), using an astrological term: "Caelestes dii catholicorum dominantur, terreni incolunt singula."

82. Cf. W. Robertson Smith, 75 ff., *passim*. In the Syrian religions as in that of Mithra, the initiates regarded each other as members of the same family, and the phrase "dear brethren" as used by our preachers, was already in use among the votaries of Jupiter Dolichenus (*fratres carissimos*, *CIL*, VI, 406 = 30758).

83. Renan mentioned this fact in his *Apotres*, p. 297 = *Journal Asiatique*, 1859, p. 259. Cf. Jalabert, *Mél. faculté orient. Beyrout*, I, 1906, p. 146.

84. This is the term (*virtutes*) used by the pagans. See the inscription *Numini et virtutibus dei aeterni* as reconstructed in *Revue de Philologie*, 1902, p. 9; *Archiv für Religionsw.*, *loc. cit.*, p. 335, n. 1 and *infra*, ch. VIII, n. 20.

85. *CIL*, VII, 759 = Bücheler, *Carm. epig.*, 24.—Cf. Lucian, *De dea Syria*, 32.

86. Macrobius, *Sat.*, I, 23, § 17: "Nominis (Adad) interpretatio significat unus unus."

87. Cicero, *Somnium Scip.*, c. 4: "Sol dux et princeps et moderator luminum reliquorum, mens mundi et temperatio." Pliny, *H. N.*, II, 6, § 12: "Sol....siderum ipsorum caelique rector. Hunc esse mundi totius animam ac planius mentem, hunc principale naturae regimen ac numen credere decet," etc. Julian of Laodicea, *Cat. codd. astr.*, I, p. 136, l. 1:

Ἥλιος βασιλεὺς καὶ ἡγεμὼν τοῦ σύμπαντος κόσμου καθεστώς, πάντων καθηγούμενος καὶ πάντων ὢν γενεσιάρχης.

88. We are here recapitulating some conclusions of a study on *La théologie solaire du paganisme romain* published in *Mémoires des savants étrangers présentés à l'Acad. des Inscr.*, XII, 2d part, pp. 447 ff., Paris, 1910.

89. The hymns of Synesius (II, 10 ff., IV, 120 ff., etc.) contain peculiar examples of the combination of the old astrological ideas with Christian theology.

VI. PERSIA.

BIBLIOGRAPHY: We shall not attempt here to give a bibliography of the works devoted to Mazdaism. We shall merely refer the reader to that of Lehmann in Chantepie de la Saussaye, *Lehrbuch der Religionsgeschichte*, II, p. 150. We should mention, in the first place, Darmesteter, *Le Zend Avesta*, 1892 ff., with introductions and commentary.—In my *Textes et monuments relatifs aux mystères de Mithra* (2 vols., 1894-1900), I, pp. xx ff., I have furnished a list of the earlier works on this subject; the conclusions of the book have been published separately without the notes, under the title: *Les Mystères de Mithra*, (2d ed., Paris and Brussels, 1902; English translation, Chicago, 1903). See also the article "Mithra" in the *Dictionnaire des antiquités* of Daremberg and Saglio, 1904.—General outlines of certain phases of this religion have been since given by Grill, *Die persische Mysterienreligion und das Christentum*, 1903; Roeses, *Ueber Mithrasdienst*, Stralsund, 1905; G. Wolff, *Ueber Mithrasdienst und Mithreen*, Frankfort, 1909; Reinach, *La morale du mithraïsme* in *Cultes, mythes*, II, 1906, pp. 220 ff.; Dill, *op. cit.*, pp. 594-626; cf. also Bigg, *op. cit.* [p. 321], 1905, p. 46 ff.; Harnack, *Ausbreitung des Christent.*, II, p. 270. Among the learned researches which we cannot enumerate here, the most important is that of Albrecht Dieterich, *Eine Mithrasliturgie*, 1903. He has endeavored with some ingenuity to show that a mystical passage inserted in a magic papyrus preserved at Paris is in reality a fragment of a Mithraic liturgy, but here I share the skepticism of Reitzenstein (*Neue Jahrb. f. das class. Altertum*, 1904, p. 192) and I have given my reasons in *Rev. de l'Instr. publ. en Belg.*, XLVII, 1904, pp. 1 ff. Dieterich answered briefly in *Archiv f. Religionswis.*, VIII, 1905, p. 502, but without convincing me. The author of the passage in question may have been more or less accurate in giving his god the external appearance of Mithra, but he certainly did not know the eschatology of the Persian mysteries. We know, for instance, through positive testimony that they taught the dogma of the passage of the soul through the seven planetary spheres, and that Mithra acted as a guide to his votaries in their ascension to the realm of the blessed. Neither the former nor the latter doctrine, however, is found in the fantastic uranography of the magician. The name of Mithra, as elsewhere that of the magi Zoroaster and Hostanes, helped to circulate an Egyptian forgery., cf. Wendland, *Die hellenistisch-römische Kultur*, 1907, p. 168, n. 1. See on this controversy Wünsch's notes in the 2d ed. of the *Mithrasliturgie*, 1910, pp. 225 ff.—A considerable number of new monuments have been published of late years (the mithreum of Saalburg by Jacobi, etc.). The most important ones are those of the temple of Sidon preserved in the collection of Clercq (De Ridder, *Marbres de la collection de C.*, 1906, pp. 52 ff.) and those of Stockstadt published by Drexel (*Der obergerm. Limes*, XXXIII, Heidelberg, 1910). In the following notes I shall only mention the works or texts which could not be utilized in my earlier researches.

1. Cf. Petr. Patricius, *Excerpta de leg.*, 12 (II, p. 393, de Boor ed.).

2. Cf. Chapot, *Les destinées de l'hellénisme au delà l'Euphrate* (*Mém. soc. antiq. de France*), 1902, pp. 207 ff.

3. Humbert in Daremberg and Saglio, *Dictionnaire*, s. v. "Amici," I, p. 228 (cf. 160). Cf. Friedländer, *Sittengesch.*, I, pp. 202 ff.

4. Cf. *L'Eternité des empereurs romains* (*Rev. d'hist. et de litt. relig.*, I), 1896, p. 442.

5. Friedländer (*loc. cit.*, p. 204) has pointed out several instances where Augustus borrowed from his distant predecessors the custom of keeping a journal of the palace, of educating the children of noble families at court, etc. Certain public institutions were undoubtedly modeled on them; for instance, the organization of the mails (Otto Hirschfeld, *Verwaltungsbeamten*, p. 190, n. 2; Rostovtzev, *Klio*, VI, p. 249 (on *angariae*); cf. Preisigke, *Die Ptolemäische Staatspost* (*Klio*, VII, p. 241), that of the secret police (Friedländer, I, p. 427).—On the Mazdean *Hvareno* who became Τύχη βασιλέως, then *Fortuna Augusti*, cf. *Mon. myst. Mithra*, I, pp. 284 ff.—Even Mommsen (*Röm. Gesch.*, V, p. 343), although pre-

disposed to look for the continuity of the Roman tradition, adds, after setting forth the rules that obtained at the court of the Parthians: "Alle Ordnungen die mit wenigen Abminderungen bei den römischen Caesaren wiederkehren und vielleicht zum Teil von diesen der älteren Grossherrschaft entlehnt sind."—Cf. also *infra,* ch. VIII, n. 19.

6. Friedländer, *loc. cit.,* p. 204; cf. p. 160.

7. Bousset, *Die Religion des Judentums im neutestam. Zeitalter,* 1903 (2d ed. 1906), pp. 453 ff., *passim.*

8. Cf. *Mon. myst. Mithra,* I, pp. 21 ff.

9. Cf. *infra,* ch. VII, pp. 188 ff.

10. *Mon. myst. Mithra,* I, pp. 9 ff., pp. 231 ff.

11. Lactantius, *De mort., persec.,* 21, 2; cf. Seeck, *Gesch. des Untergangs der antiken Welt,* II, pp. 7 ff.

12. Cf. Strzygowski, *Mschatta (Jahrb. preuss. Kunstsammlungen,* XXV), Berlin, 1904, pp. 324 ff., 371 ff.—From a communication made to the Congress of Orientalists at Copenhagen (1908) by Father Lammens, it would appear that the façade of Mschatta is the work of an Omaiyad kalif of Damascus, and Strzygowski's conclusions would, therefore, have to be modified considerably; but the influence of Sassanid art in Syria is nevertheless certain; see Dussaud, *Les Arabes en Syrie avant l'Islam,* 1907, pp. 33, 51 ff.

13. Cf. *infra,* n. 32.

14. Plutarch, *V. Pompei,* 24:

Ξενὰς δὲ θυσίας ἔθυον αὐτοὶ τὰς ἐν Ὀλύμπῳ καὶ τελετάς τινας ἀπορρήτους ἐτέλουν, ὧν ἡ τοῦ Μίθρου καὶ μέχρι δεῦρο διασῴζεται καταδειχθεῖσα πρῶτον ὑπ' ἐκείνων.

15. Lactantius Placidus ad Stat., *Theb.* IV, 717: "Quae sacra primum Persae habuerunt, a Persis Phryges, a Phrygibus Romani."

16. In the *Studia Pontica,* p. 368, I have described a grotto located near Trapezus and formerly dedicated to Mithra, but now transformed into a church. We know of no other Mithreum. A bilingual dedication to Mithra, in Greek and Aramaic, is engraved upon a rock in a wild pass near Farasha (Rhodandos) in Cappadocia. Recently it has been republished

with excellent notes by Henri Grégoire (*Comptes Rendus Acad. des Inscr.*, 1908, pp. 434 ff.), but the commentator has mentioned no trace of a temple. The text says that a strategus from Ariaramneia ἐμάγευσε Μίθρῃ. Perhaps these words must be translated according to a frequent meaning of the aorist, by "became a magus of Mithra" or "began to serve Mithra as a magus." This would lead to the conclusion that the inscription was made on the occasion of an initiation. The magus dignity was originally hereditary in the sacred caste; strangers could acquire it after the cult had assumed the form of mysteries. If the interpretation offered by us is correct the Cappadocian inscription would furnish interesting evidence of that transformation in the Orient. Moreover, we know that Tiridates of Armenia initiated Nero; see *Mon. myst. Mithra*, I, p. 239.

17. Strabo, XI, 14, § 9. On the studs of Cappadocia, cf. Grégoire, *Saints jumeaux et dieux cavaliers*, 1905, pp. 56 ff.

18. Cf. *C. R. Acad. des Inscr.*, 1905, pp. 99 ff. (note on the bilingual inscription of Aghatcha-Kalé); cf. Daremberg-Saglio-Pottier, *Dict. Antiqu.*, s. v., "Satrapa."

19. *Mon. myst. Mithra*, I, p. 10, n. 1. The argument undoubtedly dates back to Carneades, see Boll, *Studien über Claudius Ptolemäus*, 1894, pp. 181 ff.

20. Louis H. Gray (*Archiv für Religionswiss.*, VII, 1904, p. 345) has shown how these six Amshaspands passed from being divinities of the material world to the rank of moral abstractions. From an important text of Plutarch it appears that they already had this quality in Cappadocia; cf. *Mon. myst. Mithra*, II, p. 33, and Philo, *Quod omn. prob. lib.*, 11 (II, 456 M).—On Persian gods worshiped in Cappadocia, see *Mon. myst. Mithra*, I, p. 132.

21. See *supra*, n. 16 and 18.—According to Grégoire, the bilingual inscription of Farasha dates back to the first century, before or after Christ (*loc. cit.*, p. 445).

22. *Mon. myst. Mithra*, I, p. 9, n. 5.

23. Comparison of the type of Jupiter Dolichenus with the bas-reliefs of Boghaz-Keui led Kan (*De Iovis Dolicheni cultu*, Groningen, 1901, pp. 3 ff.) to see an Anatolian god in him.

The comparison of the formula *ubi ferrum nascitur* with the expression ὅπου ὁ σίδηρος τίκτεται, used in connection with the Chalybians, leads to the same conclusion, see *Revue de philologie*, XXVI, 1902, p. 281.—Still, the representations of Jupiter Dolichnus also possess a remarkable resemblance to those of the Babylonian god Ramman; cf. Jeremias in Roscher, *Lexikon der Myth.*, s. v. "Ramman," IV, col. 50 ff.

24. *Rev. archéol.* 1905, I, p. 189. Cf. *supra*, p. 373, n. 68.

25. Herod., I, 131.—On the assimilation of Baalsamin to Ahura-Mazda, cf. *supra*, p. 127, and *infra*, n. 29. At Rome, Jupiter Dolichenus was *conservator totius poli et numen praestantissimum* (*CIL*, VI, 406 = 30758).

26. Inscription of King Antiochus of Commagene (Michel, *Recueil*, No. 735), l. 43:

Πρὸς οὐρανίους Διὸς Ὠρομάσδου θρόνους θεοφιλῆ ψυχὴν προπέμψαν; cf. l. 33: Οὐρανίων ἄγχιστα θρόνων.

27. *Mon. myst. Mithra*, I, p. 87.

28. *Mon. myst. Mithra*, I, p. 333.—An inscription discovered in a mithreum at Dorstadt (Sacidava in Dacia, *CIL*, III, 7728, cf. 7729), furnishes, if I rightly understand, another proof of the relation existing between the Semitic cults and that of the Persian gods. It speaks of a "de[orum?] sacerdos creatus a Pal[myr]enis, do[mo] Macedonia, et adven[tor] huius templi." This rather obscure text becomes clear when compared with Apul., *Metam.*, XI, 26. After the hero had been initiated into the mysteries of Isis in Greece, he was received at Rome in the great temple of the Campus Martius, "fani quidem advena, religionis autem indigena." It appears also that this Macedonian, who was made a priest of their national gods (Bel, Malakbel, etc.) by a colony of Palmyrenians, was received in Dacia by the mystics of Mithra as a member of their religion.

29. At Venasa in Cappadocia, for instance, the people, even during the Christian period, celebrated a panegyric on a mountain, where the celestial Zeus, representing Baalsamin and Ahura-Mazda, was formerly worshiped (Ramsay, *Church in the Roman Empire*, 1894, pp. 142, 457). The identification of Bel with Ahura-Mazda in Cappadocia results from the Aramaic inscription of Jarpuz (Clermont-Ganneau, *Recueil*, III,

p. 59; Lidzbarski, *Ephemeris für semit. Epigraphik,* I, pp. 59 ff.). The Zeus Stratios worshiped upon a high summit near Amasia was in reality Ahura-Mazda, who in turn probably supplanted some local god (*Studia Pontica,* pp. 173 ff.).— Similarly the equation Anahita = Ishtar = Ma or Cybele for the great female divinity is accepted everywhere (*Mon. myst. Mithra,* I, p. 333), and Ma takes the epithet ἀνίκητος like Mithra (*Athen. Mitt.,* XVIII, 1893, p. 415, and XXIX, 1904, p. 169). A temple of this goddess was called ἱερὸν ᾿Αστάρτης in a decree of Anisa (Michel, *Recueil,* No. 536, l. 32).

30. The Mithra "mysteries" are not of Hellenic origin (*Mon. myst. Mithra,* I, p. 239), but their resemblance to those of Greece, which Gruppe insists upon (*Griech. Mythologie,* pp. 1596 ff.) was such that the two were bound to become confused in the Alexandrian period.

31. Harnack (*Ausbreitung des Christentums,* II, p. 271) sees in this exclusion of the Hellenic world a prime cause of the weakness of the Mithra worship in its struggle against Christianity. The mysteries of Mithra met the Greek culture with the culture of Persia, superior in some respects. But if it was capable of attracting the Roman mind by its moral qualities, it was too Asiatic, on the whole, to be accepted without repugnance by the Occidentals. The same was true of Manicheism.

32. *CIL,* III, 4413; cf. *Mon. myst. Mithra,* I, p. 281.

33. Cf. the bibliography at the head of the notes for this chapter.

34. As Plato grew older he believed that he could not explain the evils of this world without admitting the existence of an "evil soul of the world" (Zeller, *Philos. der Griechen,* II⁴, p. 973, p. 981, n. 1). But this late conception, opposed as it is to his entire system, is probably due to the influence of Oriental dualism. It is found in the Epinomis (Zeller, *ibid.,* p. 1042, n. 4), where the influence of "Chaldean" theories is undeniable; cf. Bidez, *Revue de Philologie,* XXIX, 1905, p. 319.

35. Plutarch, *De Iside,* 46 ff.; cf. Zeller, *Philos. der Griechen,* V, p. 188; Eisele, *Zur Demonologie des Plutarch (Archiv für Gesch. der Philos.,* XVII), 1903, p. 283 f.—Cf. *infra,* n. 40.

36. Arnobius, who was indebted to Cornelius Labeo for some exact information on the doctrines of the magi, says (IV, 12, p. 150, 12, Reifferscheid) : "Magi suis in accitionibus memorant antitheos saepius obrepere pro accitis, esse autem hos quosdam materiis ex crassioribus spiritus qui deos se fingant, nesciosque mendaciis et simulationibus ludant." Lactantius, the pupil of Arnobius, used the same word in speaking of Satan that a Mazdean would have used in referring to Ahriman (*Inst. divin.*, II, 9, 13, p. 144, 13, Brandt) : "Nox quam pravo illi antitheo dicimus attributam"; he is the *aemulus Dei.*—Heliodorus who has made use in his *Aethiopica* of data taken from the Mazdean beliefs (see *Monuments relatifs aux mystères de Mithra*, volume I, p. 336, n. 2) uses the Greek word in the same sense, (IV, 7, p. 105, 27, Bekker ed.) : Ἀντίθεός τις ἔοικεν ἐμποδίζειν τὴν πρᾶξιν.—The Ps.-Iamblichus, *De myster.*, III, 31, § 15, likewise speaks of δαίμονες πονηροὺς οὓς δὴ καὶ καλοῦσιν ἀντιθέους. Finally the magical papyri also knew of the existence of these deceiving spirits (Wessely, *Denksch. Akad. Wien*, XLII, p. 42, v. 702 : Πέμψον μοι τὸν ἀληθινὸν Ἀσκληπιὸν δίχα τινὸς ἀντιθέου πλανοδαίμονος).

37. In a passage to which we shall return in note 39, Porphyry (*De Abstin.*, II, 42), speaks of the demons in almost the same terms as Arnobius : Τὸ γὰρ ψεῦδος τούτοις οἰκεῖον· Βούλονται γὰρ εἶναι θεοὶ καὶ ἡ προεστῶσα αὐτῶν δύναμις δοκεῖν θεὸς εἶναι ὁ μέγιστος (cf. c. 41 : Τούτους καὶ τὸν προεστῶτα αὐτῶν) ; likewise Ps.-Iamblichus, *De myst.*, III, 30, 6 : Τὸν μέγαν ἡγεμόνα τῶν δαιμόνων.—In the *De philos. ex orac. haur.* (pp. 147 ff. Wolff), an early work in which he followed other sources than those in *De ̄Abstinentia*, Porphyry made Serapis (= Pluto) the chief of the malevolent demons. There was bound to be a connection between the Egyptian god of the underworld and the Ahriman of the Persians at an early date.—A veiled allusion to this chief of demons may be contained in Lucan, VI, 742 ff., and Plutarch who, in *De Iside*, 46, called Ahriman Hades (*supra*, p. 190; cf. *Mon. myst. Mithra*, II, p. 131, No. 3), says elsewhere (*De latenter viv.*, 6, p. 1130) : Τὸν δὲ τῆς ἐναντίας κύριον μοίρας, εἴτε θεὸς εἴτε δαίμων ἐστίν, ᾅδην ὀνομάζουσιν. Cf. Decharme, *Traditions religieuses chez les Grecs*, 1904, p. 431, n. 1.

38. The dedication *Diis angelis* recently found at Vimina-

cium (*Jahresh. Instituts in Wien,* 1905, Beiblatt, p. 6), in a
country where the Mithra worship had spread considerably
seems to me to refer to this. See Minuc. Felix, *Octav.*, 26:
"Magorum et eloquio et negotio primus Hostanes angelos, id
est ministros et nuntios Dei, eius venerationi novit.assistere."
St. Cypr., "Quod idola dii n. s.," c. 6 (p. 24, 2, Hartel): "Os-
tanes et formam Dei veri negat conspici posse et angelos veros
sedi eius dicit adsistere." Cf. Tertullian, *Apol.*, XXIII: "Magi
habentes invitatorum angelorum et daemonum adsistentem
sibi potestatem;" Arnobius, II, 35 (p. 76, 15, Reifferscheid);
Aug., *Civ. Dei*, X, 9, and the texts collected by Wolff, *Por-
phyrii de philos. ex orac. haurienda*, 1856, pp. 223 ff.; Kroll,
De orac. Chaldaicis, 1894, pp. 53; Roscher, *Die Hebdomaden-
lehre der griech. Philosophen*, Leipsic, 1906, p. 145; Abt, *Apuleius und die Zauberei*, Giessen, 1909, p. 256.

39. Porphyry, *De Abstin.*, II, 37-43, expounds a theory about
the demons, which, he says, he took from "certain Platonists"
(Πλατωνικοί τινες, Numenius and Cronius?). That these
authors, whoever they were, helped themselves freely to the
doctrines of the magi, seems to appear immediately from the
whole of Porphyry's exposition (one could almost give an
endless commentary on it with the help of the Mazdean
books) and in particular from the mention that is made of a
power commanding the spirits of evil (see *supra*, n. 37). This
conclusion is confirmed by a comparison with the passage of
Arnobius cited above (n. 36), who attributes similar theories
to the "magi," and with a chapter of the Ps.-Iamblichus (*De
mysteriis*, III, 31) which develops analogous beliefs as being
those of "Chaldean prophets."—Porphyry also cites a "Chaldean" theologian in connection with the influence of the
demons, *De regressu animae* (Aug., *Civ. Dei*, X, 9).

I conjecture that the source of all this demonology is the
book attributed to Hostanes which we find mentioned in the
second century of our era by Minucius Felix, St. Cyprian
(*supra*, n. 38), etc.; cf. Wolff, *op. cit.*, p. 138; *Mon. myst.
Mithra*, I, p. 33. As a matter of fact it would be false logic
to try to explain the evolution of demonology, which is above
everything else religious, by the development of the philosophic
theories of the Greeks (see for instance the communications
of Messrs. Stock and Glover: *Transactions of the Congress of*

History of Rel., Oxford, 1908, II, pp. 164 ff.). The influence of the popular Hellenic or foreign ideas has always been preponderant here; and the Epinomis, which contains one of the oldest accounts of the theory of demons, as proved *supra*, n. 34, was influenced by the Semitic notions about genii, the ancestors of the *djinns* and the *wélys* of Islam.

If, as we believe, the text of Porphyry really sets forth the theology of the magi, slightly modified by Platonic ideas based on popular beliefs of the Greeks and perhaps of the barbarians, we shall be able to draw interesting conclusions in regard to the mysteries of Mithra. For instance, one of the principles developed is that the gods must not be honored by the sacrifice of animated beings (ἔμψυχα), and that immolation of victims should be reserved for the demons. The same idea is found in Cornelius Labeo, (Aug., *Civ. Dei,* VIII, 13; see Arnobius, VII, 24), and possibly it was the practice of the Mithra cult. Porphyry (II, 36) speaks in this connection of rites and mysteries, but without divulging them, and it is known that in the course of its history Mazdaism passed from the bloody to the bloodless sacrifice (*Mon. myst. Mithra,* I, p. 6).

40. Cf. Plutarch, *De defectu orac.,* 10, p. 415 A:

Ἐμοὶ δὲ δοκοῦσι πλείονας λῦσαι ἀπορίας οἱ τὸ τῶν δαιμόνων γένος ἐν μέσῳ θέντες θεῶν καὶ ἀνθρώπων καὶ τρόπον τινὰ τὴν κοινωνίαν ἡμῶν συνάγον εἰς ταὐτὸ καὶ σύναπτον ἐξεύροντες· εἴτε μάγων τῶν περὶ Ζωροάστρην ὁ λόγος οὗτός ἐστι, εἴτε Θρᾴκιος...

41. Cf. Minucius Felix, 26, § 11: "Hostanes daemonas prodidit terrenos vagos humanitatis inimicos." The pagan idea, that the air was peopled with evil spirits against whom man had to strugle perpetually, persisted among the Christians; cf. Ephes., ii. 2, vi. 12, see also Prudentius, *Hamartigenia,* 514 ff.

42. Cf. Minucius Felix, *loc. cit.*: "Magi non solum sciunt daemonas, sed quidquid miraculi ludunt, per daemonas faciunt," etc. Cf. Aug., *Civ. Dei,* X, 9 and *infra,* ch. VII, n. 76.

43. *Mon. myst. Mithra,* I, pp. 139 ff.

44. Theod. Mopsuest. ap. Photius, *Bibl.* 81. Cf. *Mon. myst. Mithra,* I, p. 8.

45. Cf. Bousset, *Die Religion des Judentums im neutest. Zeitalter,* 1903, pp. 483 ff.

46. Julian, *Caesares,* p. 336 C. The term ἐντολαί is the one also used in the Greek Church for the commandments of the Lord.

47. Cf. *supra,* p. 36.

48. The remark is from Darmesteter, *Zend-Avesta,* II, p. 441.

49. Cf. Reinach, *op. cit.,* [260], pp. 230 ff.

50. Farnell, *Evolution of Religion,* p. 127.

51. Mithra is *sanctus* (*Mon. myst. Mithra,* II, p. 533), like the Syrian gods; cf. *supra,* ch. V, n. 47.

52. *Mon. myst. Mithra,* I, pp. 309 ff. The eschatology of orthodox Mazdaism has been expounded recently by Söderblom, *La vie future d'après le mazdéisme,* Paris, 1901.

53. Cf. *supra,* ch. IV, p. 100, ch. V, p. 126.

54. We have explained this theory above, p. 125. It was foreign to the religion of Zoroaster and was introduced into the mysteries of Mithra with the Chaldean astrology. Moreover, ancient mythological ideas were always mixed with this learned theology. For instance, it was an old Oriental belief that souls, being regarded as material, wore clothing (*Mon. myst. Mithra,* I, p. 15, n. 5; Bousset, *Archiv für Religionswiss.,* IV, 1901, p. 233, n. 2; *Rev. hist. des relig.,* 1899, p. 243, and especially Böklen, *Die Verwandtschaft der jüdisch-christlichen und der parsischen Eschatologie,* Göttingen, 1902, pp. 61 ff. Thence arose the notion prevalent to the end of paganism, that the soul in passing through the planetary spheres, took on the qualities of the stars "like successive tunics." Porphyry, *De abstin.,* I, 31 : 'Αποδυτέον ἄρα τοὺς πολλοὺς ἡμῖν χιτῶνας κ. τ. λ.; Macrobius, *Somnium Sc.,* I, 11, § 12: "In singulis sphaeris aetherea obvolutione vestitur"; I, 12, § 13: "Luminosi corporis amicitur accessu"; Proclus, *In Tim.,* I, 113, 8, Diehl ed. : Περιβάλλεσθαι χιτῶνας; Procl., *Opera,* Cousin ed., p. 222: "Exuendum autem nobis et tunicas quas descendentes induti sumus"; Kroll, *De orac. Chaldaïcis,* p. 51, n. 2: Ψυχὴ ἐσσαμένη νοῦν; Julian, *Or.,* II, p. 123, 22, (Hertlein). Cf. Wendland, *Die hellenistisch-römische Kultur,* p. 168 n. 1. Compare what

Hippolytus, *Philos.*, V, I, says of Isis (Ishtar?) in connection with the Naasenians. She is ἐπτάστολος, because nature also is covered with seven ethereal garments, the seven heavens of the planets; see Ps.-Apul., *Asclepius*, 34 (p. 75, 2 Thomas): "Mundum sensibilem et, quae in eo sunt, omnia a superiore illo mundo quasi ex vestimento esse contecta." I have insisted upon the persistence of this idea, because it may help us to grasp the significance attributed to a detail of the Mithra ritual in connection with which Porphyry relates nothing but contradictory interpretations. The persons initiated into the seven degrees were obliged to put on different costumes. The seven degrees of initiation successively conferred upon the mystic were symbols of the seven planetary spheres, through which the soul ascended after death (*Mon: myst. Mithra*, I, p. 316), the garments assumed by the initiates were probably considered as emblems of those "tunics" which the soul put on when descending into the lower realms and discarded on returning to heaven.

55. Renan, *Marc-Aurèle*, p. 579.

56. Anatole France, *Le mannequin d'osier*, p. 318. Cf. Reinach, *op. cit.* [p. 260], p. 232.

VII. ASTROLOGY AND MAGIC.

BIBLIOGRAPHY: Bouché-Leclercq's book *L'astrologie grecque* (Paris, 1899) makes it unnecessary to refer to the earlier works of Saumaise (*De annis climactericis*, 1648), of Seiffarth (*Beiträge zur Lit. des alten Aegypten*, II, 1883), etc. Most of the facts cited by us are taken from that monumental treatise, unless otherwise stated.—A large number of new texts has been published in the *Catalogus codicum astrologorum Graecorum* (9 vols. ready, Brussels, 1898).—Franz Boll, *Sphaera* (Leipsic, 1903) is important for the history of the Greek and barbarian constellations (see *Rev. archéol.*, 1903, I, p. 437).— De la Ville de Mirmont has furnished notes on *L'astrologie en Gaule au V*ᵉ *siècle* (*Rev. des Etudes anciennes*, 1902, pp. 115 ff.; 1903, pp. 255 ff.; 1906, p. 128). Also in book form, Bordeaux, 1904. The principal results of the latest researches have been outlined to perfection by Boll, *Die Erforschung der* *antiken Astrologie (Neue Jahrb. für das klass. Altert.,* XI), 1908, pp. 104 ff.—For the bibliography of magic, cf. *infra,* notes, 58 ff.

1. Stephan. Byzant. (*Cat. codd. astr.,* II, p. 235), I, 12: Ἐξοχωτάτη καὶ πάσης ἐπιστήμης δέσποινα. Theophil. Edess., *ibid.,* V, 1, p. 184: Ὅτι πασῶν τιμιωτέρα τεχνῶν. Vettius Valens, VI, proem. (*ibid.,* V, 2, p. 34, 7 = p. 241, 19, Kroll ed.): Τίς γὰρ οὐκ ἂν κρίναι ταύτην τὴν θεωρίαν πασῶν προὔχειν καὶ μακαριωτάτην τυγχάνειν.

2. Cf. Louis Havet, *Revue bleue,* Nov., 1905, p. 644.

3. Cf. *supra,* p. 146, p. 123.

4. Kroll, *Aus der Gesch. der Astrol. (Neue Jahrb. für das klass. Altertum,* VII), 1901, pp. 598 ff. Cf. Boll, *Cat. codd. astr.,* VII, p. 130.

5. The argumentation of Posidonius, placed at the beginning of the Tetrabiblos, inspired the defense of astrology, and it has been drawn upon considerably by authors of widely different spirit and tendencies, see Boll, *Studien über Claudius Ptolemäus,* 1894, pp. 133 ff.

6. Suetonius, Tib., 69.

7. Suetonius, *Othon,* 8; cf. *Bouché-Leclercq,* p. 556, n. 4.

8. On these edifices, cf. Maass, *Tagesgötter,* 1902. The form "Septizonia" is preferable to "Septizodia"; cf. Schürer, *Siebentägige Woche* (Extr. *Zeitschr. neutestam. Wissensch.,* VI), 1904, pp. 31, 63.

9. Friedländer, *Sittengesch.,* I, p. 364. It appears that astrology never obtained a hold on the lower classes of the rural population. It has a very insignificant place in the folklore and healing arts of the peasantry.

10. Manilius, IV, 16.—For instance *CIL,* VI, 13782, the epitaph of a Syrian freedman: "L. Caecilius L. l(ibertus) Syrus, natus mense Maio hora noctis VI, die Mercuri, vixit ann. VI dies XXXIII, mortuus est IIII Kal. Iulias hora X, elatus est h(ora) III frequentia maxima." Cf. Bucheler, *Carm. epigr.,* 1536: "Voluit hoc astrum meum."

11. Chapter Περὶ δείπνου: *Cat. codd. astr.,* IV, p. 94. The precept: "Ungues Mercurio, barbam Iove, Cypride crinem,"

ridiculed by Ausonius, VII, 29, p. 108, Piper) is well known. There are many chapters Περὶ ὀνύχων, Περὶ ἱματίων, etc.

12. *Cat. codd. astr.,* V, 1 (Rom.) p. 11, cod. 2, f. 34: Περὶ τοῦ εἰ ἔχει μέγαν ῥῖνα ὁ γεννηθείς. Πότερον πόρνη γένηται ἡ γεννηθεῖσα.

13. Varro, *De re rustica,* I, 37, 2; cf. Pliny, *Hist. nat.,* XVI, 75, § 194. Olympiod, *Comm. in Alcibiad Plat.,* p. 18 (ed. Creuzer, 1821) : Τοὺς ἱερατικῶς ζῶντας ἔστιν ἰδεῖν μὴ ἀποκειρομένους αὐξούσης τῆς σελήνης. This applies to popular superstition rather than to astrology.

14. *CIL,* VI, 27140 = Bücheler, *Carmina epigraph.,* 1163 : "Decepit utrosque | Maxima mendacis fama mathematici."

15. Palchos in the *Cat. codd. astr.,* I, pp. 106-107.

16. Manilius, IV, 386 ff., 866 ff. *passim.*

17. Vettius Valens, V, 12 (*Cat. codd. astr.,* V, 2, p. 32 = p. 239, 8, Kroll ed.) ; cf. V, 9 (*Cat.,* V, 2, p. 31, 20 = p. 222, 11 Kroll ed.).

18. Cf. Steph. Byz., *Cat. codd. astr.,* II, p. 186. He calls both στοχασμὸς ἔντεχνος. The expression is taken up again by Manuel Comnenus (*Cat.,* V, 1, p. 123, 4), and by the Arab Abou-Mashar [Apomasar] (*Cat.,* V, 2, p. 153).

19. The sacerdotal origin of astrology was well known to the ancients; see Manilius, I, 40 ff.

20. Thus in the chapter on the fixed stars which passed down to Theophilus of Edessa and a Byzantine of the ninth century, from a pagan author who wrote at Rome in 379; cf. *Cat. codd. astrol.,* V, 1, pp. 212, 218.—The same observation has been made in the manuscripts of the Cyranides, cf. F. de Mély and Ruelle, *Lapidaires grecs,* II, p. xi. n. 3.—See also *Mon. myst. Mithra,* I, pp. 31 ff.; Boll, *Die Erforsch. der antiken Astrologie,* pp. 110 ff.

21. In Vettius Valens, III, 12 (p. 150, 12 Kroll ed.) and IX, prooem. (p. 329, 20) ; cf. VI, prooem. (p. 241, 16) ; Riess, *Petosiridis et Necheps. fragm.,* fr. 1.

22. Vettius Valens, IV, 11 (*Cat. codd, astr.,* V, 2, p. 86 = p. 172, 31 ff., Kroll ed.), cf. V, 12, (*Cat., ibid.,* p. 32 = p. 238, 18 ff.), VII prooem. (*Cat.,* p. 41 = p. 263, l. 4, Kroll ed. and the note).

23. Firmicus Maternus, II, 30, VIII, prooem. and 5. Cf. Theophilus of Edessa, *Cat.*, V, 1, p. 238, 25; Julian of Laod., *Cat.*, IV, p. 104, 4.

24. *CIL*, V, 5893.—Chaeremon, an Egyptian priest, was also an astrologer.

25. Souter, *Classical Review*, 1897, p. 136; Ramsay, *Cities and Bishoprics of Phrygia*, II, p. 566, 790.

26. On the Stoic theory of sympathy see Bouché-Leclercq, pp. 28 ff., *passim*. A brilliant account will be found in Proclus, *In remp. Plat.*, II, 258 f., Kroll ed. Cf. also Clem. Alex., *Strom.*, VI, 16, p. 143 (p. 504, 21, Stähelin ed.)—Philo attributed it to the Chaldeans (*De migrat. Abrahami*, 32, II, p. 303, 5, Wendland) :

Χαλδαῖοι τῶν ἄλλων ἀνθρώπων ἐκπεπονηκέναι καὶ διαφερόντως δοκοῦσιν ἀστρονομίαν καὶ γενεθλιαλογικήν, τὰ ἐπίγεια τοῖς μετεώροις καὶ τὰ οὐράνια τοῖς ἐπὶ γῆς ἁρμοζόμενοι καὶ ὥσπερ διὰ μουσικῆς λόγων τὴν ἐμμελεστάτην συμφωνίαν τοῦ παντὸς ἐπιδεικνύμενοι τῇ τῶν μερῶν πρὸς ἄλληλα κοινωνίᾳ καὶ συμπαθείᾳ, τόποις μὲν διεζευγμένων, συγγενείᾳ δὲ οὐ διῳκισμένων.

27. Riess in Pauly-Wissowa, *Realenc.*, s. v. "Aberglaube," I, col. 38 f.

29. *Cat.*, V, 1, p. 210, where a number of other examples will be found.

30. See Boll, *Sphaera* (*passim*), and his note on the lists of animals assigned to the planets, in Roscher, *Lexikon Myth.*, s. v. "Planeten," III, col. 2534; cf. *Die Erforsch. der Astrologie*, p. 110, n. 3.

31. *Cat.*, V, 1, pp. 210 ff.

32. Cf. *supra*, ch. V. pp. 128 ff.

33. Cf. *supra*, ch. V, n. 87.

34. On worship of the sky, of the signs of the zodiac, and of the elements, cf. *Mon. myst. Mithra*, I, pp. 85 ff., 98 ff., 108 ff.

35. The magico-religious notion of sanctity, of *mana*, appeared in the idea and notation of time. This has been shown by Hubert in his profound analysis of *La représentation du temps dans la religion et la magie* (*Progr. éc. des Hautes-Etudes*), 1905 = *Mélanges hist. des rel.*, Paris, 1909, p. 190.

36. On the worship of Time see *Mon. myst. Mithra*, I, pp. 20,

74 ff.; of the seasons: *ibid.*, pp. 92 ff. There is no doubt that the veneration of time and its subdivisions (seasons, months, days, etc.) spread through the influence of astrology. Zeno had deified them; see Cicero, *Nat. D.*, II, 63 (= von Arnim, fr. 165): "Astris hod idem (i. e. vim divinam) tribuit, tum annis, mensibus, annorumque mutationibus." In conformity with the materialism of the Stoics these subdivisions of time were conceived by him as bodies (von Arnim, *loc. cit.*, II, fr. 665; cf. Zeller, *Ph. Gr.*, IV, p. 316, p. 221). The later texts have been collected by Drexler in Roscher, *Lexikon*, s. v. "Mên," II, col. 2689. See also Ambrosiaster, *Comm. in epist. Galat.*, IV, 10 (Migne, col. 381 B). Egypt had worshiped the hours, the months, and the propitious and adverse years as gods long before the Occident; see Wiedemann, *loc. cit. (infra*, n. 64) pp. 7 ff.

37. They adorn many astronomical manuscripts, particularly the *Vaticanus gr.* 1291, the archetype of which dates back to the third century of our era; cf. Boll, *Sitzungsb. Akad. München*, 1899, pp. 125 ff., 136 ff.

38. Piper, *Mythologie der christl. Kunst*, 1851, II, pp. 313 f. Cf. *Mon. myst. Mithra*, I, p. 220.

39. Bidez, *Bérose et la grande année* in the *Mélanges Paul Fredericq*, Brussels, 1904, pp. 9 ff.

40. Cf. *supra*, pp. 126, 158 f.

41. When Goethe had made the ascent of the Brocken, in 1784, during splendid weather, he expressed his admiration by writing the following verses from memory, (II, 115): "Quis caelum possit, nisi caeli munere, nosse | Et reperire deum, nisi qui pars ipse deorum est?"; cf. *Brief an Frau von Stein*, No. 518, (Schöll) 1885, quoted by Ellis in *Noctes Manilianae*, p. viii.

42. This idea in the verse of Manilius (n. 41, cf. IV, 910), and which may be found earlier in *Somnium Scipionis* (III, 4; see Macrobius, *Comment.* I, 14, § 16; "Animi societatem cum caelo et sideribus habere communem"; Pseudo-Apul., *Asclepius*, c. 6, c. 9. Firmicus Maternus, *Astrol.*, I, 5, § 10). dates back to Posidonius who made the contemplation of the sky one of the sources of the belief in God (Capelle, *Jahrb.*

für das klass. Altertum, VIII, 1905, p. 534, n. 4), and it is even older than that, for Hipparchus had already admitted a "cognationem cum homine siderum, animasque, nostras partem esse caeli" (Pliny, *Hist. nat.,* II, 26, § 95).

43. Vettius Valens, IX, 8 (*Cat. codd. astr.,* V, 2, p. 123 = p. 346, 20, Kroll ed.), VI, prooem. (*Cat.,* ibid. p. 34, p. 35, 14 = p. 242, 16, 29, Kroll ed.) ; cf. the passages of Philo collected by Cohn, *De opificio mundi,* c. 23, p. 24, and Capelle, *loc. cit.*

44. Manilius, IV, 14.

45. Cf. my article on *L'éternité des empereurs* (*Rev. hist. litt. relig.,* I), 1898, pp. 445 ff.

46. Reitzenstein, to whom belongs the credit of having shown the strength of this astrological fatalism (see *infra,* n. 57), believes that it developed in Egypt, but surely he is wrong. In this connection see the observations of Bousset, *Götting. gel. Anzeigen,* 1905, p. 704.

47. The most important work is unfortunately lost: it was the Περὶ εἱμαρμένης by Diodorus of Tarsus. Photius has left us a summary (*cod.* 223). We possess a treatise on the same subject by Gregory of Nyssa (*P. G.,* XLV, p. 145). They were supported by the Platonist Hierocles (Photius, *cod.* 214, p. 172 b.).—Many attacks on astrology are found in St. Ephraim, *Opera syriaca,* II, pp. 437 ff.; St. Basil (*Hexaem.,* VI, 5), St. Gregory of Nazianzen, St. Methodus (*Symp., P. G.,* XVII, p. 1173) ; later in St. John Chrysostom, Procopus of Gaza, etc. A curious extract from Julian of Halicarnassus has been published by Usener, *Rheinisches Mus.,* LV, 1900, p. 321.—We have spoken briefly of the Latin polemics in the *Revue d'hist. et de litt. relig.,* VIII, 1903, pp. 423 f. A work entitled *De Fato* (Bardenhewer, *Gesch. altchr. Lit.,* I, p. 315) has been attributed to Minucius Felix; Nicetas of Remesiana (about 400) wrote a book *Adversus genethlialogiam* (Gennadius, *Vir. inl.,* c. 22), but the principal adversary of the *mathematici* was St. Augustine (*Civ. Dei,* c. 1 ff.; *Epist.,* 246, ad Lampadium, etc.). See also Wendland, *Die hellenistisch-römische Kultur,* p. 172, n. 2.

48. The influence of the astrological ideas was felt by the Arabian paganism before Mohammed; see *supra,* ch. VIII, n. 57.

49. Dante, *Purg.*, XXX, 109 ff.—In the *Convivio*, II, ch. XIV, Dante expressly professes the doctrine of the influence of the stars over human affairs.—The church succeeded in extirpating the learned astrology of the Latin world almost completely at the beginning of the Middle Ages. We do not know of one astrological treatise, or of one manuscript of the Carlovingian period, but the ancient faith in the power of the stars continued in secret and gained new strength when Europe came in contact with Arabian science.

50. Bouché-Leclercq devotes a chapter to them (pp. 609 ff.).

51. Seneca, *Quaest. Nat.*, II, 35: "Expiationes et procurationes nihil aliud esse quam aegrae mentis solatia. Fata inrevocabiliter ius suum peragunt nec ulla commoventur prece." Cf. Schmidt, *Veteres philosophi quomodo iudicaverint de precibus,* Giessen, 1907, p. 34.—Vettius Valens, V, 9, (*Catal. codd. astr.*, V, 2 p. 30, 11 = p. 220, 28, Kroll ed.), professes that Ἀδύνατόν τινα εὐχαῖς ἢ θυσίαις ἐπινικῆσαι τὴν ἐξ ἀρχῆς καταβολὴν κ. τ. λ., but he seems to contradict himself, IX, 8 (p. 347, 1 ff.).

52. Suetonius, *Tib.*, 69: "Circa deos ac religiones neglegentior, quippe addictus mathematicae, plenusque persuasionis cuncta fato agi." Cf. Manilius, IV.

53. Vettius Valens, IX, 11 (*Cat. codd. astr.*, V, 2, p. 51, 8 ff. = p. 355, 15, Kroll ed.), cf. VI, prooem. (*Cat.*, p. 33 = p. 240, Kroll).

54. "Si tribuunt fata genesis, cur deos oratis?" reads a verse of Commodianus (I, 16, 5). The antinomy between the belief in fatalism and this practice did not prevent the two from existing side by side, cf. *Mon. myst. Mithra*, I, pp. 120, 311; *Revue d'hist. et de litt. relig.*, VIII, 1903, p. 431.—The peripatetic Alexander of Aphrodisias who fought fatalism in his Περὶ εἱμαρμένης, at the beginning of the third century, and who violently attacked the charlatanism and cupidity of the astrologers in another book (*De anima mantissa*, p. 180, 14, Bruns), formulated the contradiction in the popular beliefs of his time (*ibid.*, p. 182, 18):

Ποτὲ μὲν ἄνθρωποι τὸ τῆς εἱμαρμένης ὑμνοῦσιν ὡς ἀναγκαῖον, ποτὲ δὲ οὐ πάντῃ τὴν συνέχειαν αὐτῆς πιστεύουσι σώζειν· καὶ γὰρ οἱ διὰ τῶν λόγων ὑπὲρ αὐτῆς ὡς οὔσης ἀναγκαίας διατεινόμενοι σφόδρα καὶ πάντα ἀνατιθέντες αὐτῇ, ἐν ταῖς κατὰ τὸν βίον πράξεσιν οὐκ ἐοίκασιν αὐτῇ πεπιστευκέναι·

Τύχην γοῦν πολλάκις ἐπιβοῶνται, ἄλλην ὁμολογοῦντες εἶναι ταύτην αἰτίαν τῆς εἱμαρμένης· ἀλλὰ καὶ τοῖς θεοῖς οὐ διαλείπουσιν εὐχόμενοι, ὡς δυναμένου τινὸς ὑπ᾽ αὐτῶν διὰ τὰς εὐχὰς γενέσθαι καὶ παρὰ τὴν εἱμαρμένην·...καὶ μαντείαις οὐκ ὀκνοῦσι χρῆσθαι, ὡς ἐνὸν αὐτοῖς, εἰ προμάθοιεν, φυλάξασθαί τι τῶν εἱμαρμένων.....ἀπιθανώταται γοῦν εἰσιν αὐτῶν αἱ πρὸς τὴν τούτων συμφωνίαν εὑρησιλογίαι. Cf. also De Fato, c. 2 (p. 165, 26 ff. Bruns).

55. Manilius, II, 466: "Quin etiam propriis inter se legibus astra | Conveniunt, ut certa gerant commercia rerum, | Inque vicem praestant visus atque auribus haerent, | Aut odium, foedusque gerunt," etc.— Signs βλέποντα and ἀκούοντα: cf. Bouché-Leclercq, pp. 159 ff.—The planets rejoice (χαίρειν) in their mansions, etc.—Signs φωνήεντα, etc.: cf. Cat., I, pp. 164 ff.; Bouché-Leclercq, pp. 77 ff. The terminology of the driest didactic texts is saturated with mythology.

56. Saint Leo, In Nativ., VII, 3 (Migne, P. L., LIV, col. 218); Firmicus, I, 6, 7; Ambrosiaster, in the Revue d'hist. et litt. relig., VIII, 1903, p. 16.

57. Cf. Reitzenstein, Poimandres, pp. 77 ff., cf. p. 103, where a text of Zosimus attributes this theory to Zoroaster. Wendland, Die hellenistisch-röm. Kultur, 1907, p. 81. This is the meaning of the verse of the Orac. Chaldaïca: Οὐ γὰρ ὑφ᾽ εἱμαρτὴν ἀγέλην πίπτουσι θεουργοί (p. 59 Kroll). According to Arnobius (II, 62, Cornelius Labeo) the magi claimed "deo esse se gnatos nec fati obnoxios legibus."

58. Bibliography. We have no complete book on Greek and Roman magic. Maury, La magie et l'astrologie dans l'antiquité et au moyen âge, 1864, is a mere sketch. The most complete account is Hubert's art. "Magia" in the Dict. des antiquités of Daremberg, Saglio, Pottier. It contains an index of the sources and the earlier bibliography. More recent studies are: Fahz, De poet. Roman. doctrina magica, Giessen, 1903; Audollent, Defixionum tabulae, Paris, 1904; Wünsch, Antikes Zaubergerät aus Pergamon, Berlin, 1905 (important objects found dating back to the third century, A. D.); Abt, Die Apologie des Apuleius und die Zauberei, Giessen, 1908.— The superstition that is not magic, but borders upon it, is the subject of a very important article by Riess, "Aberglaube," in the Realenc. of Pauly-Wissowa. An essay by Kroll, Antiker Aberglaube, Hamburg, 1897, deserves mention.—Cf. Ch. Michel

in the *Revue d'hist. et litt. rel.*, VII, 1902, p. 184. See also *infra*, nn. 64, 65, 72.

59. The question of the principles of magic has recently been the subject of discussions started by the theories of Frazer, *The Golden Bough*, 2d ed., 1900 (cf. Goblet d'Alviella, *Revue de l'univ. de Bruxelles*, Oct. 1903). See Andrew Lang, *Magic and Religion*, London, 1901; Hubert and Mauss, *Esquisse d'une théorie générale de la magie* (*Année sociologique*, VII), 1904, p. 56; cf. *Mélanges hist. des relig.*, Paris, 1909, pp. xvii ff.; Jevons, *Magic*, in the *Transactions of the Congress for the History of Religions*, Oxford, 1908, I, p. 71. Loisy, "Magie science et religion," in *A propos d'hist. des religions*, 1911, p. 166.

60. S. Reinach, *Mythes, cultes et relig.*, II, Intr., p. xv.

61. The infiltration of magic into the liturgy under the Roman empire is shown especially in connection with the ritual of consecration of the idols, by Hock, *Griechische Weihegebräuche*, Würzburg, 1905, p. 66.—Cf. also Kroll, *Archiv für Religionsw.*, VIII, 1905, Beiheft, pp. 27 ff.

62. Friedländer, *Sittengeschichte*, I, pp. 509 f.

63. Arnobius, II, 62, cf. II, 13; Ps.-Iamblichus, *De Myst.*, VIII, 4.

64. Magic in Egypt: Budge, *Egyptian Magic*, London, 1901; Wiedemann, *Magie und Zauberei im alten Aegypten*, Leipsic, 1905 [cf. Maspero, *Rev. critique*, 1905, II, p. 166]; Otto, *Priester und Tempel*, II, p. 224; Griffith, *The Demotic Magical Papyrus of London and Leiden*, 1904 (a remarkable collection dating back to the third century of our era), and the writings analyzed by Capart, *Rev. hist. des relig.*, 1905 (Bulletin of 1904, p. 17), 1906 (Bull. of 1905, p. 92).

65. Fossey, *La magie assyrienne*, Paris, 1902. The earlier bibliography will be found p. 7. See also Hubert in Daremberg, Saglio, Pottier, *Dict. des antiq.*, s. v. "Magia," p. 1505, n. 5. Campbell Thomson, *Semitic Magic, Its Origin and Development*, London, 1908.

Traces of magical conceptions have survived even in the prayers of the orthodox Mohammedans; see the curious observations of Goldziher, *Studien, Theodor Nöldeke gewidmet,* 1906, I, pp. 302 ff. The Assyrio-Chaldean magic may be compared profitably with Hindu magic (Victor Henry, *La Magie dans l'Inde antique,* Paris, 1904).

66. There are many indications that the Chaldean magic spread over the Roman empire, probably as a consequence of the conquests of Trajan and Verus (Apul., *De Magia,* c. 38; Lucian, *Philopseudes,* c. 11; *Necyom.,* c. 6, etc. Cf. Hubert, *loc. cit.*) Those most influential in reviving these studies seem to have been two rather enigmatical personages, Julian the Chaldean, and his son Julian the Theurge, who lived under Marcus Aurelius. The latter was considered the author of the Λόγια Χαλδαϊκά, which in a measure became the Bible of the last neo-Platonists.

67. Apul., *De Magia,* c. 27. The name φιλόσοφος, *philosophus,* was finally applied to all adepts in the occult sciences.

68. The term seems to have been first used by Julian, called the Theurge, and thence to have passed to Porphyry (*Epist. Aneb.,* c. 46; Augustine, *Civ. Dei,* X, 9-10) and to the neo-Platonists.

69. Hubert, article cited, pp. 1494, n. 1; 1499 f.; 1504. Ever since magical papyri were discovered in Egypt, there has been a tendency to exaggerate the influence exercised by that country on the development of magic. It made magic prominent as we have said, but a study of these same papyri proves that elements of very different origin had combined with the native sorcery, which seems to have laid special stress upon the importance of the "barbarian names," because to the Egyptians the name had a reality quite independent of the object denoted by it, and possessed an effective force of its own (*supra,* pp. 93, 95). But that is, after all, only an incidental theory, and it is significant that in speaking of the origin of magic, Pliny (XXX, 7) names the Persians in the first place, and does not even mention the Egyptians.

70. *Mon. myst. Mithra,* I, pp. 230 ff.—Consequently Zoroaster, the undisputed master of the magi, is frequently considered a disciple of the Chaldeans or as himself coming from Babylon. The blending of Persian and Chaldean beliefs appears clearly in Lucian, *Necyom.,* 6 ff.

71. The majority of the magical formulas attributed to Democritus are the work of forgers like Bolos of Mendes (cf. Diels, *Fragmente der Vorsokratiker*, I², pp. 440 f.), but the authorship of this literature could not have been attributed to him, had not these tendencies been so favorable.

72. On Jewish magic see: Blau, *Das altjüdische Zauberwesen*, 1898; cf. Hubert, *loc. cit.*, p. 1505.

73. Pliny, *H. N.*, XXX, 1, § 6; Juvenal, VI, 548 ff. In Pliny's opinion these magicians were especially acquainted with *veneficas artes*. The toxicology of Mithridates goes back to that source (Pliny, XXV, 2, 7). Cf. Horace, *Epod.*, V, 21; Virgil, *Buc.* VIII, 95, etc.

74. Cf. *supra*, pp. 151 ff.

75. Minucius Felix, *Octavius*, 26; cf. *supra*, ch. VI, p. 152.

76. In a passage outlining the Persian demonology (see *supra*, n. 39), Porphyry tells us (*De Abst.*, II, 41):

Τούτους (sc. τοὺς δαίμονας) μάλιστα καὶ τὸν προεστῶτα αὐτῶν (c. 42, ἡ προεστῶσα αὐτῶν δύναμις = Ahriman) ἐκτιμῶσιν οἱ τὰ κακὰ διὰ τῶν γοητειῶν πραττόμενοι κ. τ. λ. Cf. Lactantius, *Divin. Inst.*, II, 14 (I, p. 164, 10, Brandt ed.); Clem. of Alexandria, *Stromat.*, III, p. 46 C, and *supra*, n. 37. The idea that the demons subsisted on the offerings and particularly on the smoke of the sacrifices agrees entirely with the old Persian and Babylonian ideas. See Yasht V, XXI, 94: What "becomes of the libations which the wicked bring to you after sunset?" "The devas receive them," etc.—In the cuneiform tablet of the deluge (see 160 ff.), the gods "smell the good odor and gather above the officiating priest like flies." (Dhorme, *Textes religieux assyro-babyloniens*, 1907, p. 115; cf. Maspero, *Hist. anc. des peuples de l'Orient*, I, p. 681.).

7. Plut., *De Iside*, c. 46.

78. The *druj Nasu* of the Mazdeans; cf. Darmesteter, *Zend-Avesta*, II, p. xi and 146 ff.

79. Cf. Lucan, *Phars.*, VI, 520 ff.

80. Mommsen, *Strafrecht*, pp. 639 ff. There is no doubt that the legislation of Augustus was directed against magic, cf. Dion, LII, 34, 3.—Manilius (II, 108) opposes to astrology the

artes quarum haud permissa facultas. Cf. also Suet., *Aug.,* 31.

81. Zachariah the Scholastic, *Vie de Sévère d'Antioche,* Kugener ed. (*Patrol. orientalis,* II), 1903, pp. 57 ff.

82. Magic at Rome in the fifth century: Wünsch, *Sethianische Verfluchungstafeln aus Rom,* Leipsic, 1898 (magical leads dated from 390 to 420); *Revue hist. litt. relig.,* VIII, 1903, p. 435, and Burchardt, *Die Zeit Constantin's,* 2d ed., 1880, pp. 236 ff.

VIII. THE TRANSFORMATION OF PAGANISM.

BIBLIOGRAPHY: The history of the destruction of paganism is a subject that has tempted many historians. Beugnot (1835), Lasaulx (1854), Schulze (Jena, 1887-1892) have tried it with varying success (see Wissowa, *Religion der Römer,* pp. 84 ff.). But hardly any one has been interested in the reconstruction of the theology of the last pagans, although material is not lacking. The meritorious studies of Gaston Boissier (*La fin du Paganisme,* Paris, 1891) treat especially the literary and moral aspects of that great transformation. Allard (*Julien l'Apostat,* I, 1900, p. 39 ff.) has furnished a summary of the religious evolution during the fourth century.

1. Socrates, *Hist. Eccl.,* IV, 32.

2. It is a notable fact that astrology scarcely penetrated at all into the rural districts (*supra,* ch. VII, n. 9), where the ancient devotions maintained themselves; see the *Vita S. Eligii,* Migne, *P. L.,* XL, col. 1172 f.—In the same way the cult of the menhirs in Gaul persisted in the Middle Ages; see d'Arbois de Jubainville, *Comptes Rendus Acad. Inscr.,* 1906, pp. 146 ff.; S. Reinach, *Mythes, cultes,* III, 1908, pp. 365 ff.

3. Aug., *Civ. Dei,* IV, 21 *et passim.* Arnobius and Lactantius had previously developed this theme.

4. On the use made of mythology during the fourth century, cf. Burckhardt, *Zeit Contantins,* 2d ed., 1880, pp. 145-147; Boissier, *La fin du paganisme,* II, pp. 276 ff. and *passim.*

5. It is well known that the poems of Prudentius (348-410), especially the Peristephanon, contain numerous attacks on paganism and the pagans.

6. Cf. *La polémique de l'Ambrosiaster contre les païens* (*Rev. hist. et litt. relig.*, VIII, 1903, pp. 418 ff.). On the personality of the author (probably the converted Jew Isaac), cf. Souter, *A Study of Ambrosiaster*, Cambridge, 1905 (*Texts and Studies*, VII) and his edition of the *Quaestiones* (Vienna, 1908), intr. p. xxiv.

7. The identity of Firmicus Maternus, the author of *De errore profanarum religionum,* and that of the writer of the eight books *Matheseos* appears to have been definitely established.

8. Maximus was Bishop of Turin about 458-465 A. D. We possess as yet only a very defective edition of the treatises *Contra Paganos* and *Contra Judaeos* (Migne, *Patr. lat.*, LVII, col. 781 ff.).

9. Particularly the *Carmen adversus paganos* written after Eugene's attempt at restoration in 394 A. D. (Riese, *Anthol. lat.*, I, 20) and the *Carmen ad senatorem ad idolorum servitutem conversum*, attributed to St. Cyprian (Hartel. ed., III, p. 302), which is probably contemporaneous with the former.

10. On this point see the judicious reflections of Paul Allard, *Julien l'Apostat*, I, 1900, p. 35.

11. Hera was the goddess of the air after the time of the Stoics ("Ηρα = ἀήρ).

12. Cf. *supra*, pp. 51, 75, 99, 120, 148. Besides the Oriental gods the only ones to retain their authority were those of the Grecian mysteries, Bacchus and Hecate, and even these were transformed by their neighbors.

13. The wife of Praetextatus, after praising his career and talents in his epitaph, adds: "Sed ista parva: tu pius mystes sacris | teletis reperta mentis arcano premis, | divumque numen multiplex doctus colis" (*CIL,* 1779 = Dessau, *Inscr. sel.,* 1259).

14. Pseudo-August. [Ambrosiaster], *Quaest. Vet. et Nov. Test.,* (p. 139, 9-11, Souter ed): "Paganos elementis esse sub-

iectos nulli dubium est....Paganos elementa colere omnibus cognitum est"; cf. 103 (p. 304, 4 Souter ed.): "Solent (pagani) ad elementa confugere dicentes haec se colere quibus gubernaculis regitur vita humana" (cf. *Rev. hist. lit. rel.*, VIII, 1903, p. 426, n. 3).—Maximus of Turin (Migne, *P. L.*, LVII, 783): "Dicunt pagani: nos solem, lunam et stellas et universa elementa colimus et veneramur." Cf. *Mon myst. Mithra*, I, p. 103, n. 4, p. 108.

15. Firmicus Maternus, *Mathes.*, VII prooem: "(Deus) qui ad fabricationem omnium elementorum diversitate composita ex contrariis et repugnantibus cuncta perfecit."

16. *Elementum* is the translation of στοιχεῖον, which has had the same meaning in Greek at least ever since the first century (see Diels, *Elementum*, 1899, pp. 44 ff., and the Septuagint, Sap. Sal., 7, 18; 19, 17. Pfister, *"Die στοιχεῖα τοῦ κόσμου in den Briefen des Paulus," Philologus*, LXIX, 1910, p. 410.—In the fourth century this meaning was generally accepted: Macrobius, *Somn. Scipionis*, I, 12, § 16: "Caeli dico et siderum, aliorumque elementorum"; cf. I, 11, § 7 ff. Martianus Capella, II, 209; Ambrosiaster, *loc. cit.*; Maximus of Turin, *loc. cit.*; Lactantius, II, 13, 2: "Elementa mundi, caelum, solem, terram, mare."—Cf. Diels, *op. cit.*, pp. 78 ff.

17. Cf. *Rev. hist. litt. rel.*, VIII, 1903, pp. 429 ff.—Until the end of the fifth century higher education in the Orient remained in the hands of the pagans. The life of Severus of Antioch, by Zachariah the Scholastic, preserved in a Syrian translation [*supra,* ch. VII, n. 81], is particularly instructive in this regard. The Christians, who were opposed to paganism and astrology, consequently manifested an aversion to the profane sciences in general, and in that way they became responsible to a serious extent for the gradual extinction of the knowledge of the past (cf. *Rev. hist. litt. rel., ibid.*, p. 431; Royer, *L'enseignement d'Ausone à Alcuin*, 1906, p. 130 ff.). But it must be said in their behalf that before them Greek philosophy had taught the vanity of every science that did not have the moral culture of the ego for its purpose, see Geffcken, *Aus der Werdezeit des Christentums*, p. 7, p. 111.

18. *Mon. myst. Mithra*, I, p. 294. Cf. *supra*, pp. 175 f.

19. Ambrosiaster, *Comm. in Epist. Pauli,* p. 58 B: "Dicentes per istos posse ire ad Deum sicut per comites pervenire ad regem" (cf. *Rev. his. lit. rel.,* VIII, 1903, p. 427).—The same idea was set forth by Maximus of Turin (*Adv. pag.,* col. 791) and by Lactantius (*Inst. div.,* II, 16, § 5 ff., p. 168 Brandt); on the celestial court, see also Arnobius, II, 36; Tertullian, *Apol.,* 24.—Zeus bore the name of king, but the Hellenic Olympus was in reality a turbulent republic. The conception of a supreme god, the sovereign of a hierarchical court, seems to have been of Persian origin, and to have been propagated by the magi and the mysteries of Mithra. The inscription of the Nemroud Dagh speaks of Διὸς Ὠρομάσδου θρόνους (*supra,* ch. VI, n. 26), and, in fact, a bas-relief shows Zeus-Oramasdes sitting on a throne, scepter in hand. The Mithra bas-reliefs likewise represent Jupiter Ormuzd on a throne, with the other gods standing around him (*Mon. myst. Mithra,* I, p. 129; II, p. 188, fig. 11); and Hostanes pictured the angels sitting around the throne of God (*supra,* ch. VI, n. 38; see Rev. iv). Moreover, the celestial god was frequently compared, not to a king in general, but to the Great King, and people spoke of his satraps; cf. Pseudo-Arist., Περὶ κόσμου, c. 6, p. 398 *a,* 10 ff. = Apul., *De mundo,* c. 26; Philo, *De opif. mundi,* c. 23, 27 (p. 24, 17; 32, 24, Cohn); Maximus of Turin, X, 9; and Capelle, *Die Schrift von der Welt* (*Neue Jahrb. für das klass. Altert.,* VIII), 1905, p. 556, n. 6. Particularly important is a passage of Celsus (Origen, *Contra Cels.,* VIII, 35) where the relation of this doctrine to the Persian demonology is shown. But the Mazdean conception must have combined, at an early date, with the old Semitic idea that Baal was the lord and master of his votaries (*supra,* p. 94 ff.). In his *Neutestamentliche Zeitgeschichte* (2d. ed., 1906, p. 364 ff.), Holtzmann insists on the fact that the people derived their conception of the kingdom of God from the pattern of the Persian monarchy. See also *supra,* p. 111.

A comparison similar to this one, which is also found among the pagans of the fourth century, is the comparison of heaven with a city (Nectarius in St. Aug., *Epist.,* 103 [Migne, *P. L.,* XXXIII, col. 386]): "Civitatem quam magnus Deus et bene meritae de eo animae habitant," etc. Compare the City of God of St. Augustine and the celestial Jerusalem of the Jews

(Bousset, *Religion des Judentums,* 1903, p. 272).—Cf. also
Manilius, V, 735 ff.

20. August., *Epist.* 16 [48] (Migne, *Pat. Lat.,* XXXIII,
col. 82) : "Equidem unum esse Deum summum sine initio, sine
prole naturae, seu patrem magnum atque magnificum, quis
tam demens, tam mente captus neget esse certissimum? Huius
nos virtutes per mundanum opus diffusas multis vocabulis in-
vocamus, quoniam nomen eius cuncti proprium videlicet ig-
noramus. Nam Deus omnibus religionibus commune nomen
est. Ita fit ut, dum eius quasi quaedam membra carptim
variis supplicationibus prosequimur, totum colere profecto vi-
deamur." And at the end: "Dii te servent, per quos et eorum
atque cunctorum mortalium communem patrem, universi mortales, quos terra sustinet, mille modis concordi discordia, veneramur et colimus." Cf. Lactantius Placidus, *Comm. in Stat.
Theb.,* IV, 516.—Another pagan (*Epist.,* 234 [21], Migne, *P.
L.,* XXXIII, col. 1031) speaks "deorum comitatu vallatus,
Dei utique potestatibus emeritus, id est eius unius et universi
et incomprehensibilis et ineffabilis infatigabilisque Creatoris
impletus virtutibus, quos (*read* quas) ut verum est angelos
dicitis vel quid alterum post Deum vel cum Deo aut a Deo
aut in Deum."

21. The two ideas are contrasted in the *Paneg. ad Constantin.
Aug.,* 313 A. D., c. 26 (p. 212, Bährens ed.) : "Summe rerum
sator, cuius tot nomina sunt quot gentium linguas esse voluisti
(quem enim te ipse dici velis, scire non possumus), sive tute
quaedam vis mensque divina es, quae toto infusa mundo omnibus miscearis elementis et sine ullo extrinsecus accedente
vigoris impulsu per te ipsa movearis, sive alique supra omne
caelum potestas es quae hoc opus tuum ex altiore naturae arce
despicias."—Compare with what we have said of *Jupiter exsuperantissimus* (p. 190).

22. Macrobius, *Sat.,* I, 17 ff.; cf. Firm. Mat., *Err. prof. rel.,*
c. 8; *Mon. myst. Mithra,* I, 338 ff. Some have supposed that
the source of Macrobius's exposition was Iamblichus.

23. Julian had intended to make all the temples centers of
moral instruction (Allard, *Julien l'Apostat,* II, 186 ff.), and
this great idea of his reign was partially realized after his
death. His homilies were little appreciated by the bantering

and frivolous Greeks of Antioch or Alexandria, but they appealed much more to Roman gravity. At Rome the rigorous mysteries of Mithra had paved the way for reform. St. Augustine, *Epist.*, 91 [202] (Migne, *P. L.*, XXXIII, col. 315), c. 408 A. D., relates that moral interpretations of the old myths were told among the pagans during his time: "Illa omnia quae antiquitus de vita deorum moribusque conscripta sunt, longe aliter sunt intelligenda atque interpretanda sapientibus. Ita vero in templis populis congregatis recitari huiuscemodi salubres interpretationes heri et nudiustertius audivimus." See also *Civ. Dei*, II, 6: "Nec nobis nescio quos susurros paucissimorum auribus anhelatos et arcana velut religione traditos iactent (pagani), quibus vitae probitas sanctitasque discatur." Compare the epitaph of Praetextatus (*CIL*, VI, 1779 = Dessau, *Inscr. sel.*, 1259): "Paulina veri et castitatis conscia | dicata templis," etc.—Firmicus Maternus (*Mathes*, II, 30) demands of the astrologer the practice of all virtues, "antistes enim deorum separatus et alienus esse debet a pravis illecebris voluptatum....Itaque purus, castus esto, etc."

24. This is clearly asserted by the verses of the epitaph cited (v. 22 ff) : "Tu me, marite, disciplinarum bono | puram ac pudicam SORTE MORTIS EXIMENS, | in templa ducis ac famulam divis dicas : | Te teste cunctis imbuor mysteriis." Cf. Aug., *Epist.*, 234 (Migne, *P. L.*, XXXIII, col. 1031, letter of a pagan to the bishop,) : "Via est in Deum melior, qua vir bonus, piis, puris iustis, castis, veris dictisque factisque probatus et deorum comitatu vallatus.... ire festinat; via est, inquam, qua purgati antiquorum sacrorum piis praeceptis expiationibusque purissimis et abstemiis observationibus decocti anima et corpore constantes deproperant."—St. Augustine(*Civ. Dei*, VI, 1 and VI, 12) opposes the pagans who assert "deos non propter praesentem vitam coli sed propter aeternam."

25. The variations of this doctrine are set forth in detail by Macrobius, *In Somn. Scip.*, I, 11, § 5 ff. According to some, the soul lived above the sphere of the moon, where the immutable realm of eternity began; according to others, in the spheres of the fixed stars where they placed the Elysian Fields (*supra*, ch. V, n. 65; see Martian, *Capella*, II, 209). The Milky Way in particular was assigned to them as their residence

(Macr., *ib.*, c. 12; cf. Favon. Eulog., *Disput. de somn. Scipionis,*
p. 1, 20 [Holder ed.]: "Bene meritis....lactei circuli lucida
ac candens habitatio deberetur"; St. Jerome, *Ep.,* 23, § 3
[Migne, *P. L.,* XXII, col. 426), in conformity with an old
Pythagorean doctrine (Gundel, *De stellarum appellatione et
relig. Romana,* 1907, p. 153 [245], as well as an Egyptian doctrine (Maspero, *Hist. des peuples de l'Orient,* I, p. 181).—According to others, finally, the soul was freed from all connection with the body and lived in the highest region of heaven,
descending first through the gates of Cancer and Capricorn,
at the intersection of the zodiac and the Milky Way, then
through the spheres of the planets. This theory, which was
that of the mysteries (*supra,* pp. 126, 152) obtained the ap-
probation of Macrobius ("quorum sectae amicior est ratio")
who explains it in detail (I, 12, § 13 ff.). Arnobius, who got
his inspiration from Cornelius Labeo (*supra,* ch. V, n. 64),
opposed it, as a widespread error (II, 16): "Dum ad corpora
labimur et properamus humana ex mundanis circulis, sequun-
tur causae quibus mali simus et pessimi." Cf. also, II, 33:
"Vos, cum primum soluti membrorum abieretis e nodis, alas
vobis adfuturas putatis quibus ad caelum pergere atque ad
sidera volare possitis," etc.). It had become so popular that
the comedy by Querolus, written in Gaul during the first
years of the fifth century, alluded to it in a mocking way, in
connection with the planets (V, 38): "Mortales vero addere
animas sive inferis nullus labor sive superis." It was still
taught, at least in part, by the Priscillianists (Aug., *De
haeres.,* 70; Priscillianus, éd. Schepss., p. 153, 15; cf. Herzog-
Hauck, *Realencycl.,* 3d ed., s. v. "Priscillian," p. 63.—We
have mentioned (*supra,* ch. V, n. 54) the origin of the belief
and of its diffusion under the empire.

26. Cf. *supra,* p. 152, and pp. 189 ff.; *Mon. myst. Mithra,* I,
p. 296.

27. This idea was spread by the Stoics (ἐκπύρωσις) and by
astrology (*supra,* p. 262); also by the Oriental religions, see
Lactantius, *Inst.,* VII, 18, and *Mon. myst. Mithra,* I, p. 310.

28. Gruppe (*Griech. Mythol.,* pp. 1488 ff.) has tried to indicate the different elements that entered into this doctrine.

29. Cf. *supra,* pp. 134 f., p. 160 and *passim.* The similarity

of the pagan theology to Christianity was strongly brought out by Arnobius, II, 13-14.—Likewise in regard to the Orient, de Wilamowitz has recently pointed out the close affinity uniting the theology of Synesius with that of Proclus (*Sitzungsb. Akad. Berlin*, XIV, 1907, pp. 280 ff.) he has also indicated how philosophy then led to Christianity.

30. M. Pichon (*Les derniers écrivains profanes*, Paris, 1906) has recently shown how the eloquence of the panegyrists unconsciously changed from paganism to monotheism. See also Maurice, *Comptes Rendus Acad. Inscriptions*, 1909, p. 165. —The vague deism of Constantine strove to reconcile the opposition of heliolatry and Christianity (Burckhardt, *Die Zeit Constantins*, pp. 353 ff.) and the emperor's letters addressed to Arius and the community of Nicomedia (Migne, *P. G.*, LXXXV, col. 1343 ff.) are, as shown by Loeschke (*Das Syntagma des Gelasius* [Rhein. Mus., LXI], 1906, p. 44), "ein merkwürdiges Produkt theologischen Dilettantismus, aufgebaut auf im wesentlichen pantheistischer Grundlage mit Hilfe weniger christlicher Termini und fast noch weniger christlicher Gedanken." I shall cite a passage in which the influence of the astrological religion is particularly noticeable (col. 1552 D): Ἰδοὺ γὰρ ὁ κόσμος μορφὴ εἴτοιν σχῆμα τυγχάνει ὤν· καὶ οἱ ἀστέρες γε χαρακτῆρας προβέβληνται· καὶ ὅλως τὸ πνεῦμα τοῦ σφαιροειδοῦς τούτου κύκλου, εἶδος τῶν ὄντων τυγχάνει ὄν, καὶ ὥσπερ μόρφωμα· καὶ ὅμως ὁ Θεὸς πανταχοῦ πάρεστι.

INDEX.

A CATALOGUE OF SELECTED DOVER BOOKS
IN ALL FIELDS OF INTEREST

A CATALOGUE OF SELECTED DOVER BOOKS
IN ALL FIELDS OF INTEREST

AMERICA'S OLD MASTERS, James T. Flexner. Four men emerged unexpectedly from provincial 18th century America to leadership in European art: Benjamin West, J. S. Copley, C. R. Peale, Gilbert Stuart. Brilliant coverage of lives and contributions. Revised, 1967 edition. 69 plates. 365pp. of text.
21806-6 Paperbound $3.00

FIRST FLOWERS OF OUR WILDERNESS: AMERICAN PAINTING, THE COLONIAL PERIOD, James T. Flexner. Painters, and regional painting traditions from earliest Colonial times up to the emergence of Copley, West and Peale Sr., Foster, Gustavus Hesselius, Feke, John Smibert and many anonymous painters in the primitive manner. Engaging presentation, with 162 illustrations. xxii + 368pp.
22180-6 Paperbound $3.50

THE LIGHT OF DISTANT SKIES: AMERICAN PAINTING, 1760-1835, James T. Flexner. The great generation of early American painters goes to Europe to learn and to teach: West, Copley, Gilbert Stuart and others. Allston, Trumbull, Morse; also contemporary American painters—primitives, derivatives, academics—who remained in America. 102 illustrations. xiii + 306pp.
22179-2 Paperbound $3.50

A HISTORY OF THE RISE AND PROGRESS OF THE ARTS OF DESIGN IN THE UNITED STATES, William Dunlap. Much the richest mine of information on early American painters, sculptors, architects, engravers, miniaturists, etc. The only source of information for scores of artists, the major primary source for many others. Unabridged reprint of rare original 1834 edition, with new introduction by James T. Flexner, and 394 new illustrations. Edited by Rita Weiss. 6⅝ x 9⅝.
21695-0, 21696-9, 21697-7 Three volumes, Paperbound $15.00

EPOCHS OF CHINESE AND JAPANESE ART, Ernest F. Fenollosa. From primitive Chinese art to the 20th century, thorough history, explanation of every important art period and form, including Japanese woodcuts; main stress on China and Japan, but Tibet, Korea also included. Still unexcelled for its detailed, rich coverage of cultural background, aesthetic elements, diffusion studies, particularly of the historical period. 2nd, 1913 edition. 242 illustrations. lii + 439pp. of text.
20364-6, 20365-4 Two volumes, Paperbound $6.00

THE GENTLE ART OF MAKING ENEMIES, James A. M. Whistler. Greatest wit of his day deflates Oscar Wilde, Ruskin, Swinburne; strikes back at inane critics, exhibitions, art journalism; aesthetics of impressionist revolution in most striking form. Highly readable classic by great painter. Reproduction of edition designed by Whistler. Introduction by Alfred Werner. xxxvi + 334pp.
21875-9 Paperbound $3.00

DESIGN BY ACCIDENT; A BOOK OF "ACCIDENTAL EFFECTS" FOR ARTISTS AND DESIGNERS, James F. O'Brien. Create your own unique, striking, imaginative effects by "controlled accident" interaction of materials: paints and lacquers, oil and water based paints, splatter, crackling materials, shatter, similar items. Everything you do will be different; first book on this limitless art, so useful to both fine artist and commercial artist. Full instructions. 192 plates showing "accidents," 8 in color. viii + 215pp. 8⅜ x 11¼. 21942-9 Paperbound $3.75

THE BOOK OF SIGNS, Rudolf Koch. Famed German type designer draws 493 beautiful symbols: religious, mystical, alchemical, imperial, property marks, runes, etc. Remarkable fusion of traditional and modern. Good for suggestions of timelessness, smartness, modernity. Text. vi + 104pp. 6⅛ x 9¼.
20162-7 Paperbound $1.50

HISTORY OF INDIAN AND INDONESIAN ART, Ananda K. Coomaraswamy. An unabridged republication of one of the finest books by a great scholar in Eastern art. Rich in descriptive material, history, social backgrounds; Sunga reliefs, Rajput paintings, Gupta temples, Burmese frescoes, textiles, jewelry, sculpture, etc. 400 photos. viii + 423pp. 6⅜ x 9¾. 21436-2 Paperbound $5.00

PRIMITIVE ART, Franz Boas. America's foremost anthropologist surveys textiles, ceramics, woodcarving, basketry, metalwork, etc.; patterns, technology, creation of symbols, style origins. All areas of world, but very full on Northwest Coast Indians. More than 350 illustrations of baskets, boxes, totem poles, weapons, etc. 378 pp.
20025-6 Paperbound $3.00

THE GENTLEMAN AND CABINET MAKER'S DIRECTOR, Thomas Chippendale. Full reprint (third edition, 1762) of most influential furniture book of all time, by master cabinetmaker. 200 plates, illustrating chairs, sofas, mirrors, tables, cabinets, plus 24 photographs of surviving pieces. Biographical introduction by N. Bienenstock. vi + 249pp. 9⅞ x 12¾. 21601-2 Paperbound $5.00

AMERICAN ANTIQUE FURNITURE, Edgar G. Miller, Jr. The basic coverage of all American furniture before 1840. Individual chapters cover type of furniture—clocks, tables, sideboards, etc.—chronologically, with inexhaustible wealth of data. More than 2100 photographs, all identified, commented on. Essential to all early American collectors. Introduction by H. E. Keyes. vi + 1106pp. 7⅞ x 10¾.
21599-7, 21600-4 Two volumes, Paperbound $11.00

PENNSYLVANIA DUTCH AMERICAN FOLK ART, Henry J. Kauffman. 279 photos, 28 drawings of tulipware, Fraktur script, painted tinware, toys, flowered furniture, quilts, samplers, hex signs, house interiors, etc. Full descriptive text. Excellent for tourist, rewarding for designer, collector. Map. 146pp. 7⅞ x 10¾.
21205-X Paperbound $3.00

EARLY NEW ENGLAND GRAVESTONE RUBBINGS, Edmund V. Gillon, Jr. 43 photographs, 226 carefully reproduced rubbings show heavily symbolic, sometimes macabre early gravestones, up to early 19th century. Remarkable early American primitive art, occasionally strikingly beautiful; always powerful. Text. xxvi + 207pp. 8⅜ x 11¼. 21380-3 Paperbound $4.00

VISUAL ILLUSIONS: THEIR CAUSES, CHARACTERISTICS, AND APPLICATIONS, Matthew Luckiesh. Thorough description and discussion of optical illusion, geometric and perspective, particularly; size and shape distortions, illusions of color, of motion; natural illusions; use of illusion in art and magic, industry, etc. Most useful today with op art, also for classical art. Scores of effects illustrated. Introduction by William H. Ittleson. 100 illustrations. xxi + 252pp.

21530-X Paperbound $2.00

A HANDBOOK OF ANATOMY FOR ART STUDENTS, Arthur Thomson. Thorough, virtually exhaustive coverage of skeletal structure, musculature, etc. Full text, supplemented by anatomical diagrams and drawings and by photographs of undraped figures. Unique in its comparison of male and female forms, pointing out differences of contour, texture, form. 211 figures, 40 drawings, 86 photographs. xx + 459pp. 5⅜ x 8⅜.

21163-0 Paperbound $3.50

150 MASTERPIECES OF DRAWING, Selected by Anthony Toney. Full page reproductions of drawings from the early 16th to the end of the 18th century, all beautifully reproduced: Rembrandt, Michelangelo, Dürer, Fragonard, Urs, Graf, Wouwerman, many others. First-rate browsing book, model book for artists. xviii + 150pp. 8⅜ x 11¼.

21032-4 Paperbound $2.50

THE LATER WORK OF AUBREY BEARDSLEY, Aubrey Beardsley. Exotic, erotic, ironic masterpieces in full maturity: Comedy Ballet, Venus and Tannhauser, Pierrot, Lysistrata, Rape of the Lock, Savoy material, Ali Baba, Volpone, etc. This material revolutionized the art world, and is still powerful, fresh, brilliant. With *The Early Work,* all Beardsley's finest work. 174 plates, 2 in color. xiv + 176pp. 8⅛ x 11.

21817-1 Paperbound $3.75

DRAWINGS OF REMBRANDT, Rembrandt van Rijn. Complete reproduction of fabulously rare edition by Lippmann and Hofstede de Groot, completely reedited, updated, improved by Prof. Seymour Slive, Fogg Museum. Portraits, Biblical sketches, landscapes, Oriental types, nudes, episodes from classical mythology—All Rembrandt's fertile genius. Also selection of drawings by his pupils and followers. "Stunning volumes," *Saturday Review.* 550 illustrations. lxxviii + 552pp. 9⅛ x 12¼.

21485-0, 21486-9 Two volumes, Paperbound $10.00

THE DISASTERS OF WAR, Francisco Goya. One of the masterpieces of Western civilization—83 etchings that record Goya's shattering, bitter reaction to the Napoleonic war that swept through Spain after the insurrection of 1808 and to war in general. Reprint of the first edition, with three additional plates from Boston's Museum of Fine Arts. All plates facsimile size. Introduction by Philip Hofer, Fogg Museum. v + 97pp. 9⅜ x 8¼.

21872-4 Paperbound $2.50

GRAPHIC WORKS OF ODILON REDON. Largest collection of Redon's graphic works ever assembled: 172 lithographs, 28 etchings and engravings, 9 drawings. These include some of his most famous works. All the plates from *Odilon Redon: oeuvre graphique complet,* plus additional plates. New introduction and caption translations by Alfred Werner. 209 illustrations. xxvii + 209pp. 9⅛ x 12¼.

21966-8 Paperbound $4.50

AMERICAN FOOD AND GAME FISHES, David S. Jordan and Barton W. Evermann. Definitive source of information, detailed and accurate enough to enable the sportsman and nature lover to identify conclusively some 1,000 species and sub-species of North American fish, sought for food or sport. Coverage of range, physiology, habits, life history, food value. Best methods of capture, interest to the angler, advice on bait, fly-fishing, etc. 338 drawings and photographs. l + 574pp. 6⅝ x 9⅜.

22196-2 Paperbound $5.00

THE FROG BOOK, Mary C. Dickerson. Complete with extensive finding keys, over 300 photographs, and an introduction to the general biology of frogs and toads, this is the classic non-technical study of Northeastern and Central species. 58 species; 290 photographs and 16 color plates. xvii + 253pp.

21973-9 Paperbound $4.00

THE MOTH BOOK: A GUIDE TO THE MOTHS OF NORTH AMERICA, William J. Holland. Classical study, eagerly sought after and used for the past 60 years. Clear identification manual to more than 2,000 different moths, largest manual in existence. General information about moths, capturing, mounting, classifying, etc., followed by species by species descriptions. 263 illustrations plus 48 color plates show almost every species, full size. 1968 edition, preface, nomenclature changes by A. E. Brower. xxiv + 479pp. of text. 6½ x 9¼.

21948-8 Paperbound $6.00

THE SEA-BEACH AT EBB-TIDE, Augusta Foote Arnold. Interested amateur can identify hundreds of marine plants and animals on coasts of North America; marine algae; seaweeds; squids; hermit crabs; horse shoe crabs; shrimps; corals; sea anemones; etc. Species descriptions cover: structure; food; reproductive cycle; size; shape; color; habitat; etc. Over 600 drawings. 85 plates. xii + 490pp.

21949-6 Paperbound $4.00

COMMON BIRD SONGS, Donald J. Borror. 33⅓ 12-inch record presents songs of 60 important birds of the eastern United States. A thorough, serious record which provides several examples for each bird, showing different types of song, individual variations, etc. Inestimable identification aid for birdwatcher. 32-page booklet gives text about birds and songs, with illustration for each bird.

21829-5 Record, book, album. Monaural. $3.50

FADS AND FALLACIES IN THE NAME OF SCIENCE, Martin Gardner. Fair, witty appraisal of cranks and quacks of science: Atlantis, Lemuria, hollow earth, flat earth, Velikovsky, orgone energy, Dianetics, flying saucers, Bridey Murphy, food fads, medical fads, perpetual motion, etc. Formerly "In the Name of Science." x + 363pp.

20394-8 Paperbound $3.00

HOAXES, Curtis D. MacDougall. Exhaustive, unbelievably rich account of great hoaxes: Locke's moon hoax, Shakespearean forgeries, sea serpents, Loch Ness monster, Cardiff giant, John Wilkes Booth's mummy, Disumbrationist school of art, dozens more; also journalism, psychology of hoaxing. 54 illustrations. xi + 338pp.

20465-0 Paperbound $3.50

"ESSENTIAL GRAMMAR" SERIES

All you really need to know about modern, colloquial grammar. Many educational shortcuts help you learn faster, understand better. Detailed cognate lists teach you to recognize similarities between English and foreign words and roots—make learning vocabulary easy and interesting. Excellent for independent study or as a supplement to record courses.

ESSENTIAL FRENCH GRAMMAR, Seymour Resnick. 2500-item cognate list. 159pp.
(EBE) 20419-7 Paperbound $1.50

ESSENTIAL GERMAN GRAMMAR, Guy Stern and Everett F. Bleiler. Unusual shortcuts on noun declension, word order, compound verbs. 124pp.
(EBE) 20422-7 Paperbound $1.25

ESSENTIAL ITALIAN GRAMMAR, Olga Ragusa. 111pp.
(EBE) 20779-X Paperbound $1.25

ESSENTIAL JAPANESE GRAMMAR, Everett F. Bleiler. In Romaji transcription; no characters needed. Japanese grammar is regular and simple. 156pp.
21027-8 Paperbound $1.50

ESSENTIAL PORTUGUESE GRAMMAR, Alexander da R. Prista. vi + 114pp.
21650-0 Paperbound $1.35

ESSENTIAL SPANISH GRAMMAR, Seymour Resnick. 2500 word cognate list. 115pp.
(EBE) 20780-3 Paperbound $1.25

ESSENTIAL ENGLISH GRAMMAR, Philip Gucker. Combines best features of modern, functional and traditional approaches. For refresher, class use, home study. x + 177pp.
21649-7 Paperbound $1.75

A PHRASE AND SENTENCE DICTIONARY OF SPOKEN SPANISH. Prepared for U. S. War Department by U. S. linguists. As above, unit is idiom, phrase or sentence rather than word. English-Spanish and Spanish-English sections contain modern equivalents of over 18,000 sentences. Introduction and appendix as above. iv + 513pp.
20495-2 Paperbound $3.50

A PHRASE AND SENTENCE DICTIONARY OF SPOKEN RUSSIAN. Dictionary prepared for U. S. War Department by U. S. linguists. Basic unit is not the word, but the idiom, phrase or sentence. English-Russian and Russian-English sections contain modern equivalents for over 30,000 phrases. Grammatical introduction covers phonetics, writing, syntax. Appendix of word lists for food, numbers, geographical names, etc. vi + 573 pp. 6⅛ x 9¼.
20496-0 Paperbound $5.50

CONVERSATIONAL CHINESE FOR BEGINNERS, Morris Swadesh. Phonetic system, beginner's course in Pai Hua Mandarin Chinese covering most important, most useful speech patterns. Emphasis on modern colloquial usage. Formerly *Chinese in Your Pocket.* xvi + 158pp.
21123-1 Paperbound $1.75

THE PRINCIPLES OF PSYCHOLOGY, William James. The famous long course, complete and unabridged. Stream of thought, time perception, memory, experimental methods—these are only some of the concerns of a work that was years ahead of its time and still valid, interesting, useful. 94 figures. Total of xviii + 1391pp.
20381-6, 20382-4 Two volumes, Paperbound $9.00

THE STRANGE STORY OF THE QUANTUM, Banesh Hoffmann. Non-mathematical but thorough explanation of work of Planck, Einstein, Bohr, Pauli, de Broglie, Schrödinger, Heisenberg, Dirac, Feynman, etc. No technical background needed. "Of books attempting such an account, this is the best," Henry Margenau, Yale. 40-page "Postscript 1959." xii + 285pp. 20518-5 Paperbound $3.00

THE RISE OF THE NEW PHYSICS, A. d'Abro. Most thorough explanation in print of central core of mathematical physics, both classical and modern; from Newton to Dirac and Heisenberg. Both history and exposition; philosophy of science, causality, explanations of higher mathematics, analytical mechanics, electromagnetism, thermodynamics, phase rule, special and general relativity, matrices. No higher mathematics needed to follow exposition, though treatment is elementary to intermediate in level. Recommended to serious student who wishes verbal understanding. 97 illustrations. xvii + 982pp. 20003-5, 20004-3 Two volumes, Paperbound$10.00

GREAT IDEAS OF OPERATIONS RESEARCH, Jagjit Singh. Easily followed non-technical explanation of mathematical tools, aims, results: statistics, linear programming, game theory, queueing theory, Monte Carlo simulation, etc. Uses only elementary mathematics. Many case studies, several analyzed in detail. Clarity, breadth make this excellent for specialist in another field who wishes background. 41 figures. x + 228pp. 21886-4 Paperbound $2.50

GREAT IDEAS OF MODERN MATHEMATICS: THEIR NATURE AND USE, Jagjit Singh. Internationally famous expositor, winner of Unesco's Kalinga Award for science popularization explains verbally such topics as differential equations, matrices, groups, sets, transformations, mathematical logic and other important modern mathematics, as well as use in physics, astrophysics, and similar fields. Superb exposition for layman, scientist in other areas. viii + 312pp.
20587-8 Paperbound $2.75

GREAT IDEAS IN INFORMATION THEORY, LANGUAGE AND CYBERNETICS, Jagjit Singh. The analog and digital computers, how they work, how they are like and unlike the human brain, the men who developed them, their future applications, computer terminology. An essential book for today, even for readers with little math. Some mathematical demonstrations included for more advanced readers. 118 figures. Tables. ix + 338pp. 21694-2 Paperbound $2.50

CHANCE, LUCK AND STATISTICS, Horace C. Levinson. Non-mathematical presentation of fundamentals of probability theory and science of statistics and their applications. Games of chance, betting odds, misuse of statistics, normal and skew distributions, birth rates, stock speculation, insurance. Enlarged edition. Formerly "The Science of Chance." xiii + 357pp. 21007-3 Paperbound $2.50

How to Know the Wild Flowers, Mrs. William Starr Dana. This is the classical book of American wildflowers (of the Eastern and Central United States), used by hundreds of thousands. Covers over 500 species, arranged in extremely easy to use color and season groups. Full descriptions, much plant lore. This Dover edition is the fullest ever compiled, with tables of nomenclature changes. 174 full-page plates by M. Satterlee. xii + 418pp. 20332-8 Paperbound $3.00

Our Plant Friends and Foes, William Atherton DuPuy. History, economic importance, essential botanical information and peculiarities of 25 common forms of plant life are provided in this book in an entertaining and charming style. Covers food plants (potatoes, apples, beans, wheat, almonds, bananas, etc.), flowers (lily, tulip, etc.), trees (pine, oak, elm, etc.), weeds, poisonous mushrooms and vines, gourds, citrus fruits, cotton, the cactus family, and much more. 108 illustrations. xiv + 290pp. 22272-1 Paperbound $2.50

How to Know the Ferns, Frances T. Parsons. Classic survey of Eastern and Central ferns, arranged according to clear, simple identification key. Excellent introduction to greatly neglected nature area. 57 illustrations and 42 plates. xvi + 215pp. 20740-4 Paperbound $2.00

Manual of the Trees of North America, Charles S. Sargent. America's foremost dendrologist provides the definitive coverage of North American trees and tree-like shrubs. 717 species fully described and illustrated: exact distribution, down to township; full botanical description; economic importance; description of subspecies and races; habitat, growth data; similar material. Necessary to every serious student of tree-life. Nomenclature revised to present. Over 100 locating keys. 783 illustrations. lii + 934pp. 20277-1, 20278-X Two volumes, Paperbound $7.00

Our Northern Shrubs, Harriet L. Keeler. Fine non-technical reference work identifying more than 225 important shrubs of Eastern and Central United States and Canada. Full text covering botanical description, habitat, plant lore, is paralleled with 205 full-page photographs of flowering or fruiting plants. Nomenclature revised by Edward G. Voss. One of few works concerned with shrubs. 205 plates, 35 drawings. xxviii + 521pp. 21989-5 Paperbound $3.75

The Mushroom Handbook, Louis C. C. Krieger. Still the best popular handbook: full descriptions of 259 species, cross references to another 200. Extremely thorough text enables you to identify, know all about any mushroom you are likely to meet in eastern and central U. S. A.: habitat, luminescence, poisonous qualities, use, folklore, etc. 32 color plates show over 50 mushrooms, also 126 other illustrations. Finding keys. vii + 560pp. 21861-9 Paperbound $4.50

Handbook of Birds of Eastern North America, Frank M. Chapman. Still much the best single-volume guide to the birds of Eastern and Central United States. Very full coverage of 675 species, with descriptions, life habits, distribution, similar data. All descriptions keyed to two-page color chart. With this single volume the average birdwatcher needs no other books. 1931 revised edition. 195 illustrations. xxxvi + 581pp. 21489-3 Paperbound $5.00

TWO LITTLE SAVAGES; BEING THE ADVENTURES OF TWO BOYS WHO LIVED AS INDIANS AND WHAT THEY LEARNED, Ernest Thompson Seton. Great classic of nature and boyhood provides a vast range of woodlore in most palatable form, a genuinely entertaining story. Two farm boys build a teepee in woods and live in it for a month, working out Indian solutions to living problems, star lore, birds and animals, plants, etc. 293 illustrations. vii + 286pp.

20985-7 Paperbound $2.50

PETER PIPER'S PRACTICAL PRINCIPLES OF PLAIN & PERFECT PRONUNCIATION. Alliterative jingles and tongue-twisters of surprising charm, that made their first appearance in America about 1830. Republished in full with the spirited woodcut illustrations from this earliest American edition. 32pp. 4½ x 6⅜.

22560-7 Paperbound $1.00

SCIENCE EXPERIMENTS AND AMUSEMENTS FOR CHILDREN, Charles Vivian. 73 easy experiments, requiring only materials found at home or easily available, such as candles, coins, steel wool, etc.; illustrate basic phenomena like vacuum, simple chemical reaction, etc. All safe. Modern, well-planned. Formerly *Science Games for Children*. 102 photos, numerous drawings. 96pp. 6⅛ x 9¼.

21856-2 Paperbound $1.25

AN INTRODUCTION TO CHESS MOVES AND TACTICS SIMPLY EXPLAINED, Leonard Barden. Informal intermediate introduction, quite strong in explaining reasons for moves. Covers basic material, tactics, important openings, traps, positional play in middle game, end game. Attempts to isolate patterns and recurrent configurations. Formerly *Chess*. 58 figures. 102pp. (USO) 21210-6 Paperbound $1.25

LASKER'S MANUAL OF CHESS, Dr. Emanuel Lasker. Lasker was not only one of the five great World Champions, he was also one of the ablest expositors, theorists, and analysts. In many ways, his Manual, permeated with his philosophy of battle, filled with keen insights, is one of the greatest works ever written on chess. Filled with analyzed games by the great players. A single-volume library that will profit almost any chess player, beginner or master. 308 diagrams. xli x 349pp.

20640-8 Paperbound $2.75

THE MASTER BOOK OF MATHEMATICAL RECREATIONS, Fred Schuh. In opinion of many the finest work ever prepared on mathematical puzzles, stunts, recreations; exhaustively thorough explanations of mathematics involved, analysis of effects, citation of puzzles and games. Mathematics involved is elementary. Translated by F. Göbel. 194 figures. xxiv + 430pp.

22134-2 Paperbound $4.00

MATHEMATICS, MAGIC AND MYSTERY, Martin Gardner. Puzzle editor for Scientific American explains mathematics behind various mystifying tricks: card tricks, stage "mind reading," coin and match tricks, counting out games, geometric dissections, etc. Probability sets, theory of numbers clearly explained. Also provides more than 400 tricks, guaranteed to work, that you can do. 135 illustrations. xii + 176pp.

20335-2 Paperbound $2.00

EAST O' THE SUN AND WEST O' THE MOON, George W. Dasent. Considered the best of all translations of these Norwegian folk tales, this collection has been enjoyed by generations of children (and folklorists too). Includes True and Untrue, Why the Sea is Salt, East O' the Sun and West O' the Moon, Why the Bear is Stumpy-Tailed, Boots and the Troll, The Cock and the Hen, Rich Peter the Pedlar, and 52 more. The only edition with all 59 tales. 77 illustrations by Erik Werenskiold and Theodor Kittelsen. xv + 418pp. 22521-6 Paperbound $3.50

GOOPS AND HOW TO BE THEM, Gelett Burgess. Classic of tongue-in-cheek humor, masquerading as etiquette book. 87 verses, twice as many cartoons, show mischievous Goops as they demonstrate to children virtues of table manners, neatness, courtesy, etc. Favorite for generations. viii + 88pp. 6½ x 9¼.
22233-0 Paperbound $1.50

ALICE'S ADVENTURES UNDER GROUND, Lewis Carroll. The first version, quite different from the final Alice in Wonderland, printed out by Carroll himself with his own illustrations. Complete facsimile of the "million dollar" manuscript Carroll gave to Alice Liddell in 1864. Introduction by Martin Gardner. viii + 96pp. Title and dedication pages in color. 21482-6 Paperbound $1.25

THE BROWNIES, THEIR BOOK, Palmer Cox. Small as mice, cunning as foxes, exuberant and full of mischief, the Brownies go to the zoo, toy shop, seashore, circus, etc., in 24 verse adventures and 266 illustrations. Long a favorite, since their first appearance in St. Nicholas Magazine. xi + 144pp. 6⅝ x 9¼.
21265-3 Paperbound $1.75

SONGS OF CHILDHOOD, Walter De La Mare. Published (under the pseudonym Walter Ramal) when De La Mare was only 29, this charming collection has long been a favorite children's book. A facsimile of the first edition in paper, the 47 poems capture the simplicity of the nursery rhyme and the ballad, including such lyrics as I Met Eve, Tartary, The Silver Penny. vii + 106pp. (USO) 21972-0 Paperbound $1.25

THE COMPLETE NONSENSE OF EDWARD LEAR, Edward Lear. The finest 19th-century humorist-cartoonist in full: all nonsense limericks, zany alphabets, Owl and Pussycat, songs, nonsense botany, and more than 500 illustrations by Lear himself. Edited by Holbrook Jackson. xxix + 287pp. (USO) 20167-8 Paperbound $2.00

BILLY WHISKERS: THE AUTOBIOGRAPHY OF A GOAT, Frances Trego Montgomery. A favorite of children since the early 20th century, here are the escapades of that rambunctious, irresistible and mischievous goat—Billy Whiskers. Much in the spirit of Peck's Bad Boy, this is a book that children never tire of reading or hearing. All the original familiar illustrations by W. H. Fry are included: 6 color plates, 18 black and white drawings. 159pp. 22345-0 Paperbound $2.00

MOTHER GOOSE MELODIES. Faithful republication of the fabulously rare Munroe and Francis "copyright 1833" Boston edition—the most important Mother Goose collection, usually referred to as the "original." Familiar rhymes plus many rare ones, with wonderful old woodcut illustrations. Edited by E. F. Bleiler. 128pp. 4½ x 6⅜. 22577-1 Paperbound $1.00

THE RED FAIRY BOOK, Andrew Lang. Lang's color fairy books have long been children's favorites. This volume includes Rapunzel, Jack and the Bean-stalk and 35 other stories, familiar and unfamiliar. 4 plates, 93 illustrations x + 367pp.
21673-X Paperbound $2.50

THE BLUE FAIRY BOOK, Andrew Lang. Lang's tales come from all countries and all times. Here are 37 tales from Grimm, the Arabian Nights, Greek Mythology, and other fascinating sources. 8 plates, 130 illustrations. xi + 390pp.
21437-0 Paperbound $2.75

HOUSEHOLD STORIES BY THE BROTHERS GRIMM. Classic English-language edition of the well-known tales — Rumpelstiltskin, Snow White, Hansel and Gretel, The Twelve Brothers, Faithful John, Rapunzel, Tom Thumb (52 stories in all). Translated into simple, straightforward English by Lucy Crane. Ornamented with headpieces, vignettes, elaborate decorative initials and a dozen full-page illustrations by Walter Crane. x + 269pp. 21080-4 Paperbound **$2.00**

THE MERRY ADVENTURES OF ROBIN HOOD, Howard Pyle. The finest modern versions of the traditional ballads and tales about the great English outlaw. Howard Pyle's complete prose version, with every word, every illustration of the first edition. Do not confuse this facsimile of the original (1883) with modern editions that change text or illustrations. 23 plates plus many page decorations. xxii + 296pp.
22043-5 Paperbound $2.75

THE STORY OF KING ARTHUR AND HIS KNIGHTS, Howard Pyle. The finest children's version of the life of King Arthur; brilliantly retold by Pyle, with 48 of his most imaginative illustrations. xviii + 313pp. 6⅛ x 9¼.
21445-1 Paperbound $2.50

THE WONDERFUL WIZARD OF OZ, L. Frank Baum. America's finest children's book in facsimile of first edition with all Denslow illustrations in full color. The edition a child should have. Introduction by Martin Gardner. 23 color plates, scores of drawings. iv + 267pp. 20691-2 Paperbound $3.50

THE MARVELOUS LAND OF OZ, L. Frank Baum. The second Oz book, every bit as imaginative as the Wizard. The hero is a boy named Tip, but the Scarecrow and the Tin Woodman are back, as is the Oz magic. 16 color plates, 120 drawings by John R. Neill. 287pp. 20692-0 Paperbound $2.50

THE MAGICAL MONARCH OF MO, L. Frank Baum. Remarkable adventures in a land even stranger than Oz. The best of Baum's books not in the Oz series. 15 color plates and dozens of drawings by Frank Verbeck. xviii + 237pp.
21892-9 Paperbound $2.25

THE BAD CHILD'S BOOK OF BEASTS, MORE BEASTS FOR WORSE CHILDREN, A MORAL ALPHABET, Hilaire Belloc. Three complete humor classics in one volume. Be kind to the frog, and do not call him names . . . and 28 other whimsical animals. Familiar favorites and some not so well known. Illustrated by Basil Blackwell. 156pp. (USO) 20749-8 Paperbound $1.50

LAST AND FIRST MEN AND STAR MAKER, TWO SCIENCE FICTION NOVELS, Olaf Stapledon. Greatest future histories in science fiction. In the first, human intelligence is the "hero," through strange paths of evolution, interplanetary invasions, incredible technologies, near extinctions and reemergences. Star Maker describes the quest of a band of star rovers for intelligence itself, through time and space: weird inhuman civilizations, crustacean minds, symbiotic worlds, etc. Complete, unabridged. v + 438pp. (USO) 21962-3 Paperbound $3.00

THREE PROPHETIC NOVELS, H. G. WELLS. Stages of a consistently planned future for mankind. *When the Sleeper Wakes,* and *A Story of the Days to Come,* anticipate *Brave New World* and *1984,* in the 21st Century; *The Time Machine,* only complete version in print, shows farther future and the end of mankind. All show Wells's greatest gifts as storyteller and novelist. Edited by E. F. Bleiler. x + 335pp. (USO) 20605-X Paperbound $3.00

THE DEVIL'S DICTIONARY, Ambrose Bierce. America's own Oscar Wilde— Ambrose Bierce—offers his barbed iconoclastic wisdom in over 1,000 definitions hailed by H. L. Mencken as "some of the most gorgeous witticisms in the English language." 145pp. 20487-1 Paperbound $1.50

MAX AND MORITZ, Wilhelm Busch. Great children's classic, father of comic strip, of two bad boys, Max and Moritz. Also Ker and Plunk (Plisch und Plumm), Cat and Mouse, Deceitful Henry, Ice-Peter, The Boy and the Pipe, and five other pieces. Original German, with English translation. Edited by H. Arthur Klein; translations by various hands and H. Arthur Klein. vi + 216pp. 20181-3 Paperbound $2.00

PIGS IS PIGS AND OTHER FAVORITES, Ellis Parker Butler. The title story is one of the best humor short stories, as Mike Flannery obfuscates biology and English. Also included, That Pup of Murchison's, The Great American Pie Company, and Perkins of Portland. 14 illustrations. v + 109pp. 21532-6 Paperbound $1.50

THE PETERKIN PAPERS, Lucretia P. Hale. It takes genius to be as stupidly mad as the Peterkins, as they decide to become wise, celebrate the "Fourth," keep a cow, and otherwise strain the resources of the Lady from Philadelphia. Basic book of American humor. 153 illustrations. 219pp. 20794-3 Paperbound $2.00

PERRAULT'S FAIRY TALES, translated by A. E. Johnson and S. R. Littlewood, with 34 full-page illustrations by Gustave Doré. All the original Perrault stories— Cinderella, Sleeping Beauty, Bluebeard, Little Red Riding Hood, Puss in Boots, Tom Thumb, etc.—with their witty verse morals and the magnificent illustrations of Doré. One of the five or six great books of European fairy tales. viii + 117pp. 8⅛ x 11. 22311-6 Paperbound $2.00

OLD HUNGARIAN FAIRY TALES, Baroness Orczy. Favorites translated and adapted by author of the *Scarlet Pimpernel.* Eight fairy tales include "The Suitors of Princess Fire-Fly," "The Twin Hunchbacks," "Mr. Cuttlefish's Love Story," and "The Enchanted Cat." This little volume of magic and adventure will captivate children as it has for generations. 90 drawings by Montagu Barstow. 96pp. (USO) 22293-4 Paperbound $1.95

POEMS OF ANNE BRADSTREET, edited with an introduction by Robert Hutchinson. A new selection of poems by America's first poet and perhaps the first significant woman poet in the English language. 48 poems display her development in works of considerable variety—love poems, domestic poems, religious meditations, formal elegies, "quaternions," etc. Notes, bibliography. viii + 222pp.

22160-1 Paperbound $2.50

THREE GOTHIC NOVELS: THE CASTLE OF OTRANTO BY HORACE WALPOLE; VATHEK BY WILLIAM BECKFORD; THE VAMPYRE BY JOHN POLIDORI, WITH FRAGMENT OF A NOVEL BY LORD BYRON, edited by E. F. Bleiler. The first Gothic novel, by Walpole; the finest Oriental tale in English, by Beckford; powerful Romantic supernatural story in versions by Polidori and Byron. All extremely important in history of literature; all still exciting, packed with supernatural thrills, ghosts, haunted castles, magic, etc. xl + 291pp.

21232-7 Paperbound $3.00

THE BEST TALES OF HOFFMANN, E. T. A. Hoffmann. 10 of Hoffmann's most important stories, in modern re-editings of standard translations: Nutcracker and the King of Mice, Signor Formica, Automata, The Sandman, Rath Krespel, The Golden Flowerpot, Master Martin the Cooper, The Mines of Falun, The King's Betrothed, A New Year's Eve Adventure. 7 illustrations by Hoffmann. Edited by E. F. Bleiler. xxxix + 419pp.

21793-0 Paperbound $3.00

GHOST AND HORROR STORIES OF AMBROSE BIERCE, Ambrose Bierce. 23 strikingly modern stories of the horrors latent in the human mind: The Eyes of the Panther, The Damned Thing, An Occurrence at Owl Creek Bridge, An Inhabitant of Carcosa, etc., plus the dream-essay, Visions of the Night. Edited by E. F. Bleiler. xxii + 199pp.

20767-6 Paperbound $2.00

BEST GHOST STORIES OF J. S. LeFANU, J. Sheridan LeFanu. Finest stories by Victorian master often considered greatest supernatural writer of all. Carmilla, Green Tea, The Haunted Baronet, The Familiar, and 12 others. Most never before available in the U. S. A. Edited by E. F. Bleiler. 8 illustrations from Victorian publications. xvii + 467pp.

20415-4 Paperbound $3.00

MATHEMATICAL FOUNDATIONS OF INFORMATION THEORY, A. I. Khinchin. Comprehensive introduction to work of Shannon, McMillan, Feinstein and Khinchin, placing these investigations on a rigorous mathematical basis. Covers entropy concept in probability theory, uniqueness theorem, Shannon's inequality, ergodic sources, the E property, martingale concept, noise, Feinstein's fundamental lemma, Shanon's first and second theorems. Translated by R. A. Silverman and M. D. Friedman. iii + 120pp.

60434-9 Paperbound $2.00

SEVEN SCIENCE FICTION NOVELS, H. G. Wells. The standard collection of the great novels. Complete, unabridged. *First Men in the Moon, Island of Dr. Moreau, War of the Worlds, Food of the Gods, Invisible Man, Time Machine, In the Days of the Comet.* Not only science fiction fans, but every educated person owes it to himself to read these novels. 1015pp. (USO) 20264-X Clothbound $6.00

JOHANN SEBASTIAN BACH, Philipp Spitta. One of the great classics of musicology, this definitive analysis of Bach's music (and life) has never been surpassed. Lucid, nontechnical analyses of hundreds of pieces (30 pages devoted to St. Matthew Passion, 26 to B Minor Mass). Also includes major analysis of 18th-century music. 450 musical examples. 40-page musical supplement. Total of xx + 1799pp.
(EUK) 22278-0, 22279-9 Two volumes, Clothbound $25.00

MOZART AND HIS PIANO CONCERTOS, Cuthbert Girdlestone. The only full-length study of an important area of Mozart's creativity. Provides detailed analyses of all 23 concertos, traces inspirational sources. 417 musical examples. Second edition. 509pp.
21271-8 Paperbound $4.50

THE PERFECT WAGNERITE: A COMMENTARY ON THE NIBLUNG'S RING, George Bernard Shaw. Brilliant and still relevant criticism in remarkable essays on Wagner's Ring cycle, Shaw's ideas on political and social ideology behind the plots, role of Leitmotifs, vocal requisites, etc. Prefaces. xxi + 136pp.
(USO) 21707-8 Paperbound $1.75

DON GIOVANNI, W. A. Mozart. Complete libretto, modern English translation; biographies of composer and librettist; accounts of early performances and critical reaction. Lavishly illustrated. All the material you need to understand and appreciate this great work. Dover Opera Guide and Libretto Series; translated and introduced by Ellen Bleiler. 92 illustrations. 209pp.
21134-7 Paperbound $2.00

BASIC ELECTRICITY, U. S. Bureau of Naval Personel. Originally a training course, best non-technical coverage of basic theory of electricity and its applications. Fundamental concepts, batteries, circuits, conductors and wiring techniques, AC and DC, inductance and capacitance, generators, motors, transformers, magnetic amplifiers, synchros, servomechanisms, etc. Also covers blue-prints, electrical diagrams, etc. Many questions, with answers. 349 illustrations. x + 448pp. $6\frac{1}{2}$ x $9\frac{1}{4}$.
20973-3 Paperbound $3.50

REPRODUCTION OF SOUND, Edgar Villchur. Thorough coverage for laymen of high fidelity systems, reproducing systems in general, needles, amplifiers, preamps, loudspeakers, feedback, explaining physical background. "A rare talent for making technicalities vividly comprehensible," R. Darrell, *High Fidelity*. 69 figures. iv + 92pp.
21515-6 Paperbound $1.35

HEAR ME TALKIN' TO YA: THE STORY OF JAZZ AS TOLD BY THE MEN WHO MADE IT, Nat Shapiro and Nat Hentoff. Louis Armstrong, Fats Waller, Jo Jones, Clarence Williams, Billy Holiday, Duke Ellington, Jelly Roll Morton and dozens of other jazz greats tell how it was in Chicago's South Side, New Orleans, depression Harlem and the modern West Coast as jazz was born and grew. xvi + 429pp.
21726-4 Paperbound $3.95

FABLES OF AESOP, translated by Sir Roger L'Estrange. A reproduction of the very rare 1931 Paris edition; a selection of the most interesting fables, together with 50 imaginative drawings by Alexander Calder. v + 128pp. $6\frac{1}{2}$x$9\frac{1}{4}$.
21780-9 Paperbound $1.50

AGAINST THE GRAIN (A REBOURS), Joris K. Huysmans. Filled with weird images, evidences of a bizarre imagination, exotic experiments with hallucinatory drugs, rich tastes and smells and the diversions of its sybarite hero Duc Jean des Esseintes, this classic novel pushed 19th-century literary decadence to its limits. Full unabridged edition. Do not confuse this with abridged editions generally sold. Introduction by Havelock Ellis. xlix + 206pp. 22190-3 Paperbound $2.50

VARIORUM SHAKESPEARE: HAMLET. Edited by Horace H. Furness; a landmark of American scholarship. Exhaustive footnotes and appendices treat all doubtful words and phrases, as well as suggested critical emendations throughout the play's history. First volume contains editor's own text, collated with all Quartos and Folios. Second volume contains full first Quarto, translations of Shakespeare's sources (Belleforest, and Saxo Grammaticus), Der Bestrafte Brudermord, and many essays on critical and historical points of interest by major authorities of past and present. Includes details of staging and costuming over the years. By far the best edition available for serious students of Shakespeare. Total of xx + 905pp. 21004-9, 21005-7, 2 volumes, Paperbound $7.00

A LIFE OF WILLIAM SHAKESPEARE, Sir Sidney Lee. This is the standard life of Shakespeare, summarizing everything known about Shakespeare and his plays. Incredibly rich in material, broad in coverage, clear and judicious, it has served thousands as the best introduction to Shakespeare. 1931 edition. 9 plates. xxix + 792pp. 21967-4 Paperbound $4.50

MASTERS OF THE DRAMA, John Gassner. Most comprehensive history of the drama in print, covering every tradition from Greeks to modern Europe and America, including India, Far East, etc. Covers more than 800 dramatists, 2000 plays, with biographical material, plot summaries, theatre history, criticism, etc. "Best of its kind in English," New Republic. 77 illustrations. xxii + 890pp. 20100-7 Clothbound $10.00

THE EVOLUTION OF THE ENGLISH LANGUAGE, George McKnight. The growth of English, from the 14th century to the present. Unusual, non-technical account presents basic information in very interesting form: sound shifts, change in grammar and syntax, vocabulary growth, similar topics. Abundantly illustrated with quotations. Formerly Modern English in the Making. xii + 590pp. 21932-1 Paperbound $3.50

AN ETYMOLOGICAL DICTIONARY OF MODERN ENGLISH, Ernest Weekley. Fullest, richest work of its sort, by foremost British lexicographer. Detailed word histories, including many colloquial and archaic words; extensive quotations. Do not confuse this with the Concise Etymological Dictionary, which is much abridged. Total of xxvii + 830pp. 6½ x 9¼. 21873-2, 21874-0 Two volumes, Paperbound $7.90

FLATLAND: A ROMANCE OF MANY DIMENSIONS, E. A. Abbott. Classic of science-fiction explores ramifications of life in a two-dimensional world, and what happens when a three-dimensional being intrudes. Amusing reading, but also useful as introduction to thought about hyperspace. Introduction by Banesh Hoffmann. 16 illustrations. xx + 103pp. 20001-9 Paperbound $1.00

THE ARCHITECTURE OF COUNTRY HOUSES, Andrew J. Downing. Together with Vaux's *Villas and Cottages* this is the basic book for Hudson River Gothic architecture of the middle Victorian period. Full, sound discussions of general aspects of housing, architecture, style, decoration, furnishing, together with scores of detailed house plans, illustrations of specific buildings, accompanied by full text. Perhaps the most influential single American architectural book. 1850 edition. Introduction by J. Stewart Johnson. 321 figures, 34 architectural designs. xvi + 560pp.
22003-6 Paperbound $5.00

LOST EXAMPLES OF COLONIAL ARCHITECTURE, John Mead Howells. Full-page photographs of buildings that have disappeared or been so altered as to be denatured, including many designed by major early American architects. 245 plates. xvii + 248pp. 7⅞ x 10¾. 21143-6 Paperbound $3.50

DOMESTIC ARCHITECTURE OF THE AMERICAN COLONIES AND OF THE EARLY REPUBLIC, Fiske Kimball. Foremost architect and restorer of Williamsburg and Monticello covers nearly 200 homes between 1620-1825. Architectural details, construction, style features, special fixtures, floor plans, etc. Generally considered finest work in its area. 219 illustrations of houses, doorways, windows, capital mantels. xx + 314pp. 7⅞ x 10¾. 21743-4 Paperbound $4.00

EARLY AMERICAN ROOMS: 1650-1858, edited by Russell Hawes Kettell. Tour of 12 rooms, each representative of a different era in American history and each furnished, decorated, designed and occupied in the style of the era. 72 plans and elevations, 8-page color section, etc., show fabrics, wall papers, arrangements, etc. Full descriptive text. xvii + 200pp. of text. 8⅜ x 11¼.
21633-0 Paperbound $5.00

THE FITZWILLIAM VIRGINAL BOOK, edited by J. Fuller Maitland and W. B. Squire. Full modern printing of famous early 17th-century ms. volume of 300 works by Morley, Byrd, Bull, Gibbons, etc. For piano or other modern keyboard instrument; easy to read format. xxxvi + 938pp. 8⅜ x 11.
21068-5, 21069-3 Two volumes, Paperbound $12.00

KEYBOARD MUSIC, Johann Sebastian Bach. Bach Gesellschaft edition. A rich selection of Bach's masterpieces for the harpsichord: the six English Suites, six French Suites, the six Partitas (Clavierübung part I), the Goldberg Variations (Clavierübung part IV), the fifteen Two-Part Inventions and the fifteen Three-Part Sinfonias. Clearly reproduced on large sheets with ample margins; eminently playable. vi + 312pp. 8⅛ x 11. 22360-4 Paperbound $5.00

THE MUSIC OF BACH: AN INTRODUCTION, Charles Sanford Terry. A fine, nontechnical introduction to Bach's music, both instrumental and vocal. Covers organ music, chamber music, passion music, other types. Analyzes themes, developments, innovations. x + 114pp. 21075-8 Paperbound $1.95

BEETHOVEN AND HIS NINE SYMPHONIES, Sir George Grove. Noted British musicologist provides best history, analysis, commentary on symphonies. Very thorough, rigorously accurate; necessary to both advanced student and amateur music lover. 436 musical passages. vii + 407 pp. 20334-4 Paperbound $4.00

ALPHABETS AND ORNAMENTS, Ernst Lehner. Well-known pictorial source for decorative alphabets, script examples, cartouches, frames, decorative title pages, calligraphic initials, borders, similar material. 14th to 19th century, mostly European. Useful in almost any graphic arts designing, varied styles. 750 illustrations. 256pp. 7 x 10. 21905-4 Paperbound $4.00

PAINTING: A CREATIVE APPROACH, Norman Colquhoun. For the beginner simple guide provides an instructive approach to painting: major stumbling blocks for beginner; overcoming them, technical points; paints and pigments; oil painting; watercolor and other media and color. New section on "plastic" paints. Glossary. Formerly *Paint Your Own Pictures.* 221pp. 22000-1 Paperbound $1.75

THE ENJOYMENT AND USE OF COLOR, Walter Sargent. Explanation of the relations between colors themselves and between colors in nature and art, including hundreds of little-known facts about color values, intensities, effects of high and low illumination, complementary colors. Many practical hints for painters, references to great masters. 7 color plates, 29 illustrations. x + 274pp. 20944-X Paperbound $3.00

THE NOTEBOOKS OF LEONARDO DA VINCI, compiled and edited by Jean Paul Richter. 1566 extracts from original manuscripts reveal the full range of Leonardo's versatile genius: all his writings on painting, sculpture, architecture, anatomy, astronomy, geography, topography, physiology, mining, music, etc., in both Italian and English, with 186 plates of manuscript pages and more than 500 additional drawings. Includes studies for the Last Supper, the lost Sforza monument, and other works. Total of xlvii + 866pp. 7⅞ x 10¾. 22572-0, 22573-9 Two volumes, Paperbound $12.00

MONTGOMERY WARD CATALOGUE OF 1895. Tea gowns, yards of flannel and pillow-case lace, stereoscopes, books of gospel hymns, the New Improved Singer Sewing Machine, side saddles, milk skimmers, straight-edged razors, high-button shoes, spittoons, and on and on . . . listing some 25,000 items, practically all illustrated. Essential to the shoppers of the 1890's, it is our truest record of the spirit of the period. Unaltered reprint of Issue No. 57, Spring and Summer 1895. Introduction by Boris Emmet. Innumerable illustrations. xiii + 624pp. 8½ x 11⅝. 22377-9 Paperbound $8.50

THE CRYSTAL PALACE EXHIBITION ILLUSTRATED CATALOGUE (LONDON, 1851). One of the wonders of the modern world—the Crystal Palace Exhibition in which all the nations of the civilized world exhibited their achievements in the arts and sciences—presented in an equally important illustrated catalogue. More than 1700 items pictured with accompanying text—ceramics, textiles, cast-iron work, carpets, pianos, sleds, razors, wall-papers, billiard tables, beehives, silverware and hundreds of other artifacts—represent the focal point of Victorian culture in the Western World. Probably the largest collection of Victorian decorative art ever assembled— indispensable for antiquarians and designers. Unabridged republication of the Art-Journal Catalogue of the Great Exhibition of 1851, with all terminal essays. New introduction by John Gloag, F.S.A. xxxiv + 426pp. 9 x 12. 22503-8 Paperbound $5.00

A HISTORY OF COSTUME, Carl Köhler. Definitive history, based on surviving pieces of clothing primarily, and paintings, statues, etc. secondarily. Highly readable text, supplemented by 594 illustrations of costumes of the ancient Mediterranean peoples, Greece and Rome, the Teutonic prehistoric period; costumes of the Middle Ages, Renaissance, Baroque, 18th and 19th centuries. Clear, measured patterns are provided for many clothing articles. Approach is practical throughout. Enlarged by Emma von Sichart. 464pp. 21030-8 Paperbound $3.50

ORIENTAL RUGS, ANTIQUE AND MODERN, Walter A. Hawley. A complete and authoritative treatise on the Oriental rug—where they are made, by whom and how, designs and symbols, characteristics in detail of the six major groups, how to distinguish them and how to buy them. Detailed technical data is provided on periods, weaves, warps, wefts, textures, sides, ends and knots, although no technical background is required for an understanding. 11 color plates, 80 halftones, 4 maps. vi + 320pp. 6⅛ x 9⅛. 22366-3 Paperbound $5.00

TEN BOOKS ON ARCHITECTURE, Vitruvius. By any standards the most important book on architecture ever written. Early Roman discussion of aesthetics of building, construction methods, orders, sites, and every other aspect of architecture has inspired, instructed architecture for about 2,000 years. Stands behind Palladio, Michelangelo, Bramante, Wren, countless others. Definitive Morris H. Morgan translation. 68 illustrations. xii + 331pp. 20645-9 Paperbound . $3.00

THE FOUR BOOKS OF ARCHITECTURE, Andrea Palladio. Translated into every major Western European language in the two centuries following its publication in 1570, this has been one of the most influential books in the history of architecture. Complete reprint of the 1738 Isaac Ware edition. New introduction by Adolf Placzek, Columbia Univ. 216 plates. xxii + 110pp. of text. 9½ x 12¾. 21308-0 Clothbound $12.50

STICKS AND STONES: A STUDY OF AMERICAN ARCHITECTURE AND CIVILIZATION, Lewis Mumford.One of the great classics of American cultural history. American architecture from the medieval-inspired earliest forms to the early 20th century; evolution of structure and style, and reciprocal influences on environment. 21 photographic illustrations. 238pp. 20202-X Paperbound $2.00

THE AMERICAN BUILDER'S COMPANION, Asher Benjamin. The most widely used early 19th century architectural style and source book, for colonial up into Greek Revival periods. Extensive development of geometry of carpentering, construction of sashes, frames, doors, stairs; plans and elevations of domestic and other buildings. Hundreds of thousands of houses were built according to this book, now invaluable to historians, architects, restorers, etc. 1827 edition. 59 plates. 114pp. 7⅞ x 10¾. 22236-5 Paperbound $4.00

DUTCH HOUSES IN THE HUDSON VALLEY BEFORE 1776, Helen Wilkinson Reynolds. The standard survey of the Dutch colonial house and outbuildings, with constructional features, decoration, and local history associated with individual homesteads. Introduction by Franklin D. Roosevelt. Map. 150 illustrations. 469pp. 6⅝ x 9¼. 21469-9 Paperbound $5.00

MATHEMATICAL PUZZLES FOR BEGINNERS AND ENTHUSIASTS, Geoffrey Mott-Smith. 189 puzzles from easy to difficult—involving arithmetic, logic, algebra, properties of digits, probability, etc.—for enjoyment and mental stimulus. Explanation of mathematical principles behind the puzzles. 135 illustrations. viii + 248pp.
20198-8 Paperbound $2.00

PAPER FOLDING FOR BEGINNERS, William D. Murray and Francis J. Rigney. Easiest book on the market, clearest instructions on making interesting, beautiful origami. Sail boats, cups, roosters, frogs that move legs, bonbon boxes, standing birds, etc. 40 projects; more than 275 diagrams and photographs. 94pp.
20713-7 Paperbound $1.00

TRICKS AND GAMES ON THE POOL TABLE, Fred Herrmann. 79 tricks and games— some solitaires, some for two or more players, some competitive games—to entertain you between formal games. Mystifying shots and throws, unusual caroms, tricks involving such props as cork, coins, a hat, etc. Formerly *Fun on the Pool Table*. 77 figures. 95pp.
21814-7 Paperbound $1.25

HAND SHADOWS TO BE THROWN UPON THE WALL: A SERIES OF NOVEL AND AMUSING FIGURES FORMED BY THE HAND, Henry Bursill. Delightful picturebook from great-grandfather's day shows how to make 18 different hand shadows: a bird that flies, duck that quacks, dog that wags his tail, camel, goose, deer, boy, turtle, etc. Only book of its sort. vi + 33pp. 6½ x 9¼. 21779-5 Paperbound $1.00

WHITTLING AND WOODCARVING, E. J. Tangerman. 18th printing of best book on market. "If you can cut a potato you can carve" toys and puzzles, chains, chessmen, caricatures, masks, frames, woodcut blocks, surface patterns, much more. Information on tools, woods, techniques. Also goes into serious wood sculpture from Middle Ages to present, East and West. 464 photos, figures. x + 293pp.
20965-2 Paperbound $2.50

HISTORY OF PHILOSOPHY, Julián Marías. Possibly the clearest, most easily followed, best planned, most useful one-volume history of philosophy on the market; neither skimpy nor overfull. Full details on system of every major philosopher and dozens of less important thinkers from pre-Socratics up to Existentialism and later. Strong on many European figures usually omitted. Has gone through dozens of editions in Europe. 1966 edition, translated by Stanley Appelbaum and Clarence Strowbridge. xviii + 505pp.
21739-6 Paperbound $3.50

YOGA: A SCIENTIFIC EVALUATION, Kovoor T. Behanan. Scientific but non-technical study of physiological results of yoga exercises; done under auspices of Yale U. Relations to Indian thought, to psychoanalysis, etc. 16 photos. xxiii + 270pp.
20505-3 Paperbound $2.50

Prices subject to change without notice.
Available at your book dealer or write for free catalogue to Dept. GI, Dover Publications, Inc., 180 Varick St., N. Y., N. Y. 10014. Dover publishes more than 150 books each year on science, elementary and advanced mathematics, biology, music, art, literary history, social sciences and other areas.